Human Rights and Chinese Thought

China poses great challenges to human rights in theory and practice. In practice, China is considered, by the measure of most Western countries, to have a patchy record of protecting individuals' human rights. In the theoretical realm, Chinese intellectuals and government officials have challenged the idea that the term "human rights" can be universally understood in one single way and have often opposed attempts by Western countries to impose international standards on Asian countries.

What should we make of these challenges – and of claims by members of other groups to have moralities of their own? *Human Rights and Chinese Thought* gives an extended answer to these questions in the first study of its kind. Stephen C. Angle integrates a full account of the development of Chinese rights discourse – reaching back to important, although neglected, origins of that discourse in seventeenth- and eighteenth-century Confucianism – with philosophical considerations of how various communities should respond to contemporary Chinese claims about the uniqueness of their human rights concepts.

Drawing on Western thinkers such as Richard Rorty, Alasdair MacIntyre, Michael Walzer, Allan Gibbard, and Robert Brandom, Angle elaborates a plausible kind of moral pluralism and demonstrates that Chinese ideas of human rights do indeed have distinctive characteristics. His conclusion is not that we should ignore one another, though. Despite our differences, Angle argues that cross-cultural moral engagement is legitimate and even morally required. International moral dialogue is a dynamic and complex process, and we all have good reasons for continuing to work toward bridging our differences.

Stephen C. Angle is Assistant Professor of Philosophy at Wesleyan University. He is the co-editor and co-translator of *The Chinese Human Rights Reader* (2001) and has published articles in *The Journal of the History of Ideas, Philosophy East and West*, and *The Journal of Chinese Philosophy*.

Cambridge Modern China Series

Edited by William Kirby, Harvard University

Human Rights and Chinese Thought

A Cross-Cultural Inquiry

STEPHEN C. ANGLE

Wesleyan University

CAMBRIDGE
UNIVERSITY PRESS

CAMBRIDGE UNIVERSITY PRESS
Cambridge, New York, Melbourne, Madrid, Cape Town, Singapore, São Paulo, Delhi

Cambridge University Press
The Edinburgh Building, Cambridge CB2 8RU, UK

Published in the United States of America by Cambridge University Press, New York

www.cambridge.org
Information on this title: www.cambridge.org/9780521007528

First published 2002

A catalogue record for this publication is available from the British Library

Library of Congress Cataloguing in Publication data
Angle, Stephen, 1964–
Human rights and Chinese thought : a cross-cultural inquiry / Stephen C. Angle.
p.   cm.
Includes bibliographical references and index.
ISBN 0-521-80971-1 – ISBN 0-521-00752-6 (pbk.)
1. Human rights – China.   I. Title.
JC599.C6 A54 2002
323´.0951 – dc21

                                                        2001043814

ISBN 978-0-521-80971-9 hardback
ISBN 978-0-521-00752-8 paperback

Transferred to digital printing 2009

For Debra, Samantha, and Rachel

Contents

Contents

Preface and Acknowledgments

The beginnings of this book lie in a chapter that I decided not to write for my dissertation. I was intrigued by what Liu Shipei had written about "*quanli*" – his term for rights – in the first years of the twentieth century. I was coming close to finishing my dissertation on the nature of cross-cultural ethical differences, and I thought that a study of the differences between Liu's concept of *quanli* and Western ideas of rights current in his day would enhance what I had already written. At some point, though, it occurred to me that if I didn't write the chapter on Liu, I could finish the dissertation that much sooner – and maybe, if I was lucky, get a job. My advisers agreed, and I filed away my notes on Liu for another occasion. My thanks once again to an excellent trio of graduate advisers, Don Munro, Peter Railton, and Allan Gibbard, both for all their help and for knowing when I should stop.

A few months later, luck had come through and I was starting a job at Wesleyan University. Soon after I got there I learned that a major East-West Philosophers' Conference was to be held the following January in Hawaii, and that Wesleyan would pay for me to go if I could get my name on the program. This sounded like too good an offer to pass up, so I called Roger Ames and asked if there was anything he could do for me. I was hoping for an easy role – discussant, something like that. Instead he suggested I give a paper. And so out came those notes on Liu Shipei. The paper I gave at the conference now forms the latter half of Chapter 6 of this book. My thanks go to Roger for getting this ball rolling.

The more I read about "*quanli*," the more intrigued I became. I was aware that one shortcoming of my dissertation had been the relatively static nature of its analysis; the development of Chinese discussions of *quanli* offered an opportunity to explore the ways that an ethical discourse in one language changed over time, in part through its (changing) interactions with various foreign discourses about rights. The opportunity to look back into Chinese history, thinking about the different sources of what I started calling "Chinese rights discourse," was also appealing because it opened up the possibility of drawing on the work I had done in graduate school on neo-Confucianism. I was finding hints in Liu's writings that he was consciously drawing on some of the neo-Confucians, and as I looked more widely, I saw more evidence of the same. My thinking about the relations between the Confucian tradition and Chinese rights discourse was dramatically enhanced by the knowledge, friendships, and conversations that grew out of my participation in two conferences on Confucianism and Human Rights organized by Ted de Bary and Tu Wei-ming. I thank them both for their personal support, and for the opportunities that their leadership provided.

For all I enjoy the neo-Confucians and their heirs in the nineteenth century, this book is about much more than looking backward. My training as a graduate student at Michigan helped me to find tools that would illuminate how we understand and engage with one another, both within and across cultures, in the present day. I believe it was my friend Jeff Kasser who first introduced me to Robert Brandom's philosophy of language, which came to play an ever-increasing role in my thinking about these subjects after I left Ann Arbor. Another stimulus to using what I had learned in graduate school to help understand our present world came in the form of a challenge: My friend Roger Hart, whose idea of "philosophers" ran more to Derrida, Lacan, and Bourdieu than to Davidson, Brandom, and Raz, questioned whether Anglo-American philosophers really could shed any light on issues that mattered in the real world. I think Roger and I have each learned from one another, and I know this book is the better for our ongoing conversations.

There is one more dimension of the book that I must explain, namely what happened between the time of Liu Shipei and the present day. Two friends in particular deserve thanks for helping me understand these hundred years – and indeed, in both cases, much more besides. The first is Peter Zarrow, whom I met at the East-West Philosophers' Conference mentioned above. Peter has been a great source of guidance and good ideas, and I will forever be in his debt for the care and insight with which he read and commented on this entire manuscript. The second is Marina Svensson. We have generated a staggering amount of email traffic between Middletown, Connecticut, and Lund, Sweden, over the last several years. Her knowledge of and passion for Chinese intellectual, cultural, and political history, particularly as it relates to human rights, never fails to impress me. She has also been a model collaborator as we have labored together to complete *The Chinese Human Rights Reader*, a collection of 63 translated essays and speeches that in many ways serves as a companion volume both to my book and to her *Debating Human Rights in China: A Conceptual and Political History*, which is due out around the same time as my book. We look at the issue of human rights in China from differing vantage points and often ask different questions, but we have come to see these differences as complementary rather than contradictory. There is no one from whom I have learned more about twentieth-century Chinese discussions of rights.

Colleagues here at Wesleyan, both in philosophy and in East Asian studies, have made this an ideal environment in which to learn and to teach. Brian Fay, Steve Horst, Bill Johnston, Don Moon, Joe Rouse, Sanford Shieh, and Vera Schwarcz, plus members of the Ethics and Politics Reading Group, have all read and commented on one or more chapters of the manuscript. More generally, the enthusiasm of my colleagues trained in Western philosophy for my work in Chinese materials has been exhilarating. Another source of inspiration and advice has been my students. All the participants in my seminars on Chinese Philosophy and Human Rights made contributions of one kind or another, for which I am very grateful. Those students who wrote senior theses or essays under my direction contributed even more directly to the development of my thinking. The work of Joe Casey, Andy Crawford, Ernest Kow, Wing Ng, and Whitney Trevelyan was particularly relevant to my own concerns, and I thank them for all they taught me.

I am grateful to both Wesleyan University and the Chiang Ching-kuo Foundation for the support they provided me as I wrote this book. The time I was afforded to focus, read, and write was invaluable. Thanks, too, to the staff of Wesleyan's Olin Library, particularly those in the Inter-Library Loan office. Virtually nothing seems to escape their reach. I would also be remiss if I did not mention the two anonymous readers for Cambridge University Press, whose scrupulous and well-informed comments did much to improve the book. My editor, Mary Child, has been a great help in bringing this project to fruition. Large parts of Chapter 6 first appeared in journal articles in *Philosophy East and West* and *The Journal of the History of Ideas*; I very much appreciate permission to reprint that material.[1]

---

[1] Stephen C. Angle (1998), Did Someone Say "Rights"? Lui Shipei's Concept of "*Quanli*," *Philosophy East and West*, 48:4, 623–625; (2000), Should We All Be More English? Liang Qichao, Rudolf von Jhering, and Rights, *Journal of the History of Ideas* 61:2, 241–261.

I turn finally to my family – those who have meant the most to me over the years I wrote the book. My mother, stepfather, and sister-in-law all read and commented on the manuscript, and even seemed to enjoy it. It has been fun talking and debating about the book's themes with everyone in the family. But the truth is, the book has really been a pretty minor presence in my life over these last seven years, at least when compared to the new and constant joys of being a parent. This book is dedicated to my wife – my co-parent and closest companion – and our two wonderful daughters.

Chronology

Classical Figures and Texts
Confucius, *Analects* (d. 479 B.C.E.)
Mencius, *Mencius* (4th c. B.C.E.)
Xunzi, *Xunzi* (ca. 310–208 B.C.E.)

Early Neo-Confucians
(Song dynasty, 960–1279; Yuan dynasty, 1279–1368)
Zhou Dunyi (1017–1073)
Zhu Xi (1130–1200)
Song Lian (1310–1381)

Later Neo-Confucians
(Ming dynasty, 1368–1644; Qing dynasty, 1644–1911)
Lü Kun (1536–1618)
Chen Que (1604–1677)
Huang Zongxi (1610–1695)
Gu Yanwu (1613–1682)
Wang Fuzhi (1619–1692)
Lü Liuliang (1629–1683)
Han Tan (1637–1704)
Dai Zhen (1723–1777)

Nineteenth-Century Figures
(Qing dynasty, 1644–1911; Opium War, 1839–1842)
Lin Zexu (1785–1850)
Wei Yuan (1794–1856)
Li Hongzhang (1823–1901)

Fukuzawa Yukichi (1835–1901)
Katō Hiroyuki (1836–1916)
Zhang Zhidong (1837–1909)
Hu Liyuan (1847–1916)
Kang Youwei (1858–1927)
He Qi (1859–1914)
Tokutomi Sohō (1863–1957)
Tan Sitong (1865–1898)

Twentieth-Century Figures
(Republic of China, 1912– ; People's Republic of China, 1949–)
Sun Yatsen (1866–1925)
Liang Qichao (1873–1929)
Chen Duxiu (1879–1942)
Liu Shipei (1884–1919)
Gao Yihan (1884–1968)
Hu Shi (1891–1962)
Luo Longji (1896–1965)

Contemporary Figures
He Hangzhou
Li Buyun
Liu Huaqiu
Luo Mingda
Wei Jingsheng
Xia Yong
Zhang Wenxian

1

Introduction

IN JUNE OF 1993, His Excellency Mr. Liu Huaqiu, head of the Chinese delegation, made the following statement in the course of his remarks to the United Nations World Conference on Human Rights in Vienna:

> The concept of human rights is a product of historical development. It is closely associated with specific social, political, and economic conditions and the specific history, culture, and values of a particular country. Different historical development stages have different human rights requirements. Countries at different development stages or with different historical traditions and cultural backgrounds also have different understanding and practice of human rights. Thus, one should not and cannot think of the human rights standard and model of certain countries as the only proper ones and demand all countries to comply with them. [Liu Huaqiu 1995, p. 214]

This statement contains two claims: first that countries can have different concepts of human rights, and second that we ought not demand that countries comply with human rights concepts different from their own. The principal goal of this book is to assess these two claims.

It is important that we know what to make of these two claims, for reasons that range from the immediate and practical to the broadly theoretical. Assessment of the two claims should influence activists and international lawyers, both within China and without. It should shape the activities of organizations that seek to transcend national boundaries, like the United Nations; if Liu is correct, the hope for global moral consensus expressed by the Universal Declaration of Human Rights may seem naive or even imperialist. Especially since the end of the cold war,

China has come to occupy a distinctive place in Western self-identities. Western media pay so much attention to China in part because it is seen as presenting an alternative, or a competitor, to ourselves.[1] Assessing Liu's claims will thus also tell us something about how to understand ourselves. Are we in the West better, or just different? Or is the matter more complicated than this simple dichotomy admits?

Of course it is more complicated. I will challenge the very notion that we can talk about "China's concept" of human rights: In the first place, people rather than countries have concepts; in the second, people often diverge in their uses of concepts, even people who are citizens of a single country. Rather than reject Liu's ideas out of hand, I will recast his claims in more careful terms. I will ask what concepts are, how they are related to communities, and how we use them to communicate. Instead of a stark choice between "different" and "better," I will develop a nuanced account of moral pluralism that recognizes the variety of ways in which we can be different from one another, the different perspectives from which we can claim to be better, and the dynamic nature of our moralities. When situated in the concrete context of debates over human rights, these abstract issues take on an immediacy that makes clear their importance not just to philosophers but also to students of cross-cultural issues quite generally.

Assessing Liu's claims will also take me rather deeply into the history of Chinese philosophy. While a common caricature portrays Chinese thought as static, I believe that all philosophical discourses are both non-monolithic and dynamic: People disagree and debate, and things change. This perspective enables me to see how certain strands of the Confucian tradition paved the way for rights discourse in China; throughout its history, in fact, Chinese rights discourse should be understood as an ongoing creative achievement, rather than a reaction to or misunderstanding of Western ideas and institutions. Only by looking at key moments in this history can we decide what to make of claims about the distinctiveness of Chinese concepts of human rights.

In the end, I do more than just assess Liu's twin claims. I am not a disinterested spectator in these matters; none of us are. I seek to act on my conclusions by engaging with contemporary Chinese rights theorists. Human rights discourses both East and West are dynamic and contested processes. By making more explicit both similarities and differences, and by judging which concepts to embrace based on the best standards I can

---

[1] See [Madsen 1995] for an enlightening account of U.S. views of China, and of ourselves.

2

find, I aim to cooperate in the development of a broader, transnational consensus.

Some of these matters, both philosophical and sinological, may seem rather distant from the issue of contemporary human rights practice. I firmly believe in their interconnection and have tried to write a book that makes these relationships clear. Many philosophers have studied little about China; many sinologists have had little contact with philosophy. I have not assumed my audience to be learned in either field, therefore, but have written about philosophy and about China in ways that should be accessible to educated readers who know little about either.

This chapter's goal is to help orient these various readers in three different ways. I begin with a historical sketch that clarifies the scope of Chinese rights discourse. I then turn to a discussion of themes from recent scholarship related to human rights in China. I am building on what I take to be the strengths of current research by other scholars, and reacting to what I see as the weaknesses; this review thus explains why the book takes the precise shape that it does. The last part of this Introduction summarizes the rest of the book and gives an initial formulation of my conclusions.

1.1 RECENT HISTORY

The word *quanli*, which has come to be the standard Chinese translation for "rights," was first used in that sense in the mid-1860s, when the missionary W. A. P. Martin employed it in his translation of Henry Wheaton's *Elements of International Law*. "*Quanli*" and related terms were used thereafter by missionaries, and gradually by Chinese intellectuals, to mean a range of things related to "rights," though I will argue in later chapters that the correspondence between *quanli* and rights is quite loose, especially in the early years of what I will nonetheless call "Chinese rights discourse." Both theoretical investigation and practical advocacy of *quanli* picked up pace at the beginning of the twentieth century. Throughout its first three decades, rights and human rights (*renquan*) were frequent topics in moral and political essays, various

---

[2] I use double quotes when I refer to a word rather than the concept expressed by that word. I italicize romanized words or concepts. "*Quanli*" is pronounced "chwan-lee." Chinese characters corresponding to all romanized words can be found in the Glossary.

rights were articulated in the earliest Chinese constitutions, and still more rights were claimed by intellectuals frustrated with one or another aspect of their government's policies.[3]

Writings on rights continued only sporadically after the early 1930s, thanks first to nearly twenty years of warfare, and then to a communist ideology that was not particularly friendly to rights-talk.[4] The past two decades, however, have been crowded with theoretical discussion and practical action both for and against human rights in China. The winter of 1978–9 witnessed the Democracy Wall movement in China, in which activists like Wei Jingsheng argued for the importance of human rights. That movement lasted for about six months before its central participants were arrested.[5] From the 1970s on, human rights played a significant role in United States foreign policy rhetoric, first focusing on the Soviet Union and then on China. In the United Nations, renewed attention was paid to the Universal Declaration of Human Rights, originally adopted in 1948, and to the two international covenants, promulgated in the late 1960s, that fleshed out its details.

In 1989 another popular movement advocating democracy and human rights arose in China, this time centering on Tiananmen Square. The brutal suppression of this movement led to sharp international condemnation of China. Partly in response, the Chinese government issued its first white paper on human rights.[6] This document rebutted various criticisms of China and argued against international meddling with the internal affairs of sovereign countries; nonetheless, it represented a new beginning for the discussion of human rights within China. Whereas many of the writings on human rights produced in China throughout the 1990s adhered very closely to the positions outlined in the white paper, some Chinese academics pushed considerably further, engaging in substantive debate with the theories of their more doctrinaire Chinese colleagues and also the theories of Western scholars.[7]

Another trend of the 1990s took shape during international meetings leading up to the 1993 United Nations World Conference on Human

---

[3] For translations of key articles in Chinese rights discourse from this period to the present, see [Angle & Svensson 2001].

[4] For detailed discussion of the rights-related discussions that did continue in this period, see [Svensson 1996, ch. 8].

[5] See [Seymour 1980] for discussion and translation of key documents.

[6] See [Information Council 1991].

[7] [Baehr et al. 1996] contains translations of a number of excellent recent papers. [Kent 1999, ch. 5] and [Weatherley 1999, ch. 6] contain helpful discussions of this period.

Rights. Leaders of some Asian nations, perhaps feeling a new confidence and sense of autonomy, argued that the United Nations' understanding of human rights was based too rigidly on the foundation of the Western liberal tradition. They called for more flexibility in the interpretation of human rights so that room could be found for what have come to be called "Asian values."[8] While the notion that all Asians share some particular set of values has been widely and justly criticized, and the motives of some of these Asian leaders (in calling for greater deference to authority, for instance) questioned, some scholars both East and West have urged that we do need to reconsider how human rights mesh with, or are interpreted within, different cultural traditions.[9]

Conflicts surrounding human rights and China seem unlikely to disappear soon. On the positive side, there is continuing dialogue of various sorts. China continues to participate in international discussions of human rights and recently signed the International Covenant on Civil and Political Rights.[10] Academic discussion of rights and human rights within China also continues, both in international conferences and in publications. On the other hand, China continues to act in ways that appear to contravene most understandings of human rights, a recent example (as of this writing) being its suppression of the Falun Gong religious movement. As a result, China continues to be criticized by Chinese dissidents abroad, by human rights non-governmental organizations like Amnesty International, and by Western governments. I hope that the work of scholars like myself can contribute to better understanding and improved dialogue, and in the end to a greater consensus on the meaning and content of human rights.

1.2 CURRENT APPROACHES: INSIGHTS AND LIMITATIONS

I now want to look more closely at a series of approaches to human rights that can be discerned in recent scholarship on the subject. I have two goals in this section: first, to try to make clear some of my intellectual debts; second, to show why I think this book is needed.

---

[8] For primary documents and scholarly analysis, see [Tang 1995].
[9] See [de Bary 1998, ch. 1] and several of the essays collected in [Bauer & Bell 1999] for astute discussion of the notion of Asian values. [Dowdle 2001] offers a sympathetic reading of the central document of Asian values advocates, the Bangkok Declaration.
[10] [Kent 1999] is a detailed study of China's participation in the international human rights dialogue.

1.2.1 Pluralism

A central issue in this book is to clarify the sense in which we can say that moralities are plural. It is widely accepted that the norms by which people regulate their lives differ, but it is hotly disputed whether more than one of these moralities can be legitimate or true or equally valid. One author whom I have found particularly helpful on these matters is Alasdair MacIntyre, who has written widely on moral traditions and on the difficulties of comparing such traditions. Two of his main claims are particularly relevant to my concerns. First, he argues that the conceptual differences between competing moral traditions can be so great that the traditions are rendered "incommensurable," which basically means that words from the moral language of one culture cannot be translated into words of another culture's moral language. MacIntyre's second claim is that genuine moral traditions can, at least sometimes, be compared and assessed through a process of comparative internal criticism. It is possible for adherents of one perspective to learn a second perspective from the inside, as a second first language, and then to see that this other perspective can solve problems or answer questions that their original perspective cannot.[11]

I have learned a great deal from MacIntyre about the importance of traditions, communities, and local standards of rationality in making up a full-fledged morality. Each of these will be discussed below as I develop my own account of what is involved in moral pluralism and what we can do about it. MacIntyre's specific account of these matters, though, is problematic, for two major reasons. First, I find his notion of incommensurability to be too blunt an instrument for dealing with the complexity and ambiguity of real cross-cultural moral conflicts. It is very difficult to refine incommensurability into a precise notion; even when this is done, it remains questionable whether the requirements for such a dramatic conceptual gulf are ever really fulfilled.[12] I prefer to think of incommensurability as the limiting case of conceptual differences, and to see all the interesting cases as falling somewhere short of this extreme.

---

[11] Each of these claims is made in more than one place, but for the first, see especially [MacIntyre 1991], and for the second [MacIntyre 1988].

[12] Fulfilled, that is, by real people speaking natural languages; it is easy to show that artificial languages can be incommensurable.

The second problem I have with MacIntyre's account is that his theoretical understanding of traditions is too static. As I will elaborate below, even when his historical studies reveal important dynamism, his theoretical account has no real role for the dynamic, mutually influencing nature of traditions, and yet it is in such dynamism, I believe, that the real opportunities for community formation and consensus-building lie. MacIntyre's stress on internal criticism – on seeing the strengths and weaknesses of other traditions from the inside – is important, but we are never comparing two unchanging entities.

The other theorist whose views I want to mention here is Richard Rorty. To say that Rorty is a pluralist is not to say that he believes in no one set of values. Rorty is deeply committed to liberal values, but he sees these values as his through the contingencies of history rather than through the necessities of Reason. Rorty writes that

> moral philosophy takes the form of an answer to the question "Who are 'we', how did we come to be what we are, and what might we become?" rather than an answer to the question "What rules should dictate my actions?" In other words, moral philosophy takes the form of historical narration and utopian speculation rather than a search for general principles. [1989, p. 60]

As will become apparent below, I am sympathetic to Rorty's emphasis on seeing moralities as historically grounded, contingent sets of values. His stress on morality being intimately linked to self-definition (who "we" are) is also insightful. Rorty's approach has two severe limitations, however. First, his rejection of "general principles" is easily taken too far, so that one is left with nothing more to say about why one holds one's values than "they are mine." It is crucial to see that this is mistaken: We always have standards for moral judgment to which we can appeal – even if we can articulate them only imperfectly – and we usually take these standards to apply not just to us, but to everyone. Moral discussions with others can push us toward refining or generalizing both our standards and our morals in ways that Rorty seems to miss.

A second problem with Rorty's account is his implication that "we" are unanimous in our commitments and univocal in our meanings. I have already suggested that the moral discourses of communities typically are much more complex, and so we need a subtler account of the relation between communities and morality. To sum up, then, this look at MacIntyre and Rorty has suggested that a satisfactory account will have to allow for a continuum of conceptual differences, for dynamic and inter-active moral traditions, for values and standards that push us toward a wider consensus, and for an understanding of "us" that acknowledges internal differences.

1.2.2 Universalism

Many who have written on human rights believe that human rights are universal. Here I want to canvass three reasons that have been given for this tenet.

Natural Rights. The idea of natural rights has a long history in Euro-pean thought, and it also played an important role in early American political thinking. In early contexts, natural rights were widely accepted to be the result of God's will. Today, few would accept that grounding for natural rights, however, and alternative attempts to say what rights humans have because of their "natures" are fraught with difficulties. Human nature is now understood to be quite plastic, our needs and values heavily influenced by the cultures within which we mature.[13] Without the premises that belief in a particular understanding of God made available, contemporary accounts of natural rights can seem forced or arbitrary. Grounding human rights on a specific account of human nature, therefore, can leave the door open for others, particularly those from other cultures, to reject one's account as parochial – or even simply as incoherent.[14]

This is not to say that justifying human rights as natural rights has no attraction. If the problematic link between nature and culture is either refuted or ignored, natural rights can seem firmer than any competing foundation for human rights. They are equally applicable to all humans, regardless of nationality. Natural rights can thus appear to be the best basis for criticism of the human rights practices of other groups – after all, we all are human, and if human rights accrue to us simply by virtue of our human nature, then surely they are universal.

---

[13] This understanding of human nature is well-grounded in contemporary biological theory. The best contemporary correlate for human nature is the human phenotype, which results from the way human genotypes are expressed in particular environments. Since culture is part of our environments, it is thus built into our phenotypes – into our natures.

[14] This point has been made by many; for a recent statement, see [Brown 1999].

International Law. A second justification for the universal application of human rights standards is the international legal consensus that has developed since World War II, as represented in United Nations documents like the Universal Declaration of Human Rights (UDHR), which was passed by the United Nations General Assembly in 1948. In addition to the UDHR and its attendant covenants, the international human rights regime is made up of numerous regional and bilateral treaties and declarations, as well as a variety of international legal institutions and their respective bodies of case law.[15]

Despite the real successes these documents represent, there are several reasons for thinking that international proclamations like these are not ideal bases for human rights discourse – or at the very least, that they cannot stand alone. We would be mistaken to think that because these documents have been signed by so many countries, there now exists a genuine legal or moral consensus in the world. The UDHR itself is not a legally binding document. The covenants and similar treaties are legally binding, but they have no more institutionalization, particularity, or enforceability than other aspects of international law. They can easily seem more like statements of aspirations or ideals than genuine legal documents. Partly because of this, and because signing these agreements can be seen as a route toward becoming a full-fledged participant in the developed world's trading regimes, it can be both easy and attractive for a nation to sign these agreements without really agreeing to them. As Ann Kent has recently put it, China's approach to the United Nations human rights regime appears to be "more instrumental than normative" [1999, p. 230]. Finally, we must remember that the documents' provisions always require interpretation, and this allows for a wide range of disagreement to be masked. In short, the consensus these documents represent may be more apparent than real – and to the extent it is a consensus, it is a quasi-legal, indirectly coerced consensus.

To say that the UDHR, the covenants, and so on are not ideal is certainly not to deny that they are tremendous accomplishments. Nor do I want to deny that they can and should have important roles in the future of international human rights discourse. They offer excellent starting points for discussion, especially in light of the fact that often-heard

---

[15] The covenants are the *International Covenant on Economic, Social, and Cultural Rights* and the *International Covenant on Civil and Political Rights*, both from 1966; China is now a signatory to both. One good source of these and related documents is [Blaustein et al. 1987]; see also the web site of the United Nations High Commissioner for Human Rights: ⟨http://www.unhchr.ch/data.htm⟩.

charges about their completely Western origin are exaggerations.[16] Working from these documents can help us to build a more genuine moral consensus on human rights issues.

A Changing World. Modernity has brought with it many things, among them the techniques and ideologies of control that have made the modern state possible, as well as the changes wrought upon traditional social structures by the international market economy. These same technological and economic changes have brought people around the globe closer together: We can both see one another more easily (thanks to television, movies, and the Internet) and influence one another more often (thanks to global markets, multinational corporations, and the ease of travel).

Some scholars have seen these changes as grounding universal human rights. Jack Donnelly, for instance, has argued that traditional, duty-based moral structures are no longer adequate to protect human dignity from the powerful forces of the modern state and economy; only observance of human rights can accomplish this. Since the modern state can be found in nations around the world, all nations need to respect human rights. He says this without glorifying the modern state. It may be an evil, but it is here, and the only protection against it is universal recognition of human rights [Donnelly 1989, pp. 60, 65, 199].

Mary Midgely has seized on another aspect of modernity – the way in which it has brought people closer together – to urge that we embrace our new neighbors with a broadened moral vision. She says that "the sheer increase in the number of humans, . . . the wide diffusion of information about them, and . . . the dramatic increase in our own technological power" have made possible an "immense enlargement of our moral scene" [Midgely 1999, p. 161]. Midgely believes that the widespread acceptance of human rights by peoples around the world, despite uncertainties that academics have about their meaning and scope, follows from enlargement of the moral scene: People have found talk of human rights useful for dealing with modern moral questions. She acknowledges that there remain some conceptual puzzles about rights and human rights, but encourages academics to take their lead from the public and deal constructively with these problems in ways that will not undermine our continuing abilities to speak and judge in terms of human rights [ibid., p. 173].

[16] See [Twiss 1999], [Morsink 1999], and, most accessibly [Glendon 2001].

I think that Donnelly and Midgely are correct to insist that our morality fit with our times. We cannot ignore political and economic realities; nor should we close our eyes to those we can now see and influence.[17] The limitation of Donnelly's approach is his insistence that the current human rights regime is the only possible, or at any rate the only practical, solution to the challenges posed by the modern state. He provides little argument for the negative side of this claim – that is, that no other system of values (and institutions) could do the job. The most he does is to express skepticism about the "political naivete" of those who promote such alternatives, or else about their motives [Donnelly 1997]. It is possible that a broad, cross-cultural consensus might reach Donnelly's conclusion, but I believe it is premature to assume that this is the only possible solution.

Midgely's point is easier to accept without qualification. The world is increasingly small, and the pressures on us (whoever "we" are) to include others within our moral compass are both real and compelling. These pressures certainly are not the only ones that globalization has brought upon us; global capitalism has at best an ambiguous relation to human rights [Santoro 2000]. Still, human rights have played important roles in the efforts of different peoples to deal with their broader moral scenes. Academics like myself cannot work in isolation from these facts. Midgely does not go as far as Donnelly and claim that the current United Nations–based understanding of human rights is the only acceptable one, but in appealing to academics to deal "constructively" with the problems they uncover, she is nonetheless asking that we keep in mind the practical effects of our work. There is always a danger that a defense of moral pluralism – even of the modest kind that I develop in Chapters 2 and 3 – can be turned into a legitimization of authoritarian politics. I am alive to that danger; in fact, I believe that my approach has the potential to strengthen, rather than weaken, the position of human rights activists in China and elsewhere.

1.2.3 Thick and Thin

The modern world has not just brought us closer together; it has also made us more aware of our differences. Although modern political and

---

[17] Richard Rorty has written about the need to embrace "human rights culture" by broadening our vision of "us," as well as the important role that "sentimental education" can play in this process; see [Rorty 1993]. Rorty underestimates the importance of reasoning and dialogue, but is correct to see the work of novelists and poets as also important.

economic forces have the tendency to strip people of their distinctive identities, this process has been strenuously resisted at both theoretical and practical levels. Liberal politics has for the most part been a willing partner in this resistance to uniformity, since tolerance is one of its central values.[18] Toleration of differences, however, might seem to sit uncomfortably alongside an insistence on universal human rights. Several theorists have sought to avoid this tension by positing that universal and particular values can exist simultaneously on different levels. As Michael Walzer has put it, we can share "thin" values – like human rights – very widely, while confining our "thick" values to smaller communities.[19]

Walzer writes that thin morality is based on a rough overlap or "reiteration" of values like "truth" and "justice." This overlap is enough to get certain kinds of criticism and certain amounts of solidarity off the ground, but these have distinct limits; real criticism, he argues, is internal to thick, grounded-in-cultural-meanings moralities. This is not to say that a minimal, roughly overlapping morality is a bad or unreal thing: It explains the fellowship we feel with demonstrators in Beijing or in Prague. But if we listen to what they say for very long, we begin to discover the distances between us and them. Using the demonstrations from 1989 as an example, Walzer notes that "when we criticize Czech communism in ways that suggest an alternative, we move quickly beyond the minimum, knowing that some of what we say will echo positively in Prague (or in this or that part of Prague) and some, perhaps, won't" [1994, p. 10].

We see here Walzer's recognition of the potential for internal complexity or contestation within the community of Prague protestors: some may have built their commitments to "justice" on grounds that resonate well with our more specific critiques, while others may not have. I will have much more to say in later chapters about the importance of this sort of inner complexity. For the time being, let us also note that Walzer

---

[18] What tolerance is, whether it is an unequivocally good thing, and how it is related to liberalism are all controversial issues on which much has been written. One particularly illuminating recent essay is [Phillips 1999]; I will discuss these issues in more detail in Chapter 3.

[19] Bernard Williams has also written of "thick" and "thin" value concepts, but with a somewhat different emphasis. Compare [Williams 1985, chs. 8–9]. Walzer himself cites Clifford Geertz's notion of "thick description" in anthropology as his inspiration; see [Walzer 1994, p. xi, fn. 1] and [Geertz 1973]. Joseph Chan applies the ideas of "thick" and "thin" to China in [Chan 2000].

does not aim at identification of a single, unchanging code of thin values. He says that thin values are embedded within thick moralities. Thin values are

> liberated . . . and appear independently, in varying degrees of thinness, only in the course of a . . . social crisis or a political confrontation – as, in the Czech case, with communist tyranny. Because (most of) the rest of us have some sense of what tyranny is and why it is wrong, the words used by the demonstrators shed whatever particular meanings they may have in the Czech language; they become widely, perhaps universally accessible. [1994, p. 3]

To make this even more concrete, he says that "what they meant by the 'Justice' inscribed on their signs . . . was simple enough: an end to arbitrary arrests, equal and impartial law enforcement, the abolition of the privileges and prerogatives of the party elite – common, garden variety justice" [1994, p. 2].

Walzer clearly is not advocating a one-size-fits-all theory of thin, universal values. Different words and concepts, in different situations, can be understood more or less thinly and can appeal more or less widely. His goal is to explain phenomena like our feeling of solidarity with protestors like those in Prague, while insisting that full-fledged criticism must take place from within. A common variation on Walzer's approach is to seek to identify a fixed set of thin values by uncovering all those values actually shared by everyone.[20] This least-common-denominator approach, though, is inadequate for at least two reasons, the second of which is a problem for Walzer as well. First, if we require universal agreement, we are likely to be confined to very vague or general notions – things like "unjustified killing is wrong." But what exactly would justify killing? Considerable diversity surely lurks behind the facade of universality. A least-common-denominator consensus risks superficiality, which of course Walzer explicitly recognizes.

The second problem is that if the values are indeed shared by everyone, the values can have only a limited critical function: They can allow criticism of practices, but not of values themselves. Whenever there is a gap between values and actual practice, there will be room for this kind of criticism. Activists seeking to ensure that their values will be institutionalized or enforced in their societies might draw encouragement from the successes of other groups in institutionalizing such values – as

---

[20] See, for instance, Parekh's discussion of "minimal universalism" in [Parekh 1999].

positive models to follow or as proof that such institutionalization is possible. If we want more than this – if we want to be able to tell others that they *ought* to be committed to human rights, even when they are not – then we will need something more than a least-common-denominator approach. In fact, no version of a least-common-denominator theory, Walzer's included, lets us criticize something that we couldn't have criticized even without recognizing the theory's (superficial) universalities. This is because the kind of criticism considered in this paragraph seems available even when values are not shared. Can't I criticize you for failing to live up to your values, whether or not I share them? Exactly how to understand such a case is admittedly rather complicated, and I will take it up in detail in Chapter 3.

John Rawls has developed a framework for what he calls "the law of peoples" that takes a different approach to determining a set of thin values. Unlike the least-common-denominator idea, Rawls starts from home. He begins, that is, by asking to what set of thin values a liberal, democratic state should be committed as its norms for international law. He then demonstrates that a certain kind of "well-ordered" but non-liberal state would *also* be committed to this same set of values, which he dubs the "law of peoples." Since his law of peoples includes the commitment to basic human rights, this leads him to conclude that "although any society must honor basic human rights, it need not be liberal" [1993, p. 43]. Rawls avoids the problems mentioned earlier for least-common-denominator understandings of thin values: The law of peoples is not universally adhered to already, so it has a wide critical function, and since it is derived from a fairly clear set of values, it should be adequately detailed.

That is not to say that I find Rawls's account ultimately successful. The central failing of his attempt to extend the law of peoples beyond liberal regimes lies in his notion of a "well-ordered" non-liberal society, which he also calls a "hierarchical society" [1993, p. 61]. It is here that the law of peoples derives its specific critical force: Although he is not prepared to say that non-liberal societies should be liberal, he is prepared to demand that they be well-ordered in their own way. The problem is that Rawls's understanding of what it takes for a non-liberal society to be well-ordered is extremely specific. It would be more perspicuous to say that his requirement is for non-liberal societies to be "legally well-ordered," since the crucial part of his definition of "well-ordered" – from which all of the important conclusions follow, including that such societies will endorse basic human rights – is having a legal system that meets

14

certain criteria. He says that these criteria are necessary for the regime to have "legitimacy in the eyes of its own people" [1993, p. 61], but he makes no attempt to substantiate this by showing why other criteria of legitimacy are unacceptable. His conception of well-ordered, therefore, rules out any number of regimes in which order and legitimacy are established through means other than a modern legal system. Since it is far from clear that the rulers or people of China, in particular, take legitimacy to rest on the legal norms that Rawls describes, I believe that his particular version of the thick–thin distinction cannot help with our problem.

Let me summarize what I think we should learn from this discussion of thick and thin values. If we are ever to take ourselves to be justified in criticizing others' values, as opposed to their mere failures to live up to their values, we need a substantive account of thin values. Least-common-denominator approaches cannot deliver such an account: It will have to start from our own thick values, in something like the way Rawls describes.[21] The process of building out from thick to thin, though, can never be completed once and for all; moralities and cultures are too dynamic for that. Distinctions of thick and thin should thus be tools in our kit, rather than providing a stand-alone solution.

1.2.4 Dialogue and Transformation

Thin values can insulate us from one another – or at least insulate our fully specified selves, complete with rich conceptions of the good, from one another. By distinguishing between thick and thin, we seem to have solved the dilemma of international cooperation in a pluralistic world, suggesting that there need be no uncomfortable rubbing-up of one set of thick values against another. In many situations this kind of insulation is a good thing. Whereas one of the reasons we articulate thin values is to give us the means to criticize egregious moral violations on the part of others, another of their functions can be to keep us from getting too involved in others' affairs. Still, such a static understanding of values is unsatisfactory. It is unrealistic, since values at both levels do change, often because of interaction with values at the other level or interaction with

---

[21] Notice that at least in this respect, Walzer's well-known criticism of Rawls for having a merely "procedural" view of morality fails to convince: The strength of Rawls's view of law of peoples, as I see it, is precisely in the way it rests on a substantive, liberal morality [Walzer 1994, pp. 11–14].

the thick values of another group. The static picture is also morally inferior, because dynamism can emerge from morally praiseworthy dialogue between groups, or from constructive reflection on the relation between thick and thin within one's own values. As Allan Gibbard has explained, many situations in which one deals with other groups on a thin basis are understood within one's group as second-best solutions: better than conflict, but worse than consensus and agreement [Gibbard 1990, pp. 242–3]. This is not to deny that we sometimes celebrate differences, in which case an ongoing disagreement may actually be preferred to consensus. Nor is it to deny that we can learn from others, which learning may continue over an extended period of time: To say that we want to work for consensus is very different from saying that we want to assimilate the others.[22] Still, one must always be ready to review the basis on which one is settling for a second-best; in many such circumstances it makes sense to work for a better solution. In Chapter 3, I will build on Gibbard's work in order to show how these stimuli to dialogue and dynamism operate.

Before moving on, it is important that I forestall a possible misunderstanding that could arise from my talk of "consensus." I do not believe that consensus is an inevitable result of conversation, even under ideal circumstances. Neither do I believe that the possibility of consensus or agreement is presupposed when we strive to communicate with one another.[23] We start from different positions, live different lives, and may never see things the same way. Despite this, we often arrive at what I will follow Gibbard in calling "norms of accommodation": These are values to which we and you commit ourselves in order to interact with one another, despite their being more shallow, or more limited, than our respective full-fledged sets of values. Thin values are an excellent example. From within each of our perspectives, it would be better if all of us lived in accord with our richer, thicker values. This is the sense in which thin values are second-best, and the sense in which we will have

---

[22] See [Fay 1996, pp. 241–2]: "Instead of trying to overcome differences or hardening them, interact with those who differ by means of these differences with an eye toward ongoing mutual learning and growth."

[23] These theses derive from the work of Jürgen Habermas; see, e.g., [Habermas 1985]. For helpful discussion of Habermas, see [Fay 1987, pp. 184–90]. When I spell out my understanding of concepts and communication in Chapter 2, it will become apparent that my view is in some sense the opposite of Habermas's: I explain how communication can take place despite pervasive disagreements and even differences in meanings.

reason to continue to work for consensus. I will have more to say about these matters in later chapters.

Some authors have specifically argued that dialogue, rather than criticism, should be the main mode of international human rights discourse. Bhikhu Parekh, for instance, has written: "If universal values are to enjoy widespread support and democratic validation and be free of ethnocentric biases, they should arise out of an open and uncoerced cross-cultural dialogue" [1999, p. 139]. Parekh says that this universality should "arise" out of the dialogue, rather than be discovered, because he imagines that a certain amount of transformation will take place in the process of reasoning out a body of values that all parties agree is the most "rationally defensible." In particular, Parekh insists that he is not advocating "teasing out the lowest common denominator of different cultural traditions"; instead, he imagines that through a process of collective reasoning we will arrive at "human universals" that all cultures can be shown to presuppose [ibid., p. 142].

Parekh's approach sounds very appealing, particularly the notion that the commitments of all parties to a conversation might be transformed through the process of dialogue. I will pursue this idea in subsequent chapters. As it stands, though, Parekh's proposal is open to some serious objections. First, other philosophers have argued that not only can cultures' moral values differ, but their standards of reasoning can differ as well.[24] This undermines the idea that a process of reasoning can be arrived at that will allow a "rationally defensible" consensus to emerge. Second, it must be admitted that Parekh's "open and uncoerced" dialogue, involving "every culture with a point of view to express," sounds a bit starry-eyed. It is perhaps revealing that while Parekh makes several proposals for human universals in the balance of his essay, he does so without the help of any cross-cultural dialogue whatsoever. Finally, Parekh seems to assume that each culture can be treated as a single unit, with a single set of values and presuppositions. To the contrary, I believe that recognition of the internal complexity of cultures and traditions must be central to a successful account of cross-cultural dialogue; these complexities can make dialogue more difficult, but they also can give us one of the keys to fruitful dialogue.

The potential rewards of recognizing internal complexity can be seen in another approach that emphasizes developing a transformative

---

[24] See [MacIntyre 1988] and [Gibbard 1990].

dialogue. David Hall and Roger Ames have argued that a specific strand of the Western tradition – American pragmatism – is the best point of departure for "our" side in discussing human rights with the Chinese [Hall & Ames 1999]. They believe that pragmatism both is superior to other strands of the Western tradition and comes closer than other elements of Western thought to the strongest elements within the Chinese intellectual tradition. They are certainly engaged in criticism here – criticizing aspects of both Western and Chinese cultures – but they do so in the service of a dialogue which they hope will lead to stronger moral consensuses both within and between the East and the West.

Hall and Ames's interpretation of the Confucianism is controversial, but I do not want to dwell on that here.[25] More relevant is criticism they have received for ignoring the impact that power relationships have on human rights dialogue: According to one critic, their efforts to show that China does have a distinctive understanding of human rights amounts to "ignoring dictators," since the claim that China has its own notion of rights has been used by the Chinese government to justify various forms of repression [Donnelly 1997]. While it is certainly true that power relations must form a part of any complete understanding of cross-cultural dialogue or criticism, I reject the idea that scholarly work revealing and explaining moral pluralism must necessarily benefit the dictators. If, as I believe, there are kernels of truth in the assertions of the Chinese government, then ignoring these truths while redoubling the volume of our claims about universal values is illegitimate and imperialistic – exactly as our Chinese critics claim. If, on the other hand, we can develop an account of moral pluralism both in general and as it applies to human rights in China, an account that nonetheless provides firm ground for critics of repression and for those who want to develop a stronger international consensus, then the dictators will have lost an important weapon in their arsenal, and we will have lost nothing.

In sum, we might do well to look for ways that dialogue, rather than bald criticism, can lead to transformed values and perhaps to consensus. In so doing, though, we must be careful not to ignore power relations nor to forget that standards of reasoning, like moral values, may vary from culture to culture. Most important, we should try to make use of the many different voices that can enter into the multiple, overlapping, sometimes conflicting dialogues that together make up contemporary rights discourse. Activists and dissidents, politicians and bureaucrats,

[25] See [Martin 1990].

scholars and students, workers and CEOs: They all count. It is no simple matter to take all these voices into account, but a model of rights discourse that gives voice only to one group is clearly inadequate.

1.2.5 History and Confucianisms

Many of the approaches I have examined so far are distinctly ahistorical: They see values, thick or thin, as grounded in current realities. Other scholars have sought to look at Chinese human rights discourse in historical perspective, or to compare human rights concepts with the ideas found in traditional Confucianism. I believe that there are important insights within each of these perspectives. If one rejects the idea that there is a single (thick) morality for all humans – based on either Reason or human nature – then it is natural to think that culture and history have a great deal to do with morality. As I discussed earlier in the context of Richard Rorty's writings, moralities can be seen as the dynamic products of traditions of moral discourse in particular social and physical contexts. If it is true that moralities are dynamic, then even if we can identify a thick or thin universal morality today, its universality must be, in a certain sense, a coincidence. Its universality must be owed to the particular set of circumstances in which peoples around the globe find themselves, and to the ways in which their traditions of moral discourse have adapted to these circumstances.[26] If this is all true, our hypothesized universal consensus may be very fragile. We would do well to understand what has brought it about and how we might maintain it. To the extent that we have not yet achieved such a moral consensus, a historical consciousness might help us to see why this is so and might help us to see where and how such a consensus might be reached. In particular, a historical perspective may be needed to fully assess the first of Liu Huaqiu's claims, namely that China has a different concept of human rights than those of other countries. It makes sense to look at the history of rights discourse in China to see whether this is true, and if so, why. Researching this history is also helpful for two other reasons. First, we will see that the Chinese rights tradition has rich resources that thinkers today can call upon: Over the last hundred and more years, rights have been discussed and conceptualized in a variety of ways, opening up a range of "Chinese" perspectives on rights. Second, reviewing the history of

---

[26] Donnelly's theory that human rights are required by the modern state and global market economy is at least the beginning of an explanation of universalism along these lines.

Chinese rights discourse helps us to appreciate the wisdom of seeing moral traditions as contingent and rooted in historical particularity.

The range and diversity of Chinese rights discourse have been little appreciated by contemporary scholars, nor by the wider public, both within China and without.[27] Even those scholars who have paid attention to this earlier rights discourse have tended to give it either brief or narrow treatment. Ann Kent, for instance, spends only seven pages of her *Between Freedom and Subsistence* on the years from 1860 to 1949 and writes so as to minimize the creative aspects of the discourse [Kent 1993, pp. 37–42]. The views of Liang Qichao (1873–1929) on rights and democracy inform an important part of Andrew Nathan's *Chinese Democracy*, but Nathan pays little attention to Liang's contemporaries and to later pre-communist thinkers [Nathan 1985]. In addition, the connections that have been drawn between rights discourse and native traditions have tended to be of a negative, restricting variety. Nathan believes that the two forces motivating intellectual change in early-twentieth-century China were (1) deep concern with the plight of China and (2) a sense that Western nations had better – more successful – political and moral values. Since the changes that followed from those motivations were limited by what Kent calls a "Chinese filter" [Kent 1993, p. 37], however, the Western ideas were transplanted imperfectly onto Chinese soil, and ideas like democracy and human rights did not put down deep roots.[28]

I believe that such interpretations are of significant importance in understanding Chinese concepts of rights, but they also distort our view by leaving out an important side of the picture. It is crucial to add that the Chinese tradition has also played a positive, constructive role in motivating thinkers to develop rights (*quanli*) concepts. To see this, one needs to appreciate some of the important differences that existed within Confucianism as it developed into the tradition now called neo-Confucianism. Like all traditions, neo-Confucianism was internally diverse, with a number of adherents emphasizing the importance of

---

[27] There are signs that this neglect may be ending. Marina Svensson's *Debating Human Rights in China*, based on her groundbreaking Ph.D. dissertation, surveys a large number of authors in impressive detail [Svensson 2002]. In addition, two collections of Chinese essays on rights from earlier in this century have appeared, one in China and one on the Internet. See [Liu Junning 1998] and ⟨http://www.igc.apc.org/hric/educ/big5/qishi/mulu.html⟩. Svensson's and my translation work, finally, should help to further open up the subject; see [Angle & Svensson 2001].

[28] An even more recent example of the tendencies discussed in this paragraph is [Weatherley 1999], on which see [Angle 2000].

fulfilling people's desires, as I will show in Chapter 4. Some Chinese rights thinkers in both the nineteenth and early twentieth centuries quite consciously drew on, and were motivated by, this strand of the neo-Confucian tradition. Only when we give this link to tradition its due can we begin to understand the world the way Chinese thinkers did; only then can we see them as creative and critical, rather than merely passive, reactive, and constrained.[29]

While little work has been done on the relationship between the neo-Confucian tradition and rights discourse,[30] a number of scholars have argued that the values of classical Confucianism – that is, the earlier Confucian tradition dating from the fifth through third centuries B.C.E. – are compatible with, or even actively promote, human rights. One problem with much of this work is that it implies an equation of classical Confucianism with the whole of Chinese tradition and seems to assume that Chinese moral discourse is static. A recent essay, for example, argues that each and every provision of the UDHR is either positively endorsed by, or at least compatible with, classical Confucianism [Chen 1999]. So what if this is true? There are no classical Confucians alive today, nor have there been for centuries. If the question of whether Chinese culture is compatible with human rights is to be relevant, we need to look to more recent Chinese culture, in all its complexity. A second major problem with claims that a concern for rights can be found in classical Confucianism is that they interpret both Confucian texts and ideas of rights very loosely. Rights have a distinctive conceptual structure that sets them apart from other moral commitments, like duties or ideals. The humanistic ideals found in the populist chapters of the *Analects* certainly resonate with some of the ideals expressed in the more general assertions of the UDHR, but this is very different from finding "rights" in the *Analects*.[31] There is one perspective, though, from which I see these kinds of comparisons as potentially important. To the extent that contemporary Chinese thinkers are attempting to construct a new

---

[29] Compare the similar methodological proposal put forward in [Lydia Liu 1995, pp. 26–7]. Like Liu, I applaud what Paul Cohen has called a "China-centered approach" to Chinese history: to read Chinese history from within, while neither ignoring nor overemphasizing the role of non-Chinese actors, events, and texts. See [Cohen 1984].

[30] The works of Wm. Theodore de Bary are the principal exception. See [1988] and especially [1998]. Ron-guey Chu also explores connections between neo-Confucian ideas and rights in [Chu 1998], and see the suggestive final chapter of [Wood 1995].

[31] The same can be said of other classical works like the *Mencius*. For "populism" in certain chapters of the *Analects*, see [Brooks & Brooks 1998]. See also [Donnelly 1989, ch. 3] for further criticism of the idea that Confucianism contains rights claims.

Chinese moral discourse on top of the ruins of communism, reacquaintance with the *Analects* and other classical works, together with the rediscovery of rights discourse from earlier in this century, may be very healthy.[32]

1.3 THIS BOOK

The two claims this book aims to assess are, once again: (1) Countries can have different concepts of human rights, and (2) we ought not demand that countries comply with human rights concepts different from their own. The specific way I go about assessing these claims is based upon the contemporary human rights theorizing reviewed in the previous section. This literature has rich offerings in some areas; in other areas, it is sparse or unreliable. What it means for one concept of rights to be different from another is rarely explained, nor are the many differences within nations or traditions taken into account. The resources that neo-Confucianism contributed to Chinese rights discourse are inadequately explored. With only a few recent exceptions, the history of China's actual rights discourse is neglected. All of these issues are critical for understanding whether, and in what ways, distinctive concepts of human rights can be found in China. I also need to make clear what I mean by moral pluralism, and how it relates to the idea that Chinese concepts of rights may be distinctively different from various views in the West. Finally, I have suggested earlier that dialogue and mutual openness are valuable strategies for overcoming pluralism when pluralism is found to be problematic. I would do well, then, to open up such a dialogue with contemporary Chinese rights theorists.

I will begin, in Chapter 2, by developing the ideas of Robert Brandom in order to introduce a way of thinking about what concepts are, how they depend on social norms, and how they can differ from one another. Brandom's account makes it easy to see how despite differences, we can still communicate, if we want to; his emphasis on communication as a cooperative practice meshes very nicely with the view of cross-cultural moral dialogue I develop in subsequent chapters. Brandom's work is of fundamental significance to understanding claims about conceptual difference and thus about pluralism, but its highly technical nature can

---

[32] Joseph Chan [Chan 1999] and Randall Peerenboom [Peerenboom 1993] aim to contribute to this constructive project. For a challenging critique of this project, see [Ci 1999].

make this difficult for non-specialists to appreciate. A central goal of this chapter is to open Brandom up to non-philosophers.

In order to assess Liu Huaqiu's second claim, I need to explore the consequences to which pluralism can lead. Chapter 3 builds on the excellent foundation provided by Allan Gibbard, laying out the issues and options facing those who encounter a group with seemingly different moral commitments. The conclusions of this chapter are relatively abstract, which means both that they are applicable well beyond the debate over China and human rights and also that we have to wait until later chapters to fill in concrete details before the considerations offered in this chapter can offer us advice on whether or not we can apply our standards of human rights to the Chinese.

I next turn to the more historical part of the book, starting with a look, in Chapter 4, at the neo-Confucian debate over legitimate desires. In these debates we find an important, though underappreciated, origin of Chinese rights discourse. This chapter tells the story of a robust strand of the neo-Confucian tradition as it develops through the sixteenth, seventeenth, and eighteenth centuries. In Chapter 5, I look at the various nineteenth-century origins of Chinese rights discourse. I focus on the early uses of terms like "*quanli*" and "*minquan*," which corresponded, at least partially, to "rights" and "people's rights." The story is complex, with missionaries, international diplomats, Japanese liberals, and Chinese scholars all playing roles. These origins, coupled with the role that neo-Confucianism plays in developments described in the following chapter, all help to make concrete the idea that moral discourses have messy, complicated, and contingent histories. Universal consensus is something that people have to work for, rather than something they can assume.

The longest essay on rights by a Chinese thinker until well into the twentieth century was "On Rights Consciousness" by Liang Qichao, written in 1902. Chapter 6 examines that essay as well as the important moral and political writings of Liang's contemporary, Liu Shipei. Both Liang and Liu explicitly draw on Western thinkers – Liang on the German legal philosopher Rudolf von Jhering, Liu on the French thinker Jean-Jacques Rousseau – and part of my goal here is to compare the roles that foreign and developing Chinese concepts of rights play in their writings. While I do not believe that Liang and Liu were simply continuing neo-Confucianism, I will argue that the interest that they and others had in rights makes much more sense when we see it in the context of neo-Confucian concerns.

Chapter 7 is based on essays written in the three decades after those discussed in the previous chapter, and presents a series of perspectives on the dynamism of Chinese rights discourse. In order to illustrate one way in which Chinese and Western rights discourses can converge, I also consider in this chapter the views of the American philosopher John Dewey, whose ideas resonated well with those of many Chinese when Dewey traveled to China in 1919. The chapter concludes with a discussion of the range of Marxist perspectives on rights, both in abstract theory and on the ground in China.

My main goal in Chapter 8 is to discuss and then engage with the rights theories that have been developed in China in the past decade. This entails a significant detour into contemporary European and American rights theory, without which any effort at substantial engagement on my part – grounded, as I am, in contemporary European and American philosophy – would be shallow or disingenuous. The challenges I raise are not just for Chinese thinkers, though; I believe that there are genuine, weighty challenges to the ways that we think about rights implicit in the works of both contemporary Chinese theorists and their predecessors fifty years earlier. This chapter represents an early move in a dialogue that has the potential, I believe, to influence the thinking – and rights concepts – of people East and West.

I summarize my conclusions in Chapter 9. I have shown the existence in China of a distinctive discourse about rights: one with its own concepts, motivation, and trajectory. This is by no means to deny that Chinese rights discourse has been related in various ways to, and influenced at many different times by, the whole range of European and American rights discourses. I emphasize the dynamic, interactive, and internally contested nature of Chinese rights discourse, while at the same time noting the existence of recurring themes and value orientations. These continuities include a view of rights as means to valuable ends, rather than as ends in themselves; a tight relationship between rights and interests; a belief that legitimate interests can all be harmonized; and a simultaneous commitment to political and economic rights.

I therefore agree, at least to a significant degree, with Liu Huaqiu's assertion that China's rights discourse is conceptually distinctive. I am also sympathetic to part of his normative claim: We need to be careful of our grounds before demanding that others comply with our moralities. Any group that wants to deny that others can engage with their values, though, also needs an account of the basis for their denial, and I show that such reasons are difficult to produce. In the typical case –

including the present issue over human rights – there is more than enough on which to base a dialogue. I argue that there is a great deal we can say to one another, sometimes as one nation to another, but more often as members of one sub-group to another. The more lines of engagement that can be established, the more hope there is for reaching a broader consensus. This diversity of roles and interests within all nations party to these issues must be recognized and exploited. It makes sense that the engagement I undertake in Chapter 8 is with Chinese intellectuals and scholars, for I am an intellectual and a scholar. The framework within which I make these efforts toward dialogue, though, is much broader: It will require the efforts not simply of scholars, but also of women and men from many walks of life if it is to succeed in meeting the challenge that China poses to us, and that we pose to China.

2

Languages, Concepts, and Pluralism

WHAT EXACTLY DOES IT MEAN to say that speakers of one language have a different concept of rights than speakers of another? If their concepts are different, can they still communicate with one another? Is it even true that all speakers of a given language share the same concepts – especially of loaded terms like "rights"? To pursue the issues at the heart of this book, we need answers to these questions. First, we need a framework for talking about concepts that is precise enough to bear philosophical weight but not so technical as to be impenetrable to non-specialists. With that in hand, we can turn to the question of pluralism: that is, the claim that there is more than one legitimate morality. Doing justice to claims like those of Liu Huaqiu requires that we think carefully about what moral pluralism is, and about what its implications might be.

To do this, I proceed as follows. Section 2.1 aims to motivate the analytical framework within which I will discuss concepts, a framework that draws on the recent work of Robert Brandom. One of the chief goals of the section is to defend the idea that there are always conceptual differences between us, even if we speak the same language, but this need not stand in the way of successful communication. This is an uncommon view, but I will show that it overcomes a long-standing objection to conceptual pluralism and is thus uniquely well suited to my larger project in this work. Section 2.2 asks what it can mean, on this picture, for communication to fail, which leads to an account of the various degrees of conceptual distance that can separate speakers or languages from one another. In the final section, I apply these ideas specifically to moral pluralism. The understanding of pluralism that I develop emphasizes its contingency, flexibility, and openness to cross-cultural

26

engagement. Each of these factors will be exploited in the chapters to follow.

2.1.1 Language and Concept

Language is first of all something we do. We utter sentences and these sentences have consequences. I say "How are you?" and you respond "Fine." You say "Please pass the salt" and I pick up the salt shaker and hand it to you. I say "It's raining," you grumble "The weatherman's wrong again," and I chuckle. And so on. When I say that language is something *we* do, the "we" is important: languages are social practices engaged in by groups of people. Like all social practices, languages are governed by norms. Not every utterance counts as a good or acceptable instance of a given language. If you and I are speaking English and I say "Mail at the post office is," then while you probably will understand me, you will also recognize my having made an error. If the social situation is appropriate, you may correct me, saying "You mean 'The mail is at the post office,' right?" Of course there may have been a point to my saying what I did; perhaps I was making fun of the sentence structure of the German language, with which we both were struggling earlier that day. The joke's working, though, still depends on the sentence's not having proper English structure.

Language use is also open-ended. Very many English sentences have been uttered, to be sure, but there are many more perfectly good English sentences that have not yet been heard. This is so even if we leave the stock of English words fixed. The complete story of a language, therefore, must account for not just the words and sentences people in a given community have uttered, but also those that they could utter and still count as speaking (or writing) correctly. And things are more complicated still. It probably goes without saying that languages are not static: Words can be added or subtracted, meanings can expand, contract, or change altogether, new syntactic patterns become accepted while others are abandoned, and so on. The English spoken today is markedly different from the English of one hundred years ago, yet we still call both English, while there are other, older languages like Middle English to which we give separate names. We also make distinctions more fine-grained than these national languages, as various words can have different meanings depending on the particular community to which the speaker belongs. Sometimes whether or not something counts as correct usage is contested, based on whether or not one allows that a new language has been created.[1] In any event, it seems clear that distinguishing between languages is bound up with norms, power relations, and self-understandings.[2]

One of the most important tools we have to understand language and its attendant norms is the concept. Thinking about things in terms of concepts helps us to talk more clearly about what words and sentences in a given language mean, as well as to say what it is that sentences or words uttered by different speakers, or in different languages, share. Consider the English word "snow" and the French word "*neige.*" We all agree that the two words mean the same thing, but philosophers have noticed that meaning is a complex notion made up of several aspects, and have introduced vocabulary to express these different facets. We can say, for instance, that "snow" and "*neige*" both *refer* to the same *objects.* When I say "snow," or when a French speaker says "*neige,*" we are each speaking about the same thing. *Reference,* that is, is a relation that applies between words and objects. On the other hand, we can say that both words *express* the same *concept.* Other ways to put this would be to say that English and French speakers both conceptualize the same stuff (snow) in the same ways or that their sentences about snow have the same conceptual content.

Questions of reference and concept are not always so clear. Consider the following example, which will help us clarify what concepts are. Imagine a conversation between two students in Beijing; one, Ms. Wang, is a senior at Beijing University; the other, Mr. Smith, is an American studying for the year in the city. In the course of a discussion about politics, Wang says "*Ren ren dou you shengcun quan,*" and when Smith seems unsure of her meaning, offers "All people have a right to subsistence" as a translation of her Chinese sentence. Smith immediately denies this, asserting "People do not have a right to subsistence." Wang is mystified, wondering in English, "But isn't this absolutely central to what 'rights' are? Are we even talking about the same things?" She continues:

---

[1] One example of this is the controversy currently surrounding instruction in Ebonics: It is clear that part of what is at stake is the degree to which members of the African-American community, and others, want African-Americans to understand themselves as a distinct community.

[2] For a fascinating look at some of these dimensions of linguistic activity, see [Bourdieu 1974].

The right to subsistence means the right to the minimal benefits needed to live a decent life: things like food, clothing, and shelter. It's simply obvious that such benefits are central to having rights – to what "rights" mean. In Chinese, the second character making up the word "*quanli*," which we translate as "rights," is "*li*," which means "benefit." (The first, "*quan*," means "power.") Our rights simply are, in part, our legitimate benefits. And what could be more legitimate than the things needed for subsistence?

Mr. Smith answers her as follows:

I'm not sure how much stock I put in etymology. Lots of things go in briefcases other than legal briefs. I think we should look to current use to see what our words mean. Still, since – as you've explained it to me – "*quanli*" was explicitly coined as a neologism, perhaps its roots do have significance. In any event, the relation between "rights" and benefits is not something that I am comfortable settling just as a matter of definition. The word "rights" is related to earlier European traditions about "*ius*," which has connotations of power but not of benefit. Some philosophers think that rights must be beneficial to people, but others have argued that while rights are typically beneficial, the notion of a protected choice comes closer to covering the essence of rights.

My main reason for rejecting your idea of a "right to subsistence" is not that I reject any connection between "right" and benefits, but rather that I believe rights to be conceptually linked to duties that others hold, and so-called positive rights like your "right to subsistence" have no clear duty-holders to back them up. How can we be sure who has the duty to fulfill the right? And what about conflicts between this right and others, like the right to private property? Without a duty-holder, there can be no right. I feel that only negative rights – rights to freedom from interference, wherein each and every individual has a duty not to interfere – are genuine rights. The rest is all inflated rhetoric.

Ms. Wang's response to this opens up other areas of disagreement:

I agree that there are important relations between rights and duties, but as I understand it, the central issue is that in order to enjoy rights, one must also shoulder duties. Certainly in most cases, at least, there are also duty-holders in the sense you specify, but I don't understand your resistance to positive rights. Depending on the context, the duty-holders in such cases can be the state, the nation, or even all humanity. Do you deny that groups can have duties and rights?

I'm also concerned about your suggestion that rights to subsistence might conflict with other rights. I gather your idea is that in order to fulfill someone's right to subsistence, someone else's private property might have to be redistributed? I see that as no conflict at all: No one has a right to so much property that others are left without subsistence. Such benefits are simply not legitimate, and thus not rights at all. Rights, after all, aim at harmonizing people's interests.

We will leave the discussion here and reflect on what the two have said.

Ms. Wang and Mr. Smith are imaginary, but the words I have put into their mouths are not arbitrary. The ideas about the meaning of "*quanli*" and "rights" that they express have roots in many aspects of Chinese and American moral discourse, respectively.[3] This is not to say that either of these discourses is univocal, uncontested, or static. As I will discuss later, these moral discourses themselves contain differences over the meanings of words, contestations over which meanings are most appropriate, and the continuous dynamism associated with any live moral discourse. Our understanding of concepts and of pluralism will have to account for these complexities. The views I have attributed to Ms. Wang and Mr. Smith are selected from these internally complex discourses. The views are representative, in the sense that they are based on ideas or commitments prominent in the two respective communities, but they are not definitive of those two communities. It is not, after all, the purpose of this chapter to debate the meaning(s) of "rights," but to think through what the implications of multiple meanings could be.

2.1.2 Pushes toward Holism

Let us consider, then, the dialogue between Wang and Smith. There appear to be large areas of overlap and agreement. Despite Wang's puzzle over "rights," for the most part they seem to be having little trouble communicating: Their statements seem quite responsive to one another. Still, there are substantial disagreements about what rights are. Some of the questions raised by the dialogue are

---

[3] I draw here on a range of authors from both countries; see Chapter 8 for more detail.

[A] Is it part of the concept of rights that rights are benefits?

[B] Is it part of the concept of rights that these benefits are legitimate?

[C] Does the concept of rights make sense only alongside duties?

[D] If so, are they duties shouldered by the rights-holder, or duties held by others? Are these even the same sense of "duty"?

[E] Can rights conflict with one another? If not, is it part of the very concept of rights that they cannot, or is it a contingent fact about our world?

In order to answer these types of questions, we must get clear on what it means to be "part of the concept of rights." These questions aim at establishing whether Wang and Smith are using a common concept, but disagree about some of its characteristics, or are using different concepts, in which case we may decide that "rights" is an inadequate translation for "*quanli*" – even if it does better than any other English word.

Before going further, it would be well to consider an objection that may arise at this point: Isn't it obvious that they are talking about the same thing, but have political differences? Why should we be tempted to think that their differences are caused by their respective languages when we all know how deeply politics and self-interests inform debates such as this one (and here, no doubt, the objector has in mind actual exchanges between representatives of the Chinese and U.S. governments)? In response, let me emphasize that I am not advocating linguistic determinism – the view that our various commitments are determined by our language. We use language in pursuit of various goals, and language is bound up with other things we do, the things that others do, and our material world in countless ways. No one of these "determines" the others; all influence one another. The language we use turns out to be a particularly good lens through which to view our commitments, but it cannot be understood on its own. There are many kinds of evidence we can draw on in interpretation: actions, structures of power, comparative living standards, and so on. We do not have to simply take people at their word. Neither should we dismiss everything that people say, though, out of an assumption that we already understand the way the world works. I rely primarily on language, but strive to remain cognizant of the changing contexts that influence what we mean by what we say.

That said, I am not going to pay much attention to the contexts of Wang and Smith, because they are imaginary. My goal at the moment is not to answer the questions raised above, but to think about what is at stake in answering these types of questions. A first approximation of an answer is that when one makes explicit what is, and what is not, part of one's concepts, one is articulating norms for a community to which one belongs. That is, when Wang suggests that part of the concept of rights is that rights are benefits, she is saying that part of being a member of her community (which community she has in mind – Beijing University, China, the whole world, etc. – need not detain us for the moment) is to take it as given that rights include "legitimate benefits." If this were not part of the concept, that would mean that community members could disagree about that particular aspect without ceasing to be community members.

We are rarely very explicit about these matters. It is also important to note that individuals' roles in determining such things are more complicated than I have so far made it seem: Words are not the only things that influence community membership, and people who are by other standards members of the same community may come to disagree, implicitly or explicitly, about how they should use their words. I will deal with such complexities below. Now let us return to Wang and Smith, and to the question of what they mean.

For Wang to decide whether Smith shares her concept of rights, she must strive to answer the kinds of questions listed above, and perhaps many more. In order to be sure what Smith's words "People do not have a right to subsistence" mean – what concepts his words express – she has to consider their relation to large numbers of other words. What other sentences does he seem to hold true? What inferences involving rights does he endorse? It can seem that only if she has an interpretation that works for a substantial chunk of his vocabulary can she confidently interpret any of it.

This is the insight that has pushed many philosophers to conclude that conceptual meaning is holistic: it depends on a web of connections among many concepts. This is not yet to have said with any clarity or precision what holism is, but it may be enough to begin to see one of the main problems to which holist theories of meaning give rise. Suppose that the meanings of concepts are mutually determined by the relations they bear to one another, so that what I mean by "rights" depends on what I mean by "duty," by "interest," by "harmony," and so on. What "duty" means, in turn, depends on its own web of related concepts; it is easy to see that one doesn't have to go through very many steps before some superficially quite unrelated ideas will turn out to be implicated in one another's meanings. This suggests, in turn, that even small differences in meaning will quickly ramify throughout an individual's web of concepts. If I understand "harmony" differently from you, holism would seem to suggest that my concepts of rights, and thus of interest, and so on, will all differ from yours.

The reason that philosophers have seen this to be problematic is that most believe that successful communication involves coming to share something with another. I attempt to communicate my thought that snow is white to you by saying "Snow is white," and I succeed if you come to understand that I believe that snow is white.[4] However, given the plausible hypothesis that we all differ, at least slightly, from one another in at least some concepts, then if we adopt holism, it would seem that you can never come to understand my meaning. You will always understand what I say in terms at least slightly different from my own. "Snow" or "white" will mean something different to you than to me, so you will fail to come to share the meaning I intended. Communication is impossible.

One way that philosophers have tried to rescue holism is to say that communication is really about coming to share similar, rather than identical, meanings and beliefs. A problem with this response is the difficulty of saying with any precision what counts as having "similar" beliefs [Fodor & Lepore 1992, pp. 17f.]. My strategy will instead be to rely on a different understanding of what communication is about. To see how this works, we will first have to examine more closely what conceptual content itself is, and how it emerges in linguistic practice.

2.1.3 A Shared Practice

Let's begin with the connection between conceptual meaning and commitment. Suppose I tell you that "The earth is flat." I have thereby expressed a whole range of commitments. I have committed myself to the earth's being flat, to at least some planets being flat, to the earth's not being spherical, and so on. I might not recognize all of the things to which I've committed myself; if I knew nothing of fifteenth-century history, for instance, I might not know that I was now committed to "Columbus was wrong." We can tell that I have expressed these commitments, though, and also see how crucial they are to linguistic practice, if we consider the following scenario. You challenge me, saying, "Oh, you think some planets are flat?" I respond "No, but the earth is flat." Puzzled, you respond "Isn't the earth a planet?" "Sure it is," say I. Were

---

[4] For an influential effort to spell out this idea more carefully, see [Grice 1989].

the conversation to continue on these lines – my seeming to accept commitments but to disavow many of their entailments – you'd probably give up trying to talk with me. I am not playing by the rules.

This is not to say that there is one inflexible set of rules defining what words mean. Meanings change over time, and the commitments that one person or group expresses with a given sentence may not entirely overlap with those of another. Still, unless we express a fairly stable set of commitments, our ability to make sense to one another – to communicate – will disappear. (If you are not convinced of this, look back at the previous paragraph and consider how many commitments my statements were still honoring!) In this light, we can see concepts as relatively stable patterns of commitments that are appropriately held by speakers across a given community.[5]

This centrality of commitment to linguistic practice is part of what has led Robert Brandom, a leading contemporary philosopher, to characterize conceptual content in terms of inferential structure. He asks what the difference is between a parrot's being trained to make the noise "red" when shown a red object, on the one hand, and a person's reporting that an object is "red," on the other. Brandom writes that "The parrot does not treat 'That's red' as incompatible with 'That's green,' nor as following from 'That's scarlet' and entailing 'That's colored.' Insofar as the repeatable response is not, for the parrot, caught up in practical proprieties of inference and justification, . . . it is not a conceptual or cognitive matter at all. . . . Concepts are essentially inferentially articulated" [Brandom 1994, p. 89]. The parrot's "That's red" does not express any kind of commitment; a person's report of "That's red," by contrast, commits him or her to the propriety of concluding, among other things, "That's colored."

It should be clear that this theory immediately commits one to holism about meaning, as sketched above. If conceptual content is determined by inferential structure, then what I mean by "That's red" depends on what I mean by "That's colored," and so on. Brandom's appealing account of conceptual content, that is, leads us headlong into difficulties about communication. Brandom recognizes that his account runs into problems, so long as communication is thought to be about coming to share common meanings, and so he proposes that "the paradigm of com-

---

[5] For a related view, see Bjørn Ramberg's discussion of viscous patterns of practice [Ramberg 1989, p. 112].

munication as joint possession of some common thing [be] relinquished in favor of – or modified in the direction of – a paradigm of communication as a kind of cooperation in practice" [Brandom 1994, p. 485]. One of the central themes of Brandom's understanding of language is emphasizing its embeddedness in linguistic practice. Communication is possible because we are all able to engage in the shared practice of interpreting one another and ourselves.[6]

How does this work? Brandom conceptualizes linguistic practice as a scorekeeping activity: We keep track of which commitments each participant in a conversation, including ourselves, has taken on.[7] Some of these attributions of commitment are prompted by explicit performances, whether linguistic (I say "The sun is shining") or practical (I pick up a Frisbee and step toward the door). Others depend on implicit inferential relations, for instance when I attribute to you the commitment that "It is not cloudy" after you've announced that the sun is shining. Sometimes, when things are particularly complicated or vexed, we even make our scorekeeping explicit. For the most part, scorekeeping takes place informally or implicitly, though we are ready to make it explicit should confusion arise.

Already lurking in Brandom's claim that inferential significance is relative to an individual's whole set of commitments is the idea that linguistic scorekeeping will be perspectival. If the same sentence can mean different things to you and me, it only makes sense that the commitments I attribute based on that sentence's utterance will differ from those you attribute. For each participant in communicative practice, therefore, linguistic scorekeepers will have to keep "two sets of books" [Brandom 1994, p. 488]. In the simple case where only two people – Ms. A and Mr. B – are involved, that is, A must do her best to keep track of what commitments she believes follow from what B says and does, as well as what commitments B takes to follow from what he has said and done. And this is only the beginning: A also needs to keep score on her own commitments, both from her own and from B's perspectives, and of course all this applies to B as well.

---

[6] In a famous paper, Donald Davidson gestures toward a similar solution, though without yet taking the crucial step of abandoning the idea that communication involves coming to share something. See [Davidson 1986, esp. p. 445].

[7] This is a simplification: We attribute not just commitments, but also entitlements. Brandom also details the different ways in which these two types of normative status can be inherited, as well as explaining the role of discursive authority and responsibility in these entitlements. See [1994, pp. 168–70].

To make this more concrete, let us revisit Ms. Wang and Mr. Smith. Suppose that one December day, Smith says to Wang "Out on the street this morning I passed by a beggar. The poor fellow didn't have a coat and really seemed to be suffering." How does Wang interpret this? In her book for Smith, she marks down a new score, namely that Smith is committed to having seen a beggar who was suffering, and to the inferential consequences that follow from that and whatever other relevant commitments Smith has. Most of these inferential consequences also get noted down in the second book that Wang keeps on Smith, in which Wang records what actually (from her perspective) follows from Smith's explicit commitments. In both of these books, for instance, she records the further commitment that Smith left his dorm room that morning, since (1) she presumes Smith would take this to follow from his being out on the street, and (2) she similarly takes it to follow from his statement. So long as she has no reason to suspect that Smith is deceiving her, in fact, she may well inherit both of these commitments (that there was a beggar on the street, and that Smith went out) from Smith.

So far, the score Wang records in each book is the same. As I mentioned above, though, the books can diverge. For instance, what if Wang knew that students pretending to be beggars frequent the streets outside of Smith's dorm. In this case, she'll score her second book on Smith – the one that keeps track of what actually follows – differently from the first, perhaps recording only the commitment to having passed a person in rags asking for money. If she were to put the discrepancy between the two books into words, she might say "Smith believes he saw a beggar, but I know better."

2.1.4 Objectivity

This example points to a crucial issue we must face, namely the status of objectivity in these various attributions. I have made Wang out to know something that Smith did not, namely that fake beggars frequent his environs. But couldn't it still have been a beggar? Isn't the only difference between the two books the perspective of the scorekeeper? Nothing about the second book magically renders it "correct," capturing the "actual" facts of the matter, right?

True enough, but the difference in perspective turns out to be critical, undergirding the very idea of objective truth. From your perspective or my perspective, there is nothing special about Wang's perspective, even if it turns out that she is right, at least about the presence of a beggar that morning. From Wang's perspective, though, her perspective is indeed special, for it is from her perspective that she thinks of how things actually are, as opposed to how others (or even herself) merely believe them to be. Or rather, it is in the context of comparing her perspective with that of another, as inevitably occurs in communication, that the difference between how someone takes things to be, and how they objectively are, first emerges.[8] The difference between Wang and Smith over the presence of beggars is not merely subjective; Wang's scorebooks do not simply record that "he's committed to one thing and I'm committed to another." As Wang sees it, Smith's inference from person in rags to beggar is wrong, not just different. Even if Wang turns out to be wrong about the beggar, the difference between something's being held true, on one hand, and in fact being true, on the other, survives unscathed.

If objectivity emerges in the way Brandom claims, then it is essentially social, or as Brandom puts it, "Objectivity appears as a feature of the structure of discursive intersubjectivity" [Brandom 1994, p. 599]. It is only in the context of linguistic interrelations with one another that talk of objective truth becomes intelligible. Brandom stresses, though, that

> traditionally intersubjectivity has been understood in the *I–we* way, which focuses on the contrast between the commitments of *one* individual and the commitments of the *community* (collectively), or those shared by *all* individuals (distributively). In the ... account offered here, by contrast, intersubjectivity is understood in a perspectival *I–thou* fashion, which focuses on the relation between commitments *undertaken* by a scorekeeper interpreting others and the commitments *attributed* by that scorekeeper to those others. [1994, p. 599]

The shared practice of discursive scorekeeping thus makes possible both communication and objectivity, though it does not guarantee that the former will be successful nor the latter ever be secured. The fact that each of us regularly takes our commitments to be rightly held, rather than just held, gives rise to the idea of objectivity. And, says Brandom, there is nothing more to objectivity than this type of "perspectival form":

---

[8] I agree with Brandom's suggestion that his account of objectivity provides a detailed way of making sense of one of Davidson's most important claims, namely that "the concepts of objective truth and error necessarily emerge in the context of interpretation" [Davidson 1984b (1975), pp. 169–70]. See [Brandom 1994, p. 599].

"What is shared by all discursive perspectives is *that* there is a difference between what is objectively correct in the way of concept application and what is merely taken to be so, not *what* it is – the structure, not the content" [ibid., p. 600].

Brandom's account of objectivity has two important corollaries which will be exploited in the balance of this book. First, notice that for all Brandom has said, practical commitments (like ethical or political norms) are as amenable to objectivity as any other commitments. This will certainly require further discussion, but on its face suggests that ethical and political disputes – even those between different countries or cultures – might have "objective" solutions. This need not mean that one morality will turn out to be the objectively best for all peoples in all times; the mere fact that we treat scientific concepts as objective does not mean that we are confident that we have at last discovered eternal truths about nature. As I discuss in more detail later, treating something objectively is perfectly compatible with subsequently discovering that we were wrong – or even that in certain circumstances, some things are better for some people than for others.

Second, since Brandom privileges no particular perspective on the "objectively correct," his account is neutral between competing conceptions of how we ought to best discover the way things are. This means both that parties to a dispute may need to articulate and defend their epistemological theories, and that no culture's epistemological norms will enter a dispute with an advantage. Brandom's approach meshes well with the approach I take when I turn, in the next chapter, to examining what we ought to do when faced with pluralism. The upshot is that Brandom's account contains elements traditionally associated with both relativist and absolutist theories, and thus can lay the groundwork for a perspective occupying the middle ground between these two unpromising extremes.

If the previous several paragraphs have been successful, then I will have convinced my readers that Brandom's account of communicative practice (1) is a plausible theoretical reconstruction of what always goes on during communication, albeit usually in the background, and (2) succeeds in resolving the problem that communication had seemed to pose for holist accounts of meaning. It is important to see, though, that this account does not magically guarantee that communication will always succeed. It is true that we are all, often without recognizing it, adept interpreters who regularly handle potential obstacles – new words, nicknames, malapropisms – to successful communicative practice without slipping.[9] Still, communication can break down, in contexts both pedestrian and bizarre. In the next section, I will explore the nature and ramifications of communicative failures, because such breakdowns will help us to understand the range of cases in which one's concepts can be different from those of another.

2.2 CONCEPTUAL DISTANCES

2.2.1 Breakdowns in Communication

On the old, communication-is-coming-to-share-something view, it was easy to say what a failure to communicate was: We failed to share the crucial something. If the something was taken to be conceptual content, for instance, then communication succeeded whenever the conceptual content I understood you to be asserting exactly matched the content you in fact intended to assert, and failed otherwise. For this view to get off the ground, content must be construed non-holistically, and I find the many attempts to do so unpromising. But perhaps it can yet be made to work. I bring up these theories not because I think they are correct, but rather to illustrate that their way of characterizing communicative failure is not open to Brandom. On his account, after all, we always fail to share conceptual contents, at least to some degree. So it would seem that failure – and for that matter, success – in communication must be spelled out differently.

Let us return to the conversation between Wang and Smith. When Smith denied that people had subsistence rights, Wang realized she was unsure how to interpret his sentence; in the terms developed earlier, she was unsure how to score his sentence. Part of this realization included the possibility that she may have partially misunderstood earlier exchanges with him involving "rights," or "subsistence," or even "people." Without further conversation, she could not be sure whether (1) he had said something false, but they were having no problems communicating, or (2) communication, at least in that instance and perhaps

---

[9] See [Davidson 1986]. While Davidson's picture accords well with Brandom's in many respects, it should be clear that Brandom would reject Davidson's contention that successful communication occurs when two people come to share "passing theories." See [Davidson 1986, pp. 442–3].

even in prior instances, had broken down. We imagined that she began to explain her confusion, but that as they tried to sort things out, their situation got ever more puzzling, which might well have led her to worry that she had in fact been misunderstanding him on a whole range of related subjects (like duties, interests, and harmony). Let us now imagine that they dropped the conversation there, at least for the time being. Perhaps it was time for dinner.

As this example suggests, failures of communication are rarely all-or-nothing affairs. They can vary in both obviousness and degree of failure. The most extreme cases are characterized by the blank stare: We've been talking along happily when you utter something that I can make no sense of at all. In such cases it is both completely obvious that communication has broken down and that the breakdown is complete, since I have no way to clarify what you meant other than to ask you to say it in a different way. The "rights" case is less extreme, though as our two conversants continued to talk it became increasingly obvious that there was a problem – and perhaps less clear how to continue. There are at least two stages of failure: first, the initial recognition or initial worry, and second, any subsequent exploration or attempt to overcome the failure. Whether the first phase counts as "recognition" or "worry" depends largely on the obviousness of failure, while the nature of the second stage will depend, in part, on the degree of failure.

In this light, let us look at the issue driving this section: How can Brandom explain communicative failure? He cannot avail himself of the abstract failure-to-share-content criterion, but our consideration of the "rights" case shows that there are other, more practical criteria that suggest themselves. Are we simply at a loss when it comes to trying to "score" our interlocutor's utterance? Do we have no idea how to begin unraveling the mystery? These both correspond to the blank stare case. Most situations will of course be less extreme, with cases of minor puzzlement about side issues – often put aside and soon forgotten – representing the opposite end of the spectrum. In keeping with Brandom's overall orientation, criteria of success and failure in communication turn out to be practical.

What we make of failures – that is, the interrelated issues of making sense of the failure and deciding what to do about it – will depend in part on normative matters. The way we score another's utterances will depend on what commitments we take her to hold, and this will depend to a significant degree on the community to which we take her to belong. Part of belonging to a community is sharing many commitments with others in the community. This is of course a complicated matter; we typically belong to multiple, overlapping communities, as I will discuss in subsequent chapters. Given the detail in which I will treat these issues later, I will not dwell on them at length here. In the present context, it suffices to note that the recognition of a failure of communication could be followed by the realization that our interlocutor is in a sense a different person than we had thought. She may actually not have certain commitments that we had been confidently attributing to her, and we may understand this as her not belonging, after all, to some particular community ("liberals" or "Americans" or whatever). On the other hand, after working out where our conversation had gone awry, we may see her as speaking differently from others in her community, but with good reason – we may agree with her that she's got a better sense of the underlying motivation or norms of the community in question than does the mainstream. However we end up understanding the situation, I think it should be clear that our commitments and our understandings of what different communities demand of their members will weigh heavily in our responses to breakdowns of communication.

2.2.2 *Words Matter*

We now understand something of what could count, in Brandom's eyes, as communicative failure. Let us turn to the question of why such failures occur at all. Languages are often very malleable. History demonstrates this, and philosophy gives us no reason to doubt that it will continue. An important theme of this book, though, will be the degree to which languages are, and often remain, different from one another. The words our language contains at a particular point in time can matter.

One way to see how words matter is to reflect on the nature of the "commitments" that make up the various "scores" involved in linguistic practice. At one point Brandom notes that "almost everyone is committed and entitled to such claims as that $2 + 2 = 4$, that red is a color, and that there have been black dogs" [Brandom 1994, p. 185]. That is, we as interpreters will invariably attribute such commitments and entitlements to almost anyone. Notice that we use our language, our words, to make these attributions. Indeed, how could it be otherwise? Unless Brandom were to posit some pre-linguistic scorekeeping facility, which would run counter to his most fundamental themes, scorekeeping has to take place in whatever language(s) we have available.

Even when we both speak the same language, this is periodically relevant: Imagine yourself on an art gallery tour being told that "In the next room we'll see a series of paintings with fuliginous backgrounds." Without much context, you may well be at a loss to score that utterance. Communication will have (momentarily) broken down, though the sentence may have still "communicated" things to you in a broader sense – confirming, perhaps, that this guide is pretentious and not particularly interested in communicating well with his audience. Once you reach the next room, of course, you may well be able to score the utterance, adding a new word to your vocabulary in the process.

When dealing with an interlocutor (or text) using a different language, especially one emerging from a significantly different cultural context, vocabulary issues can be even more salient. One of the issues in the "rights" case, recall, was that Wang became unsure whether her words were adequate to score Smith's utterance – in particular, whether "*quanli*" adequately corresponded to "rights." There is a range of senses, from simple to increasingly radical, in which this could be true. The simplest case is analogous to what happened with "fuliginous": I have other words that can capture the same meaning – can play the same inferential role – but just did not know which ones to use.

More radical cases arise when one cannot, or cannot easily, match one's interlocutor's words with one or more of one's own words, even given plenty of time to investigate. Students of languages and cultures distant from their own regularly run into terms in the language under study that resist easy translation. Let me begin with cases in which the foreigners use some object, or ascribe some property, or perform some action that has no correlate in our practices. I'll call this a missing-word case. Imagine yourself a missionary in seventeenth-century China, wondering what the objects on a friendly Confucian scholar's desk are. The scholar utters "*Zhe shi yige yantai*" while pointing at the round stone on which he mixes dry ink with water when preparing to write calligraphy. You are fairly sure that "*zhe shi yige...*" correlates with our demonstrative "this is a ..."; the question is, What to do about "*yantai*"? I am imagining that "inkstone" is not, at this point in time, part of our language, whether or not that corresponds to the actual histories of English and of Western writing technology.

The obvious step at this point is to add a new word to our language. Make up a word like "inkstone," letting it denote just what the Chinese refer to by "*yantai*," and the problem would seem to be solved.[10] Donald Davidson has written that "even when the metalanguage is different from the object language, the theory exerts no pressure for improvement, clarification, or analysis of individual words, except when, by accident of vocabulary, straightforward translation fails" [Davidson 1984a (1967), p. 33]. The presumed fact that English lacked the word "inkstone" is no mere accident, of course; English had no word for it because English speakers had no need for the concept, given that they had never employed inkstones. Adding the word to our language now that we have encountered inkstones, though, seems perfectly straightforward.

One of the features of simple missing-word problems is their isolated nature. There is relatively little spillover into other concepts, often because of basic similarities between the foreigner's practices and our own. This is not to suggest that *yantai* is isolated from other concepts, but rather that the problem *yantai* presents is isolated. There are certainly differences between Chinese calligraphic practice and contemporary American calligraphic practices, but with a few minor adjustments (like the introduction of "inkstone"), the latter's vocabulary can readily be used to score utterances concerned with the former.

Brandom has pointed out that sometimes even what looks like the addition of a single word can be problematic. The following example will help to make the point. Brandom writes that "When the prosecutor at Oscar Wilde's trial asked him to say under oath whether a particular passage in one of his works did or did not constitute blasphemy, Wilde replied 'Blasphemy is not one of my words'" [Brandom 1994, p. 126]. Wilde recognized, that is, that using the word "blasphemy" brought with it certain commitments that he rejected, even if he were to deny that a particular passage was blasphemous. Brandom labels the process of reflecting on and making explicit the commitments entailed by our words "expressive rationality." As Brandom puts it (rather grandly):

> In Reason's fight against thought debased by prejudice and propaganda, the first rule is that material inferential commitments that are potentially controversial should be made explicit as claims, exposing them both as vulnerable to reasoned challenge and as in need of reasoned defense. [1994, p. 126]

---

[10] In some cases one might introduce a phrase to correspond to the "missing object," depending in large part on accepted practice in one's (meta-) language.

My project in this book can be seen as in part the application of expressive rationality to different communities' rights discourses.

"Inkstone" is unlikely to raise anyone's hackles, in part because of the ways it ties to commitments and practices that we already endorse. It is when problems are less isolated that the most radical conceptual differences occur. This is perhaps most likely when dealing with a vocabulary of inter-defined theoretical terms, such as that associated with scientific, ethical, or political practices. It has thus been primarily in studies of these types of practices that theorists have spoken of the most extreme kind of conceptual difference, incommensurability. In her pioneering *Patterns of Culture*, for instance, Ruth Benedict wrote that different cultures travel along "different roads in pursuit of different ends, and these ends and these means in one society cannot be judged in terms of those of another society, because they are incommensurable" [Benedict 1934, p. 223]. Thomas Kuhn and others have similarly argued that scientific practices and their attendant vocabularies can be mutually incommensurable [Kuhn 1970, 1983].

Incommensurability is a tricky, often problematic, notion. I see it as a limiting case of conceptual differences, applicable (if at all) when divergences of practice and vocabulary are so pervasive that the task of enriching one's language, and so being able to score an interlocutor's utterances, seems hopeless. As Kuhn has put it, the question is no longer of enriching one's language, but of learning the other's language – and perhaps then teaching that language to still others [Kuhn 1983]. Even this understanding of incommensurability, though, risks treating language as overly static. "Incommensurable" sounds like a relation that stands for all time: If language A is incommensurable with language B, then sentences of the one can *never* be correctly translated into the other. Given how much languages can change over time, this is a very strong claim which is never adequately defended. While I believe that there can be a variety of reasons why people's linguistic practices can resist change, it nonetheless seems preferable to say that languages are "incommensu-*rate*" rather than "incommensur*able*."[11]

Interesting, real-world cases where there is the potential for communication to fail tend to fall in between the extremes represented by missing words and incommensurate languages. In the remaining chapters of this book I will rely on Brandom's conception of language to

---

[11] For more discussion, see [Angle 1994].

understand the changing relations between Chinese and Western rights discourses, and I will exploit his notion of expressive rationality as I seek a method of constructive, legitimate engagement across cultural and conceptual differences. One important step in that direction will be to better understand how conceptual differences can give rise to moral pluralism, to which I now turn.

2.3 PLURALISM

If speakers of different moral languages systematically use concepts that differ significantly from one another, then they are liable to talk past one another. This is the simple idea behind the understanding of pluralism that I will endorse. The spectrum of conceptual differences that we have just examined opens up the possibility of moral pluralism. Consider the initial dialogue between Wang and Smith. Depending on how the questions that dialogue raised are answered, Wang and Smith may come to see that they are using a common concept, but disagree about certain of its characteristics, or they may decide that their concepts are actually different, and that "rights" is an inadequate translation for "*quanli*."

I need to emphasize how important this kind of decision can be. If the two are disagreeing about a common concept, then one of them is mistaken. It would be like you and I visiting an art museum, and after taking a tour, disagreeing about whether, for a painting to count as fuliginous, it had to have predominantly gray hues. Neither of us had ever heard the word before the tour guide used it, and we each came to a different understanding, each taking on and attributing different commitments to one another and the tour guide. Neither of us intends to create a new word, of course; we are seeking to grasp a concept that is new to us but familiar to art museum tour guides. There is no temptation in a case like this to conclude that we are using different concepts; if we want to resolve the dispute, we can simply swallow our pride and ask the tour guide who is correct.

In the case of "fuliginous," it seems clear that there is a single concept because there is a single community using it: Their practices embody the norms which determine what commitments can appropriately be attributed when someone uses the word. In an opposite kind of case, it is equally clear that two different (though perhaps overlapping) communities are involved. Consider how silly it would be, for instance, for two people to argue about whether a "foul ball" (in baseball) had to be disgusting, as in "foul odor." The two words may have had a common origin, but they have come to be mere homonyms, expressing two very different concepts, each appropriate to its own context.

Our question is, Where does Ms. Wang's and Mr. Smith's dispute lie on the spectrum between these two extremes? I say that it is a spectrum, and not simply two options, in part because of the dynamic character of linguistic practice. All of our practices change over time, thanks to both conscious interventions and less conscious evolutions. As the previous paragraphs have implied, one of the decisive factors in these changes will be changes in the communities of which we see ourselves as members. Part of being a baseball player or a baseball fan is coming to use "foul" in a new way, alongside the old way. In some cases, becoming a member of a different group might put pressure on one to give up one's old way of speaking. One of my friends in college had grown up in a small, homogeneous community near the Rocky Mountains. It wasn't long after becoming a member of the diverse student body at an east-coast university that he realized certain words he used, often in jokes, were making others uncomfortable, and he was led to reflect on the inferential connections that others, at least, drew from his utterances. He very likely was reflecting at the same time on the inferential proprieties to which his concepts were committing him. He soon stopped using the words, no longer willing to countenance their implications. As we saw earlier, Brandom calls this expressive rationality. It is at least part of the process that Wang and Smith may be prompted to undergo as a result of their encounter. As a result of complexities like this, assessing the dispute between Wang and Smith will require more than just answers to the questions I posed earlier. Determining whether they disagree about a shared concept, or are using two different concepts, is in significant part a practical question about with which communities they identify, and thus to which norms they are subject.

At one end of the spectrum, we might imagine two communities with moralities that are undeniably different and expressed in different languages, but which speakers of each language can readily understand and translate into their own language. Since a long-lived language like English or Chinese has been used over the centuries to express a variety of moralities, it is perhaps unsurprising that speakers of such languages often can express in their own language the claims made by adherents of quite different moralities. Although "rights" may be the dominant idiom of Western morality at the end of the millennium, we still find in our vocabularies resources with which to discuss ideals of virtue, charity, chivalry, honor, and many others.[12] If we were to encounter a community speaking the language and committed to the ideals of Victorian England, we could easily understand them, even as we objected (perhaps) to their paternalism.

At the other extreme are cases in which moral languages are so different that some philosophers have labeled them "incommensurable." Originally, "incommensurable" meant that two distances could not be measured on a single scale. Under the influence of philosophers like Kuhn and MacIntyre, its application has been extended to words of one language being inexpressible in another's terms. While I think there is considerable value to the arguments that have been made in the name of incommensurability, I have found such discussions to suffer from a number of important failings. First, as explained earlier, most accounts of incommensurability treat language as overly static; it is preferable to say that languages are "incommensurate" rather than "incommensurable." A second problem with incommensurability is that it is too blunt an instrument. Arguments for it tend to be all-or-nothing: Either two languages are incommensurate, or they are not. This is unsatisfactory both because it gives one insufficient room to analyze the whole range of conceptual differences that can exist between languages, and because it introduces an artificial precision into what is ultimately a messy, practical question. The practical nature of incommensurability is a third issue that is often missed, though Mario Biagioli, at least, has paid it considerable attention. Biagioli argues that Galileo and his Scholastic rivals purposely kept their claims incommensurable from one another in order to preserve their socio-professional communities [Biagioli 1990]. Whether or not this case is best understood in terms of full-blown incommensurate languages, it nicely illustrates the ways in which the commitments of one's community can help to shape the words one uses.

As far as I am concerned, incommensurateness is simply the limiting case of conceptual distance. If communication breaks down between two people in the way that I sketched earlier, and resists sustained efforts to reestablish it, then we may suspect that the people's languages are incommensurate with one another. Perhaps this failure of communication is confinable to certain fields of discourse and to certain fragments of the respective languages; it may be, for instance, that we are able to communicate about baking but not about morality. Radical failures of

---

[12] See [Stout 1988] for a helpful discussion of this idea.

communication are unlikely to be too local, though, since when the problem is confined to a few words, a bit of linguistic enrichment will more often than not solve the problem, as we saw earlier in the missing-word case.

Locating people and their communities on the spectrum of conceptual differences is not a simple matter, and I feel it serves no purpose to artificially place Smith and Wang somewhere on the continuum. They are, after all, merely a thought experiment, however much they are derived from things people have actually said. I will draw on the tools and ideas of this section in my subsequent discussions of whether or not the moralities containing different communities' rights concepts are plural, as Liu Huaqiu claims.

3

The Consequences of Pluralism

THE LESSON OF THE LAST CHAPTER has been that if there is moral pluralism in our world, it is there because the concepts with which different groups make moral judgments are different from one another – perhaps radically so, perhaps in more mundane ways. This is not to say that our languages determine what we think; rather, it is our practices and the commitments they entail that shape our languages. As our commitments change, so too can the meanings of our words, or even the words we use themselves. One of the goals of this chapter is to think about the ways in which these changes can occur as we interact with one another.

Chapter 2 was motivated in large part by Liu Huaqiu's claim that the Chinese concept of rights differed from corresponding Western concepts. In order to know what to make of this claim, we needed to understand better what it means for concepts to differ from one another. We came to see concepts as emerging from relatively stable agreements in a community's norms, rather than as single, unchanging things that people had to share for communication to succeed. Concepts are more messy and complicated than Liu's formulation envisioned.

This chapter is motivated by the second of Liu's claims – that since the Chinese have a concept of rights different from those of their persistent critics, they should not be held accountable to these concepts different from their own. We can generalize his idea: There is a plurality of sets of moral concepts, and one is bound only by those sets that are like one's own. This second claim takes pluralism for granted, and derives from it an important practical conclusion. For the purposes of this chapter, I will grant the claim's premise and consider whether Liu's conclusion follows. We will see that just as in the previous chapter, things are more messy and complicated – and more interesting – than Liu imagines.

49

To say this is not yet to say that moral pluralism currently exists in our world, and in particular I have not yet argued that the moralities of China and the United States are actually plural. If what I have said above is correct, the actual existence of moral pluralism is not something that can be established through *a priori* argument. It must be argued case by case based on concrete situations. We also need to recognize that the existence of pluralism in a particular case is itself a normative question: Groups A and B may disagree on whether they should be understood as part of a single community subject to a single set of norms, or as two separate communities each with its own morality. I will argue in subsequent chapters that at various stages in their development, there have existed significant conceptual distances between Chinese and Western moralities, and this despite the degrees to which adherents of the different moralities come to engage with one another. In my concluding chapters I will suggest that some important differences remain, though diversity and contestation internal to both Chinese and Western communities make sweeping conclusions problematic. A central goal of the present chapter is to show in an abstract way how substantial, constructive engagement is possible even if differences between moralities persist; in the book's last two chapters, I will look at concrete ways in which such engagement can be undertaken.

What, then, are the consequences of pluralism? The short answer is, It depends. It depends on the structure and content of our values, and on theirs; on what costs we pay for interfering with them, and for not interfering; and on the relations of power between us and them, among many other things. It also depends on what we take the implications of pluralism to be for our commitment to our own values. Does moral pluralism mean that our own morality loses its grip on us? I will argue that it should not, though reflecting on pluralism may cause that grip to relax ever so slightly. After this, I will turn to the various strategies that we can adopt toward others with different moralities, which range from static attitudes like ignoring, repressing, or accommodating, to various kinds of more dynamic engagement. In fact, we can often do more than one of these things simultaneously. In the chapter's final section, I will look at the possibilities for, and implications of, divided communities (both ours and theirs) and multiple strategies.

3.1 OUR OWN VALUES

Is skepticism, subjectivism, or even nihilism a sensible response to pluralism? I believe not. They are overreactions to pluralism, reactions based on the unrealistic expectation that there should be a single set of concepts to which all people should adhere. I will argue that we can retain commitment to our own values through reliance on local justifications similar to those advocated by the well-known pragmatist philosopher Richard Rorty. In fact, we can do better than Rorty recognizes, since a certain kind of general argument is available to defend our values. I conclude this section by urging that we not fall prey to hubris and expect too much from our justifications. We must not rely too much on our common "human natures," for in that direction lies either closing our eyes to pluralism or embracing skepticism.

I begin with the following suggestion from Richard Rorty:

> Deweyan pragmatists urge us to think of ourselves as part of a pageant of historical progress which will gradually encompass all of the human race, and are willing to argue that the vocabulary which 20th century Western social democrats use is the best vocabulary the race has come up with so far (by, e.g., arguing that the vocabulary of the Cashinahua cannot be combined with modern technology, and that abandoning that technology is too high a price to pay for the benefits the Cashinahuas enjoy). . . . Pragmatists hope, but have no metaphysical justification for believing, that future universal histories of humanity will describe 20th century Western social democrats in favorable terms. But they admit that we have no very clear idea what those terms will be. [Rorty 1991, p. 219]

Rorty describes the beginnings of an argument that a twentieth-century Western social democrat like himself might make to explain why he was committed to his moral vocabulary and values instead of to those of the Cashinahua.[1] It is a local justificatory story, since it only applies to a potential choice between Rorty's values and those of one alternative. Some of the considerations offered in defense of social democratic vocabulary and values, of course, might be used repeatedly in other local

---

[1] Rorty uses the Cashinahua, a group of around 2000 in Brazil and Peru, as an arbitrary example of a pre-modern society. Interestingly enough, there exists a rough translation of the Universal Declaration of Human Rights into the Cashinahua language; see ⟨http://www.unhchr.ch/udhr/lang/cbs.htm⟩, accessed 3/13/01.

justificatory arguments, but there need be no general justification that shows one's own system to be superior to all possible rivals.

In another essay, Rorty recommends that we "see the choice between vocabularies as made neither within a neutral and universal meta-vocabulary nor by an attempt to fight one's way past appearances to the real, but simply by playing the old off against the new" [Rorty 1989, p. 73]. Rorty maintains that good liberals should "regard the justification of liberal society simply as a matter of historical comparison with other attempts at social organization – those of the past and those imagined by utopians" [ibid., p. 53]. According to Rorty, such justifications should be like "choices of friends or heroes. Such choices are not made by reference to criteria. They cannot be preceded by presuppositionless critical reflection, conducted in no particular language and outside any particular context" [ibid., p. 54].

There is much to what Rorty says: Historical comparison is important and "presuppositionless critical reflection" is not. Still, these ways of articulating the sense in which evaluative arguments are not general present us with a false dichotomy. It is true that stressing modern technology, for example, appeals to the values and costs recognized by Western social democrats themselves. It may well be that Rorty's argument would get no grip on current members of the Cashinahua people. Be this as it may, it is crucial that there is more that we can say to ourselves about why we are committed to our own values, which may or may not be the case for friends and heroes, depending on what we take friendship or hero worship to entail.

First of all, it is clear that the moral values we embrace bear relations to one another and to a variety of non-moral matters. Rorty himself, for instance, finds cruelty to be "the worst thing we do" [1989, p. xv]. Even if we agree with his subsequent assertion that for "liberal ironists" like himself, "there is no answer to the question 'Why not be cruel?'," we can still insist that even for such "ironists," there are important relations between "avoid cruelty" and other values. To give one example, it is apparent that on Rorty's telling, we can give reasons why we should endorse some values: In response to "Why not torture?" we might answer "Because it is cruel." These relations do not ground "presuppositionless critical reflection" on why we value what we do, but they do allow us to say rather a lot about why we value X rather than Y, or why avoiding B carries more weight with us than avoiding A. We will see later that not only can this sort of discussion help us to understand our values and why we care about the things we do, but it can also lead to productive engagement with those committed to other moralities.

Rorty might agree with my argument in the previous paragraph, but he will still insist that there is no answer to "Why not be cruel?" I do not believe that there is a single context-, community-, and tradition-independent answer, but Allan Gibbard has shown that reasoning about moral and other norms often depends on appeals to what he calls "epistemic norms." Epistemic norms are the standards we use for evaluating what to believe: When should we give credence to another's claims? When are we willing to grant authority to another's commitments, such that we can inherit entitlement to those same commitments? In one example, Gibbard imagines himself arguing with an "ideally coherent anorexic" who believes that it "makes sense to starve herself to death for the sake of a trim figure" [Gibbard 1990, p. 192]. Now suppose the anorexic were to challenge Gibbard: "How do you know that I'm being irrational? What's your justification?" Gibbard writes that

> I of course can issue the same challenge to her, and the mutual challenges may do nothing to advance the conversation. They may be met with mutual dogmatism. Or instead they may undermine the confidence of both of us, leaving us normative skeptics. They may, on the other hand, allow for some further assessment of our opposing normative claims. She, after all, can lay claim to one special source of normative authority: it is she who is living her life; it is she who experiences what it is really like to be in her circumstance. I must answer this epistemological argument with one that favors my own normative authority, or else I must give up the claim I have been asserting. This may in the end not resolve our fundamental disagreement, but then again it might. [1990, p. 193]

How might the dispute be resolved? If Gibbard comes to realize that the anorexic has a convincing story she can tell explaining how she knows that she's being reasonable, and he has no such story for himself, he might give in. Not to give in would be dogmatic, since it would mean refusing to grant the anorexic epistemic legitimacy, despite the fact that she meets all the requirements of his own epistemic norms.

This is not to imply that dogma has no legitimate place in cross-cultural moral encounters. In general, I can imagine as many as three different reactions to other communities' epistemic norms. The first is that we either share their norms or at least see theirs as plausible; in either case, we choose to treat them as competent normative judges, to borrow Gibbard's terminology. This means that we expect them to be moved by the same issues that move us, and also that we expect to find considerations they offer coherent and sometimes convincing. I say "sometimes" because granting others competence is not the same as deeming them infallible: Just as we make mistakes and change our minds about normative issues, which can after all be very complex, so they, too, may not have thought things through as clearly as we – or they – might desire. Granting normative competence lays the groundwork for sub-stantive engagement between our morality and theirs, in ways that I will discuss later.

A second type of reaction, still not dogmatic, would be to have rea-sons for thinking someone else's epistemic standards to be inferior to one's own. Call this a clash of epistemologies. For example, Alasdair MacIntyre has imagined an encounter between adherents of ancient Confucian ethics, with its focus on "ritual propriety (*li*)," and classical Aristotelian ethics [MacIntyre 1991]. What might happen if MacIntyre's Aristotelians tried to convince the Confucians to abandon judging things in terms of *li*?

The epistemic norms to which the Confucians might appeal in order to justify or explain the importance of *li* would include giving authority to the words of sages, both as recorded in the various classics and as con-firmed by the spontaneous reactions of properly trained contemporary Confucians. Aristotelians might insist on reasoning from certain first principles which are necessary for objectivity, an objectivity which, MacIntyre says, "is already itself understood in a specifically Aristotelian way as both presupposing and employing formal and teleological princi-ples alien to many rival modes of thought" [1991, pp. 108–9]. We can see that Confucians would very likely be unmoved by the Aristotelians' appeal to objectivity. The epistemic norms that the two groups recognize as governing their ethical discourses are different enough to provide no push toward mutual accommodation. As far as the Confucians are con-cerned, the Aristotelians abide by inferior standards, and vice versa. Such an inconclusive result to a debate over proper epistemic norms would tend to lessen or even sever mutual interaction, just like a thoroughly dogmatic response.

What, then, of plain dogma? Can we simply refuse to grant others normative authority even if we lack a story about why they judge poorly? This brings us back to the case of the anorexic: what if she says she is applying the same sort of epistemic norms that I endorse? Can I nonetheless reject her conclusions? Gibbard argues convincingly that there is a coherent way in which I can do this, though it has significant consequences. I can treat normative judgments via-à-vis the anorexic as "parochial." This means to deny others potential normative competence simply on the grounds that they are not "one of us" [Gibbard 1990, pp. 206–8]. Parochialism does not rest on generic qualifications that they might fulfill, but simply fail to, like being trained in the Confucian classics. The examples of treating people parochially that come readily to mind often have racist or nationalist overtones: During World War II, perhaps some Americans refused to grant normative competence to Japanese-Americans simply because they weren't adequately "American," rather than because of any genuine fear that they were spying for America's wartime enemy.[2]

Parochialism can be coherent – though it does seem morally noxious from where I sit – so long as it is not relied on to make demands on those to whom one is denying competence. To continue my example, Americans can coherently explain to one another why they are refusing to heed the moral judgments of the Japanese-Americans whom they have interned by saying that "they are not competent judges of these things, because they are not real Americans." It might well be immoral by these Americans' own lights to act this way, but it is not incoherent. What they cannot do is make demands on the Japanese-Americans themselves. Gibbard explains that such demands "have an air of brow-beating. [We would be asking them] to accept what [we] say, but for no reason [they] could accept in the same terms. We are inhibited, normally, from making such demands. We are embarrassed if we are shown to have made them" [1990, p. 207]. In short, to treat others parochially cuts us off from ordinary normative discussion with them.

We can respond dogmatically to Gibbard's anorexic, if we have no other means to resist her claims, but doing so brings with it the costs just outlined for parochialism. Returning to the main theme of this section, I see no reason why an encounter such as Gibbard has described might lead us to become "normative skeptics." In a spirit similar to that of Rorty's imaginary dialogue with members of the Cashinahua, we can readily come up with reasons why our beliefs and values about eating, nutrition, and self-image are superior to those of the anorexic, even if these are not reasons that convince her – even if, in a very extreme case,

---

[2] For a related discussion, see Chad Hansen's discussion of the "Asian Values Excuse" in [Hansen 1997].

we have no recourse but parochialism. So long as we are consistent in applying our own moral and epistemic standards, the simple knowledge that other moralities – and other epistemologies – exist should not undermine our own commitments. Still, if we engage with these alternative moralities, it is possible that we will come to view them as at least in part superior to our own. Such possibilities are part of granting normative competence to others.

Local justifications, while adequate to ground continued commitment to our values, do nonetheless lead to some limits on that commitment. Rorty writes: "Pragmatists hope, but have no metaphysical justification for believing, that future universal histories of humanity will describe 20th century Western social democrats in favorable terms." Why can't pragmatists be more certain? Rorty argues that the limited commitment he describes is the best we can achieve while at the same time recognizing that how we got here is the result of a contingent historical process. Social changes and other processes over which we have little control can greatly influence the morality to which future people and even our future selves will be committed. I'll call this attitude *long-term fallibilism*. We don't know how things are going to turn out in the long term. We could turn out to be a moral dead end. We may be very confident that we have improved on those who preceded us, by recognizing the immorality of slavery, for instance. We nonetheless feel that the presence of other groups with other moralities, many of them with histories equal to or longer than our own and to whom we cannot give reasons to give up their way of judging the world, requires that we remain open to the possibility that in the long term our morality will be abandoned.

Long-term fallibilism is a familiar attitude in many fields of human endeavor. The histories of science and medicine, for instance, should make it very clear that the particular theories or treatments upon which current practitioners rely could well turn out to be mistaken. Currently used cancer therapies might turn out to be doing more harm than good; the latest "discoveries" in subatomic physics might be relying on fundamental misconceptions. This does not lead to abandoning medicine or physics, though: Theorists do well to be open-minded, but are nonetheless committed to their current ways of thinking and acting. Reflecting on morality in the face of pluralism – and indeed, our own moral tradition's complex history – should lead us to a similar attitude.

One reason to be still more sanguine about our values derives from qualifying Rorty's assumption that the world's many different moralities are segregated from one another, each representing a choice of language, culture, life. In the preceding chapter I have described a broader range of conceptual differences according to which some moralities overlap more and some less. As we move through the Chinese rights tradition in the chapters that follow, we will also see how dynamic moralities can be, as well as how complex their interrelations with other moralities can become. Because of overlaps and interactions, it becomes less easy to see distinct moralities as belonging to an "us" and a "them." It is at least possible, in many cases, to argue that we and they compose a single community, at least on some issues. Instead of Rorty's local, bilateral justifications, overlap and interaction thus push us toward more general justifications as we think about one another as belonging, partly and contingently, to overlapping communities. I will pursue some of the implications of this thought further in this chapter's final section.

3.2 STATIC ATTITUDES

Moralities can be plural, and yet we can remain committed to our own values. What, then, are we to make of those committed to other moralities? Gibbard suggests that there are three possibilities: We can strive to ignore them, we can seek to coerce them into accepting our values, or we can endeavor to work out some means of accommodating the differences. The differences between these depend on several factors, including power, costs, and the contents of one's own values. These three strategies have in common the assumption of a primarily static relationship between us and them. Even repression, which aims to force them to share our values, looks to a single, unchanging solution to our differences with them. After I have discussed these static strategies, I will turn in the next section to the more dynamic and open-ended idea of engagement.

3.2.1 Ignoring

There is a range of situations in which we might want to simply ignore a group with a morality different from our own. Most benign – at least in the short term – are cases in which groups have relatively little to do with one another. Gibbard calls this "isolation," writing that "groups are isolated on a topic if they can disagree on it without much loss – as they count losses" [1990, p. 235]. Whether this is possible depends on how much and what kinds of interaction groups have with one another. Relations between European nations and China prior to the Opium War

(1839–1842) provide an interesting example of isolation. There were certain kinds of interactions between these groups. Narrowly defined commercial transactions took place in restricted areas; a few diplomatic missions were received in Beijing; small numbers of missionaries were allowed to teach and translate. The diplomatic missions were treated primarily as curiosities on both sides. European traders were willing to abide by the limits put on their commerce; significant engagement with one another's values was not necessary. The case of the Jesuit missionaries is perhaps a partial exception to overall isolation, reminding us that it is important to consider internal complexities in all cross-cultural situations. The Jesuits worked assiduously to create a moral language that would bridge Christian and Chinese values and beliefs. While it is difficult to point to any direct influences on Chinese moral thinking, leading Jesuits were certainly participants in seventeenth-century China's moral discourse, at least to some extent. Since the Jesuits' influence was small, we can still say that on the whole the relation between the larger groups was one of isolation.[3]

Isolation, then, is ignoring another group when it is easy to do so. Sometimes it is much harder to ignore another, but it may nonetheless seem like the only choice. Consider two groups, one with dramatically less power than the other. Good examples might be the relations between Americans of the nineteenth century's westward expansion, on the one hand, and various native American nations, on the other. In some cases the latter tried to settle – often with limited success – for some manner of accommodation with the former's values. In others cases, though, native Americans sought simply to ignore those with whom they would not accommodate and whom they had not the power to repress. Ignoring was not completely passive, of course; it often involved great costs associated with relocation. In the end, it was not a viable strategy, given the extent of the white men's ambitions.

The long-term success of ignoring others depends on multiple factors, many of them associated with the dynamics of power, as both of the preceding examples suggest. It may have been the obvious strategy for China prior to the Opium War, but the different fates of China and Japan in the hundred years since then suggest that isolation can turn into more costly ignoring almost without one realizing it.

---

[3] It is worth adding that the Jesuits' understanding of Chinese thought was transmitted back to Europe and exerted a detectable, but again small, influence on European moral discourse. See [Jensen 1997].

3.2.2 Repressing

If we do not (or cannot) ignore others, and yet we persist in judging differently from them, then we must choose whether to attempt repression or to seek some kind of accommodation. Gibbard defines repression as "coercion held illegitimate by the people coerced" [1990, p. 236]. As he notes, not all coercion is repressive in this sense. Two nations might agree to allow themselves to be coerced by an international organization like the International Criminal Court or the World Trade Organization as part of a scheme of accommodation; I will discuss this kind of possibility below. Repression is also closely bound up with power relations, since successful repression depends on being able to impose it on an unwilling other. Native Americans waging war against white settlers might be best conceptualized as attempting repression, since they were neither ignoring nor accommodating their enemies. Repression may have been the last, best hope for the survival of their way of life, but because of technological- and demographic-based imbalances of power, it failed.

Gibbard argues that "repression is always a bad. It shifts the basis of normative discussion, and it subverts a valuable kind of respect we may have for each other" [1990, p. 237]. Gibbard believes that discussion over moral and other norms normally takes place in an atmosphere free of threats, wherein each participant is free to say whatever he or she would like. When repression is threatened, normative discussion loses this autonomy, which is a cost to all involved. He also maintains that it is "part of our discursive nature" to value respecting others, in the sense of being willing to "treat others in ways they themselves find legitimate" [1990, p. 238].

What should we make of these claims? First, note that Gibbard has not asserted that repression is always *wrong*, nor that it is always worse than some other, non-repressive alternative. As the example of native Americans showed, people may find that, in certain circumstances, repressing others is their best option. Still, Gibbard insists, repression is never without cost even to the repressors – not to mention the repressees: it "shifts the basis of normative discussion" and "subverts a valuable kind of respect." The latter claim Gibbard ties explicitly to our "nature" in a way I find problematic.[4] He takes an unsupported leap from

---

[4] In most of his book, Gibbard handles evolutionary explanations quite deftly; this attempt to derive a specific normative conclusion from human nature is uncharacteristic.

his observation that all humans engage in discussion of norms to the con-clusion that all people must value discussions which "treat others in ways [these others] themselves find legitimate." This ignores Gibbard's own insight, discussed in greater detail later, that groups sometimes refuse to accord others the status of potentially competent normative judges. Even groups who fully endorse the egalitarian, respect-based model of nor-mative discussion favored by Gibbard may still recognize that a parent subverts no valuable respect when he or she "represses" small children.[5] Some groups will place more importance than others on explicitly hier-archical relationships, but it is easy enough to see that adults occupying different roles in a society might be accorded different degrees of normative competence. If only scholars trained in the dialectic, to borrow one of Gibbard's own examples, are competent moral judges, then why should it trouble such a scholar to insist that a non-initiate bend to his will?

We cannot conclude from our "natures" that normative discussions ought to be carried out in an atmosphere of egalitarian respect. Gibbard's assertion that such discussions are "normally" carried on free from threats also deserves closer scrutiny. Coercion comes in many vari-eties. Power imbalances are surely a common feature of normative encounters, and it can often be difficult to disentangle what is voluntary and what is not, what is held illegitimate and what is not. Consider Chinese endeavors to gain access to favorable trading relations with various developed nations. Supposing for a moment that the Chinese can be thought of as a single group and that they have distinctly dif-ferent notions of human rights than do the developed nations, can we not imagine them voluntarily agreeing to being treated in a way they find illegitimate – to being repressed – because the costs of not being able to trade would be still greater? What attitude ought members of developed countries have toward such a result? They may well think it inferior to a voluntary *and* non-repressive agreement, perhaps in part because it strikes them as lacking in the kind of respect with which Gibbard is concerned. But this seems to be only a contingent possibility and not one, to return to the theme of the previous paragraph, that can have roots in our natures. The World Trade Organization is a long

---

[5] Given the value placed on respect in such groups, the relationship between parent and child presumably will be an evolving one, with egalitarian respect playing an increasingly important role as the child matures.

way from the hunter-gatherer environments in which our ancestors evolved.[6]

I have been disagreeing with Gibbard's assertion that repression must always be a bad, but I certainly agree that it will typically have costs. It may of course undermine the sort of respect that Gibbard emphasized, supposing that we value such respect. Depending on how we go about coercing the others, it will probably have other costs as well, though these will vary with power relations, among other things. Other groups may come to fear that they, too, will be repressed, leading to long-term problems for us. Repression may also sit very uncomfortably alongside simultaneous engagement with the same group on normative issues. I will discuss engagement below, and then turn in the final section of the chapter to more detailed consideration of which strategies can be pursued together – and why we might prefer some combinations to others.

3.2.3 Accommodating

If we cannot or will not live apart, and cannot or will not repress the other, some form of accommodation must be reached. This is true even if we also pursue a policy of engagement which aims at reaching consensus. We must have a means for dealing with current differences, whatever the long-term prognosis. In English the best-known words for describing accommodation are "tolerance" and "toleration," and in Europe and the United States the most famous cases of tolerance concern religion. While most scholars agree on the historical causes of religious toleration, there is widespread disagreement on the proper scope and meaning of toleration today. This disagreement is readily explicable when one realizes that there are good reasons for viewing practices that could well be called toleration from both broad and narrow perspectives, as we will see. I will follow Gibbard's lead – though differing with him significantly on the specifics – by distinguishing *accommodation*, as a broad phenomenon, from *tolerance*, which will be defined more narrowly. Tolerance is a special case of accommodation. Even then,

---

[6] Sociobiological accounts often ignore the enormous differences between the environments in which humans evolved, and that which we now inhabit; given that phenotypes are the results of the ways that genotypes express themselves in particular environments, these differences can be extremely important. See [Kitcher 1985] for discussion.

as we will see, there are reasons not to insist on too firm a distinction between tolerance and other flavors of accommodation.

In order for the relationship between two groups to count as accommodation, two conditions must be fulfilled. First, they must significantly and persistently disagree with one another. Second, they must nonetheless prefer to interact in accord with norms of accommodation, rather than try to repress one another. In the typical case, both sides will compromise to arrive at shared norms of accommodation, but I see no reason why this is essential. If only one side finds that it must commit to a new, inferior (from its perspective) set of values in order to get by, this is still accommodation rather than repression as long as the side that compromised did so willingly, as a result of a process it found legitimate. The difference between such an accommodation and the voluntary agreement to be repressed that I discussed earlier is slight but significant. In both cases, it likely will be the less powerful side that changes its values; the difference is over whether the compromiser has any genuine commitment to the new values. In the case of an accommodation they do: They see the accommodation as a legitimate basis on which to interact. In the case of repression, they do not, and presumably will ignore the new values whenever they can get away with it. I do not claim that this distinction is always clear in the real world, particularly because groups are never as unified as my discussion in these paragraphs has been assuming.

One of the most interesting forms that norms of accommodation can take is a set of thin values on which there is (or appears to be) mutual agreement, despite disagreement at the level of thick values. As I discussed in the book's Introduction, thin values are moral and political commitments that have shed most of their ties to specific moral traditions, languages, and histories. It is hoped that different groups can agree on certain thin values, despite disagreeing on the thicker reasons why one ought to be committed to those values. I also explained in the Introduction that there are two different ways in which thin values can be derived. One approach, which I found problematic for several reasons, is to look for lowest-common-denominator values. The alternative is to build a thin set of values out of a specific thick morality. I found Rawls's specific implementation of this strategy to be unconvincing, but concluded that it held more promise than the lowest-common-denominator option. We can now see that two or more groups' arriving at a shared set of thin values is a particular case of the more general phenomenon of accommodation. If we and they, in consultation with one another, arrive at a set of values on which we are willing to agree, and on the basis of which we can fruitfully interact, then we have constructed thin values to serve as our norms of accommodation.

I noted in the Introduction that dealing with one another based upon thin values – and more generally based on norms of accommodation – should in most cases be understood as a second-best solution: better than repression or isolation, but worse than arriving at a thicker consensus. I do not base this claim on any confidence in or commitment to One Truth on which all moral discussion must ultimately converge; I do not even hold that we must imagine the possibility of such a Truth for our discussions to make sense. Instead, we should view accommodations as second-bests for two more pragmatic reasons. First, if without any coercion from us, they arrive at thick values which more closely approximate our own, despite their different historical, cultural, and other experiences, that should give us added confidence in the viability of our own values – not enough to overcome our long-term fallibilist attitude, but a comfort nonetheless. Second, to the extent that their thick values move away from ours, they may cease to feel justified in endorsing the thin norms of accommodation. Accommodation relies, recall, on each group's internal sense that accommodation is better than the alternatives. If the ways they evaluate those alternatives change, then the grounds for the accommodation may fall away. Merely thin agreement, in short, is more fragile than robust consensus.

These considerations push us toward finding a thick enough moral consensus to sustain rich interactions over the long term, but I want to note that a consensus which falls short of full agreement may be adequate, and may in fact be preferable to full agreement for other, equally pragmatic reasons. Complete unanimity might be tedious; it might cause us to lose out on chances for learning from different perspectives and different experiences. I am comfortable allowing for such possibilities since I have offered pragmatic reasons why I believe we will tend to find accommodations to be second-best, rather than metaphysical reasons why we have to do so.

Gibbard identifies two types of accommodation, modus vivendi and toleration. On Gibbard's telling, the two have much in common: They both represent groups seeking agreement on second-best norms in order to avoid paying the costs associated with failure to agree. In both cases, the costs one avoids through accommodation may include losses in war, expenses of policing repression, and lost cooperation [Gibbard 1990, p. 244]. It is avoiding these costs that motivates a modus vivendi. As we have already seen, Gibbard also believes that repression is costly because of the lost mutual respect it entails. When one's motivation for accommodation begins to center on restoring such mutual respect, Gibbard argues, then genuine toleration becomes possible:

> The initial pressures [toward accommodation] may be those of a modus vivendi, and those pressures may continue to help sustain the arrangement. Part of the reward of accommodation, though, is this kind of mutual respect. In time it may seem enough to justify the accommodation. Groups then have achieved toleration. [1990, pp. 244–5]

Toleration, we might say, comes from seeing moral value in the accommodation, rather than just an avoidance of harms. The qualifications I have already made about Gibbard's understanding of respect still hold; I cannot agree with him that this is something we must all value. Still, it does seem like a value many moralities today endorse, and thus a likely motive for accommodation.

The distinction we see in Gibbard between a positive, moral motivation for accommodation and a negative, prudential motivation is mirrored in an essay by Bernard Williams. He argues that to the extent someone values individual autonomy, toleration will also be valuable to that person, since only by letting others make their own choices does one respect their autonomy. He emphasizes, though, that this positive evaluation of tolerance is based on the acceptance of other substantive values (like autonomy); toleration does not "rise above the battle of values" [Williams 1996, p. 25]. He elaborates:

> The people whom the liberal is particularly required to tolerate are precisely those who are unlikely to share the liberal's view of the good of autonomy, which is the basis of the toleration, to the extent that this expresses a value. The liberal has not, in this representation of toleration, given them a reason to value toleration if they do not already share his other values. [ibid.]

Williams, in other words, understands more clearly than Gibbard the possibility of someone's not seeing positive value in tolerance. Williams takes comfort, though, in the fact that there are motivations for what he calls the "practice of toleration" other than actually finding toleration to be a value. In particular, he suggests that the "practice of toleration" can be "underlaid by . . . an understood balance of power" [Williams 1996, p. 22]. By this he means a "Hobbesian equilibrium, under which the accep-

tance of one group by the other is the best that either of them can get"
[ibid., p. 21]. A "practice of toleration" undergirded by such an equilibrium is thus much the same as Gibbard's modus vivendi.

Of the static attitudes surveyed in this section, accommodation is obviously the most attractive, given the difficulty or undesirability of achieving isolation in the contemporary world. In most situations it will not
make sense to settle solely on one of these static strategies, however.
Values change, sometimes as a result of conscious efforts and sometimes
as collateral effects of economic, social, or other sorts of processes. To
the extent that it is possible to influence the direction of these changes,
we ought to endeavor to do so, lest we end up in situations less desirable
(from our perspectives) than the current moment. I call active efforts to
influence the values of others *engagement*, and I now turn to a discussion of the types and logics of engagement.

3.3 DYNAMIC ENGAGEMENT

In this section I explore issues related to the questions of whether and
how we can engage with members of a community whose morality is different from our own. When the conceptual distance between moralities
is great, only limited kinds of engagement will be possible, which I discuss
first. More substantial engagement requires communicating well enough
to judge whether to accord others normative competence, on the basis
of which genuinely open, reasoned discussion can take place. I end with
consideration of non-discursive kinds of engagement and of the norms
that ought to govern such practices.

3.3.1 *Pragmatic Disagreement*

A good first step is to see whether we can understand their moral reasoning well enough to assess it in our terms. If not, then there is considerably less room for reasoning, though other types of engagement may
still be possible, which I will discuss later. Suppose that we recognize that
they condemn an action which we endorse, but that there is considerable
difference in what each side takes the action to be. The concepts
expressed by verbs and adverbs, after all, are no less inferentially articulated than other concepts. We may find ourselves unsure how to translate the word – or make sense of the concept – with which they have
categorized an action. In such a case we may not, at least for the time
being, be in literal disagreement with them, since we are not sure what

to make of their concept in our terms. So long as we can conclude that they are condemning that which we endorse, we are still in *pragmatic* disagreement.

If we find ourselves in pragmatic disagreement with them but unable to communicate effectively about wherein or why we differ, it seems clear that there is little room for our convincing them that they are mistaken. Situations like this, which I doubt are very common, are the most radical of conceptual differences; I have suggested above that we call the two languages "incommensurate" in such cases. There are only two possible routes to reasoning with them in a case like this. First, linguistic innovation on one or both sides might render the two languages adequately commensurate for communication to succeed. Such changes may be intentional or not, and they may be consciously resisted by those with a stake in the current social-conceptual order.[7] Once they occur, engagement along the lines sketched below can take place.

Another option is to learn their language from the ground up – to acquire a "second first language," as Alasdair MacIntyre has put it [1988, p. 374] – and then to criticize their moral standpoint from the inside. I will deal with this *internal* criticism in a moment, since it applies even when conceptual differences are far less radical. The idea that we might learn their language and then reason with them also suggests another possibility: If we have learned their language and their value system like natives, aren't we perfectly placed to decide between the two systems? Shouldn't such a bilingual be able to judge which moral assessment best applies to the action, whether or not the languages are incommensurate? MacIntyre has discussed such a case, which he calls a "boundary situation":

> Consider the predicament of someone who lives in a time and place where he or she is a full member of two linguistic communities, speaking one language, Zuni, say, or Irish, exclusively to the older members of his family and village and Spanish or English, say, to those from the world outside, who seek to engage him or her in a way of life in the exclusively Spanish- or English-speaking world. [MacIntyre 1989, pp. 184–5]

Granting for discussion that English and Irish moral languages are incommensurate, and supposing that there is some action over which English and Irish speakers come into pragmatic ethical conflict, could

---

[7] For discussion of these complexities, see [Angle in press] and [Biagioli 1990].

someone in such a boundary situation weigh the conflicting reasons he or she is given by speakers of the two languages?

It certainly seems possible for someone in a boundary situation to be gripped by two very different sets of ethical standards. Sometimes the person will in effect be able to live two lives, holding himself or herself to one set of standards when in their village and another when dealing with business people from London. Immigrants or exiles may also find themselves in similar situations. I'll call such people *moral schizophrenics*. If the moral schizophrenic is lucky, no circumstance will arise to force an important choice in which the two sets of standards conflict. When a choice must be made, though, there can be no simple weighing of one reason versus another. The choice will often demand that one renounce one way of life in favor of the other, but not because one can see that the chosen path is superior to the path not taken. The choice instead has the character of a leap, an existential commitment. Some people may be able to leap back and forth between perspectives for a period of time – perhaps Oskar Schindler was one of these? – but I suspect that for most, such a fluidity in basic moral commitments would prove psychologically untenable. When we offer reasons to such people, therefore, we are not attempting to convince them of the independent, rational superiority of our way of judging. We are attempting to woo them into looking at it from our moral perspective rather than from the competing perspective.

Suppose that this is all that can be said in the case of incommensurate languages. In most cases, though, communication is less problematic. We may not be supremely confident that we are understanding them correctly, but the snags that we are hitting seem minor (at worst). Their terms are different from ours, but as I suggested earlier, languages like English have considerable histories which give us resources for understanding and translating others. We may recognize their moral concepts as ones from our past. In some such cases, we will have arguments ready to deploy against the use of such notions; in others, social changes may simply have made the older concepts irrelevant to us. Even then, we may be prepared to argue why our current categories, and our corresponding evaluation of the action in question, are better. Let me turn now to consider these and other types of more reasoned engagement.

3.3.2 Substantive Engagement

There are many ways to engage with members of a group whose morality differs from our own. We can talk, negotiate, tell stories, take tours, study, and so on. We can do these things together and separately, in our land and in theirs. As we will see in subsequent chapters, engagement of these various kinds pervades Chinese rights discourse in the twentieth century. Many of these things can be done while simultaneously pursuing one of the other strategies explored earlier; this is especially so since groups are rarely monolithic. In the next section I will explore the possibilities for and ramifications of multiple strategies. Can one really engage and repress, for instance, at the same time? Here I will confine myself to the grounds and dynamics of engagement.

Engagement can take three forms. Full-fledged engagement requires that I grant you competence as a normative judge. Since engagement aims at changing your norms, in order not to repress you, I need to give you reasons that you will accept in your terms. Therefore, I must work under the premise that your terms are adequately akin to my terms, and that you and I can recognize the same kinds of reasons. If this is so, then in principle you might realize something that I had missed, yet ought to see and accept. Full-fledged engagement may begin with the goal of changing your values, but it can end up changing both of ours, or even only mine.

I have purposely left some important clauses in the preceding paragraph vague, because whether our terms are "adequately" similar and whether our reasons are of the same "kinds" are not things that can be known for sure prior to engaging with one another. This type of engagement, that is, can be carried out between two people or groups whose moralities are somewhat different from one another. Pluralism need not bar engagement. I pointed out earlier that communities with rich traditions of moral reasoning can often draw on or modify resources from earlier, or currently non-canonical, moments in their moral discourse in order to understand and evaluate foreign claims. Engagement can also involve learning: I may have no concept that corresponds to one of yours, but I may be able and willing to learn it and use it to enrich my moral language. I may even be willing to use it in place of current concepts. Perhaps, after reflecting on the commitments and entitlements entailed by my current vocabulary, I come to embrace the entailments of your concept rather than those of mine. This process, which as we saw earlier Brandom calls "expressive rationality," can lead to the revision of my moral language. At least, if a result of the engagement is that people in my community come to speak in the new way, then we can say that "our" moral language has changed. If revisions that I feel are necessary are resisted by my home community, this should be understood as a (partial) splintering of my community, with my coming to share some of your norms and vocabulary.

Rather than pursue this issue of a divided community just yet, let me turn to the second kind of engagement, namely internal criticism. The idea here is that either because I explicitly deny you normative competence or because I simply cannot understand you well enough (in my terms) to grant it, I may be ineligible for full-fledged engagement. Still, thanks perhaps to careful study on my part, I may be able to engage with your norms on your terms. My criticism, that is, is completely internal to your system of values. For you to accept my internal criticism as potentially valid, of course, you must be willing to grant me normative competence based on your own standards, and it may take some work on my part to convince you that I merit such acceptance. Unless your attitude toward me is simply parochial, though, it should be possible in principle for me to earn the right to engage your norms from the inside.

One value of internal criticism is that it assures us that even radical differences need not stand in the way of some kind of reasoned engagement with others. Of course there are no guarantees that internal criticism will issue in any particular result. Alasdair MacIntyre has argued that in certain circumstances, internal criticism can lead to the rational choice of one tradition over another. He says that when one tradition fails by its own lights, and a second tradition not only does not fail (internally), but also has the resources to explain why the first tradition failed, then adherents of the first tradition can reasonably choose to switch their allegiance to the second tradition [MacIntyre 1988].

MacIntyre's argument seems quite reasonable, and may even be right. For better or worse, though, choices are hardly ever all-or-nothing decisions between two traditions, as MacIntyre's own historical studies show. Traditions and moralities are not monolithic; despite the degree to which one aspect can be systematically related to another, whole moralities do not stand or fall as integral entities. Criticism, revision, and other changes are always more piecemeal, so a single vision of how reasoned cross-cultural criticism goes on must be inadequate. As I will discuss in this chapter's last section, internally contested concepts and communities make these matters still more complicated, and as we will see in the next several chapters, the development of rights discourse in China was in fact more complicated in just the ways this chapter should lead one to expect.

Finally, I want to discuss the possibility of non-discursive engagement: tourism, trade (perhaps especially in cultural products like books and movies), employment by multinational business firms, and so on. Richard Rorty has argued that this is in fact the most important kind, or even the sole valuable kind, of engagement. He calls it "sentimental education," and argues that in today's world, "most of the work in changing moral intuitions is being done by manipulating our feelings rather than by increasing our knowledge" [Rorty 1993, p. 118]. I agree with Rorty that non-discursive engagement can be effective, but I must add two qualifications. First, it is evident that the various forms of discursive engagement considered earlier are important and clearly legitimate. Second, we must ask what attitude "they" might have toward non-discursive engagement of Rorty's or some other kind. If they find it illegitimate, does it therefore count as repression? If so, are there any differences between this form of repression and those based on discursive demands? Suppose that some of them object to Hollywood movies, but others stand in line to see them. How should we feel? Such complexities lead us directly into the question of how to handle divided communities.

3.4 MULTIPLE STRATEGIES AND DIVIDED COMMUNITIES

At the heart of my understanding of concepts and norms is the idea that people can have different commitments, and even mean different things, without ceasing to be able to communicate nor ceasing to be parts of larger communities. In this section I make explicit some of the ways in which communities can be divided over how to react to pluralism. I also explore the parallel issue of how even single individuals – not to mention whole communities – can simultaneously pursue more than one strategy with respect to foreign moral claims. There are two ways to conceptualize divisions within a community: top-down and bottom-up. If we look down from the top, we see a large community (perhaps a nation) which is internally divided along multiple, overlapping dimensions of class, race, profession, gender, wealth, education, politics, and so on. Looking up from the bottom, we see numerous small communities which both overlap with others and are subsumed into ever-larger communities. As the community-level grows higher, the attachment of individuals to the larger community's goals and norms tends to progressively weaken. People typically care more about what happens in their family, neighborhood, religious group, or labor union than what happens in state or federal politics, not to mention United Nations deliberations. In any event, the bottom-up and top-down perspectives complement one another, and I will draw on both.

One more introductory remark: Divisions within the communities we will examine are often not as severe as one might expect. When we look at the views of Chinese activists from the 1978–9 Democracy Wall movement, for instance, we will find substantial overlap with the norms expressed by the Communist Party leadership. The activists endorsed the leadership's "Four Modernization" aims, desiring only to add a fifth – democratization. Without meaning to minimize the significance of this so-called Fifth Modernization, the joint commitment to agricultural, industrial, military, and technological modernization was real and significant. Without such commonalities, it would be difficult to speak of a single community at all. Rather than an internally contested group, we would be faced with fundamental splintering, which probably is best understood as more than one group masquerading as a single group. Even here, trajectories matter: The "United" in "United Nations" might be thought of as such a masquerade, but it really expresses an aspiration more than any self-delusion.

Turning now to my two main questions, I think it is clear that there are significant similarities between the multiple-strategies case and the divided-community case. The former imagines that a certain "us" will simultaneously adopt more than one attitude toward a particular "them." The latter supposes that we (or they) will be internally divided, and so will have different reactions to a single strategy: Some may find a certain demand repressive, others tolerate it, and still others simply endorse it. But this is structurally similar to the multiple-strategy case, since in that instance we are considering making multiple simultaneous demands, for instance a set of three, one of which they might find repressive, one they might tolerate, and the third they might endorse.

Some combinations raise few if any complications. Accommodation and one or more varieties of engagement, for instance, go naturally together. The accommodation serves as a provisional bridge across the differences in moralities, possibly thought of as a set of thin values to which all can commit and in accord with which all can interact. Much of what passes across this bridge can be seen as non-discursive engagement: We inevitably influence one another when we cooperate on business deals, travel in one another's lands and learn about our respective cultures, and so on. At the same time, accommodation can serve as a bridge to more explicit engagement between scholars, governments, activists, and others. As we saw earlier, this can take place either with or without the mutual granting of normative competence. Two or more decades ago, the bourgeois-class background of the typical American scholar might have disqualified him or her, in the eyes of many Chinese colleagues, from normative competence. As a result of changes in Chinese epistemic standards, this criterion is less likely to be in play today, though I can certainly make no blanket prediction about the commitments of all individuals. In any event, engagement based on mutual openness with the goal of finding greater consensus is perfectly compatible with current accommodation.

Internal criticism deserves some separate discussion, in part because it is unlikely to be undertaken by many of "us" at a time. By "internal criticism," recall, I mean our working inside their morality, based on meeting their standards for normative competence – all this without essential reference to how any of the claims we make within their morality might relate to those we make in our own voices back at home. Travelers, expatriates, and scholars are perhaps the most likely to be able and willing to engage in such criticism. Because of the relative isolation of such people within their own communities, it is particularly easy to imagine other members of their larger community simultaneously pursuing other strategies, including those incompatible with accommodation, like repression or parochialism. Another obvious possibility is that the rest of the internal critics' own community might be more or less happily isolated from the foreigners.

One of the options that divided communities and multiple strategies make possible is something I will call horizontal engagement between sub-communities. If we imagine all the different sub-groups of a nation-sized community piled on top of one another, facing a similar pile that corresponds to another nation, some of the individual groups may have bonds with groups horizontally across from them – in the other nation – that are as strong as or stronger than the vertical ties they have to others in their nation.[8] Perhaps Chinese feminists share a great deal with American feminists; they may have commitments in common that others in their nations do not share. Business executives, military officials, democratic activists – all are examples of groups that may have such horizontal connections that can open up possibilities for engagement. What makes this possibility especially interesting is that each group also has opportunities for pursuing vertical engagement with other groups in their home society. To the extent that open engagement pushes toward consensus, as I argued earlier, the two-dimensional engagement I am

---

[8] For the purposes of this image, I ignore the degree to which different sub-communities will overlap and interpenetrate one another.

describing, perhaps reiterated among many different pairs of groups, will provide some momentum toward consensus between the two larger groups.

There is no reason to assume, of course, that all the pressures that these horizontal ties bring to bear on moral discussions within their home societies will push in the same direction. The question of whether the United States should grant China most-favored-nation trade status was vexed for at least two decades, with no firm consensus, and with different groups – influenced, no doubt, by the views of their analogues in China – pushing in different directions. My account does not enable me to confidently predict that overlapping horizontal engagement will lead every time to a satisfying consensus. It does seem to be one of our best hopes, though. It turns one of the most troubling obstacles to cross-cultural communication and engagement – namely, internal contestation and complexity – into a virtue. Whether it will help us forward in a particular case cannot be known in advance. Instead of dwelling further on this matter, I turn now to Chinese rights discourse itself. The next chapters illustrate many of the attitudes I have surveyed here, from initial isolation in the seventeenth and eighteenth centuries, to repression and accommodation in the nineteenth, to increasing engagement in the twentieth. Engagement is not the only strategy relevant to the twentieth and early twenty-first centuries, of course; Liu Huaqiu's argument makes clear that he is concerned about repressive impositions of other standards on China. In my concluding chapters, I will return to Liu's claims and suggest some ways that Sino-Western dialogues on rights can be advanced.

4

The Shift toward Legitimate Desires in Neo-Confucianism

I BEGIN FROM THE UNCONTROVERSIAL fact that prior to the nineteenth century, Chinese had no word that we can translate as "rights." There were, to be sure, concepts whose meanings partially overlapped with the meaning of rights. There were ideas and institutions whose roles might be argued to have served functions similar to those served by rights. I begin from the lack of a single translation because my first task is to explain what the subject matter of this chapter is: If not "rights," then what?

Suppose that instead of assuming that "*quanli*" meant rights, we ask what the word would mean to an audience of educated Chinese in the nineteenth century who did not benefit from special glosses or explanations. They probably would take it to mean what the characters had been used to mean for 2000 and more years: power and benefit.[1] To say that "one ought to enjoy *quanli*," then, would just mean that one ought to enjoy powers and benefits. What would our hypothetical audience make of this notion? The more thought we give to this question, the more questions we realize must be answered before we can be sure of any assessment. After all, what powers and what benefits are we talking about? Must anything have been done to make the recipients merit the rewards? Does it make a difference who the people are – what roles they play in society?

One obvious source of answers to these questions on which our audience could draw is Confucianism. The point of this thought experiment, in fact, is simply to motivate an examination of what the Confucian tradition has had to say about what powers and benefits we should enjoy, and why. This is important because, as I will argue in later chapters, to a

---

[1] I will explore the history of the term "*quanli*" more thoroughly in the next chapter.

74

great extent I think that early users of *"quanli"* did mean something pretty close to what our audience from the previous paragraph would have assumed, and the theory and practical wisdom about *quan* and *li* on which the early users drew was largely Confucian. Confucianism can thus be a starting point in our exploration of *quanli* discourse.

Much of the discussion will focus on desires rather than on *quan* and *li*, because Confucian analysis tended to center on our motivations and characters rather than on our specific goals. Instead of asking which, among the many objects of our desires, should be fulfilled, Confucians ask which types of desires (if any) we should have. Answers to this question are varied because Confucianism has been, throughout its long history, a live and contested philosophical tradition. In fact, I will show that questions about desires are among the most troubling ones to neo-Confucian philosophers – that is, to those individuals who contributed to the revival of Confucian philosophy from the beginning of the Song dynasty (960–1279) on into the modern era.[2]

This chapter is divided into two sections. I begin with early neo-Confucianism. Here we will see a doctrine advocating "no desires" which – whatever its merits – was easily used by power-holders to call for the suppression of people's desires. Then I will turn to representatives of the strand within the Confucian tradition that valorized desires, stressing desires' fundamental place in any satisfactory account of human moral psychology. These thinkers were critics of the earlier neo-Confucians, as well as of contemporaries who continued to advocate theses unfriendly to desires. We will see in the next two chapters that nineteenth- and early-twentieth-century advocates of *quanli* share important convictions with, and in some cases draw explicitly on, these pro-desire Confucians. They are thus an important source of what I am calling Chinese rights discourse. Recognizing that the discourse has roots this deep in Chinese traditions will help us, in later chapters, to assess claims about distinctive Chinese concepts of rights.

4.1 NEO-CONFUCIANISM AGAINST DESIRE?

There is significant scholarly disagreement about how ascetic Song-dynasty neo-Confucianism was. Certainly slogans like "no desire" don't

---

[2] Study of Confucian texts never vanished in China, but after its great flourishing in the classical period, Confucian thought languished for several centuries while Buddhism and Daoism captured the intellectual imagination of China's elites. Note that I use the term "neo-Confucian" very broadly, thus sidestepping some scholarly controversies.

sound like they place very much importance on the fulfillment of every-day wants and desires, but several interpreters have argued that super-ficial readings of this and other slogans miss the real point of neo-Confucianism. In this section I will show that such apologists for neo-Confucianism do indeed have a point: Early neo-Confucians like Zhou Dunyi and Zhu Xi do not advocate extreme self-denial. Even on the most charitable reading, though, Zhou and Zhu suffer from two important weaknesses: (1) They write in ways almost calling out to be misinterpreted, and are thus easily bent to the needs of power-holders. (2) They fail to provide a satisfactory account of the positive roles that desires can play in proper action. This latter failing reinforces the ease with which they can be read as thoroughgoing opponents of desire.

I shall begin with Zhou Dunyi (1017–73) because it was he who first raised the slogan of "no desire (*wuyu*)" among the thinkers spearheading the Confucian revival during the Song dynasty. While not all Song Confucians agreed with Zhou's anti-desire stance, his view was widely influential and was endorsed a century later by neo-Confucianism's great synthesizer, Zhu Xi (1130–1200). It was at Zhou's slogan, in addition, that some of the harshest criticism of later Confu-cians – thinkers like Chen Que and Dai Zhen, whose views we will encounter later – was leveled.[3]

Zhou is best known for two texts: the *Diagram of the Supreme Ulti-mate Explained* and *Comprehending the Book of Changes*. Both deal largely with abstract metaphysics, but both add comments on the nature of sagehood that bring up the notion of "desire." In the *Diagram Explained*, for instance, we find:

> The sage settles [human affairs] using the mean, correctness, human-ity, and righteousness. . . . He regards tranquility as fundamental.
> (Having no desire, he will be tranquil.) He establishes himself as the ultimate standard for man. [Zhou 1990, p. 6; Zhu & Lu 1967, p. 6, somewhat altered]

Similarly, in *Comprehending the Book of Changes*, Zhou explains that there is an "essential way" to learn to be a sage:

---

[3] Zhou's standing in the neo-Confucian tradition has been a matter of controversy. Zhu Xi made him out to be one of the tradition's founders. Some scholars have questioned this [Graham 1958, pp. 152–75]. More recently, Zhou's role has been assessed more pos-itively [Tillman 1992, pp. 60, 115]. For my purposes, the important point is that since Zhu Xi, Confucians themselves have taken Zhou to be an important source of neo-Confucian ideas and values, on which there is no disagreement.

Unity is the essential way. Unity is [having] no desire. If one has no desire, then one is vacuous while tranquil, straight while active. Being vacuous while tranquil, one becomes intelligent and hence penetrating; being straight while active, one becomes impartial and hence all-embracing. Being intelligent, penetrating, impartial, and all-embracing, one is almost a sage. [Zhou 1990, p. 29; Zhu & Lu 1967, p. 123]

What does he mean by saying that those on the path to sagehood should have "no desire (*wuyu*)"?

It is easy to read the first of these passages as advocating an extreme passivity – not desiring anything and thus being "tranquil" – but when we consider the second passage's mention of being "straight while active," we see that the idea is more complicated than this. Commentators have long understood that the idea of "tranquility" in the first passage is different from, and more fundamental than, the "tranquility" mentioned in the second. Fundamental tranquility comes from having no desires and leads to "unity."

We can better appreciate what Zhou is up to if we consider a few more passages from *Comprehending the Book of Changes*. To begin with, here is what Zhou says about the proper role of music in calming desires:

In ancient times, sage-kings instituted ceremonies and moral education. . . . Consequently, all people were in perfect harmony and all things were in concord. Thereupon the sage-kings created music to give expression to the winds coming from the eight directions[4] and to calm (*ping*) the feelings of the people. This is the reason why the sound of music is quiescent (*dan*) and not hurtful, harmonious and not licentious. As it enters the ear and affects the heart, everyone becomes quiescent and harmonious. Because of quiescence, one's desires will be calmed; because of harmony, one's impetuousness will disappear. [Zhou 1990, p. 28; Zhu & Lu 1967, p. 218, somewhat altered]

Zhou contrasts this with more recent rulers, who "indulge their desires without restraint" and replace the ancients' music with modern music, music which is "seductive, licentious, depressive, and complaining," and which "arouses desires and increases bitterness without end" [ibid.]. Although rulers might not like hearing themselves charged with

---

[4] According to Chan, this refers to "people's sentiments" [Zhu & Lu 1967, p. 218, fn. 3].

indulgence, it takes little imagination to see that they might like the idea of people who are unified and "quiescent." I will expand on this theme later.

Even more extreme than Zhou's description of the proper effect of music is his picture of Yanzi, Confucius's favorite student. Zhou cites the *Analects*'s description of Yanzi ("having only a single dish of rice, a single gourd of drink, and living in a narrow lane; others could not have endured this distress, but he did not allow his joy to be affected" [6:9]) and comments:

> Wealth and honor are what people love.[5] Yanzi did not love or seek them but instead enjoyed poverty. What does this tell us about his unique heart? There are high honors and enormous wealth that one can love and seek after, but Yanzi was unlike others since he could see what was truly great and forget what was really small. He saw the great, so his mind was at peace. His mind was at peace, so there was nothing he lacked. Lacking nothing, he treated wealth, honor, poverty, and humble station in the same way. As he treated them in the same way, he could transform them and equalize them. This is why Yanzi was regarded as second to the sage. [Zhou 1990, p. 31; Chan 1963, p. 475, somewhat altered]

This same idea, that wealth and station are as nothing to the sage, is repeated in chapter 33 of *Comprehending the Book of Changes*.[6]

When we put all these passages together, it certainly sounds like some desires that most of us have are ones which the sage should not have at all. If we lack these desires, we will be calm, tranquil, quiescent, and lack for nothing, though we may be desperately hungry and living in filth. This discouragement of actively seeking to fulfill one's desires – even including those for food and shelter, apparently – could not be more different from the attitude toward desires that will help to generate concern with *quanli*. Before we get to that, though, we need to look at the way that these ideas are expressed by Zhou's most important advocate, Zhu Xi.

Interpreters of Zhu Xi's views on desires and benefit face a problem very different from that faced by those who seek to make sense of Zhou's

---

[5] Contrast *Analects* 4:5, which says that all people desire wealth and honor, but these should only be sought in the right ways.

[6] Given that Zhou will be accused of being too influenced by Daoism by later critics, it is striking how much similarity there is between this description of Yanzi and that found in chapters 4 and 6 of the Daoist classic *Zhuangzi*; see [Graham 1981, esp. pp. 68–9 and 92].

ideas: Zhu was prolific, and there is a wealth of material from which to work. His enormous body of commentaries, recorded sayings, and essays represents a remarkable effort to synthesize the writings of earlier neo-Confucians into a single vision. It is easy to misinterpret Zhu if one takes passages out of context – as was sometimes done by his later critics, as we will see. When given a careful, sympathetic reading, the material all hangs together quite well. In brief, while some passages tempt one to read Zhu as advocating the radical reduction of desires, a balanced interpretation finds Zhu favoring the idea of the hierarchical ordering of desires. His view is thus not as extreme as Zhou's. Still, I argue later in the chapter that Zhu's critics were on to something: Zhu does not find an adequate place in his account of human psychology for people's everyday desires.

The easiest way to misunderstand Zhu is to read him as opposed to all satisfaction of human desires – as, in other words, advocating a radically ascetic doctrine. This kind of misreading is encouraged by the many times that Zhu contrasts "human desires (*renyu*)" with "heaven's pattern (*tianli*)." "Heaven's pattern" is his ultimate standard of value, the pattern in accord with which all things harmoniously flourish. "Human desires" can look quite bad by comparison, as when Zhu says:

> A mind that has never known right learning is muddied by human desire. Having known right learning, then the heaven's pattern will naturally issue forth and be seen, and human desire will gradually be eradicated. This is truly a good thing. [Zhu 1974 (1710), p. 99; 1991, p. 106, slightly altered]

A great deal hangs on what Zhu means here by "human desire," of course. In another passage, he begins to make that clear, as well as to clarify his understanding of Zhou's "no desire" doctrine:

> Zhou [Dunyi] said that one should have fewer and fewer desires until one has none, for he was afraid that people thought it enough to have few desires. . . . But the task of having no desire depends on one's ability to have few desires. No one but the sage can reach the point of having no desire. [Someone then asked:] "But what are we to make of this word 'desire'?" [Zhu replied:] "There are different [meanings]. This [idea of] having few desires – that is with respect to those [desires] that are improper: things like selfish desires. As for being hungry and desiring to eat or being thirsty and desiring to

drink, are these desires that one can be without?" [Zhu 1983, p. 2414; Chan 1963, p. 155, slightly altered]

One thing we see in this passage is Zhu's recognition that Zhou's teachings are difficult, suitable only for very advanced students. Still, sages do, in some sense, reach the state of having "no desire." In this connection it is important to see that there are two different kinds of desires, one good and one bad. A plausible suggestion, which will be confirmed as we examine more evidence, is to understand the "human desires" that Zhu directs us to "eradicate" as indicating our bad desires. This has not yet said what characterizes those bad desires, but it does at least make clear that we need not read Zhu as advocating that we rid ourselves of the desires to eat and drink.

Before trying to pin down what it is that makes certain desires bad, let us look at a fascinating passage in which it is clear that some of our desires are good. In response to the suggestion that the "human mind is the mind of human desires,"[7] Zhu says:

If the human mind is so very bad, our bodies would have to be completely eliminated before the mind of the way became clear. . . .[8] The human mind is our body with consciousness and desires, as in the case of "I desire humanity" and "I follow what my heart desires."[9] When "the desire of our nature" is "affected by external things and becomes activated,"[10] how can we avoid that desire? Only when external temptation causes us to fail will it be harmful. . . . Take the case of food. When one is hungry or thirsty and desires to eat one's fill, that is the human mind. However, there must be moral pattern in it. There are [times] one should eat and [times] one should not. . . . This is the correctness of the mind of the way. [Zhu 1983, ch. 62, sec. 41; Chan 1989, p. 202]

---

[7] Zhu's predecessor Cheng Yi (1033–1107), for whose ideas Zhu had the highest respect, introduced the idea of distinguishing the "human mind (*renxin*)" from the "way mind (*daoxin*)" in order to solve certain epistemological difficulties. See [Graham 1958, p. 64] for helpful discussion.

[8] Chan badly misses the point of this phrase in his translation; see [Chan 1989, p. 202].

[9] "I desire humanity" and "I follow what my heart desires" are attributed to Confucius in *Analects* 7:30 and 2:4, respectively.

[10] Both the phrases "the desire of our nature (*xing zhi yu*)" and "affected by external things and becomes activated" come from the *Book of Music*. Interestingly enough, it is possible that in the *Book of Music*, the "*yu*" of "*xing zhi yu*" is a copyist's error; see discussion in [Dai 1990a, p. 110, fn. 4]. Ewell there suggests that proper neo-Confucians would find "*xing zhi yu*" so bizarre as to be ungrammatical; clearly, he is mistaken about Zhu Xi on this score.

This is one of three passages in Zhu's massive *Classified Conversations* that invoke the phrase "desire of the nature (*xing zhi yu*)," a quotation from the *Book of Music*. Since elsewhere Zhu identifies "nature" with "heaven's pattern," his acknowledging that the nature has desires is equivalent to acknowledging that these desires are essential to our ethical well-being. These are desires, examples of which include not only "I desire humaneness" but also appropriate desires to eat and drink, which we should never be without.

When the three preceding passages are considered together, I think we can see that desires, as well as the closely related idea of the embodied self, can be vexing for neo-Confucians. This is especially true for Zhu, who more than any other writer of his day seeks to synthesize the writings both of his immediate predecessors and of classical thinkers. He is committed to a distinction between human desires and heavenly pattern and to Zhou's "no desire" thesis, on one hand, and to the correctness of "desir[ing] humaneness" and the existence of "desires of the nature," on the other. I do not want to argue that his attempt to make sense of all this is a disaster; indeed, I think Zhu's philosophical system is a remarkable achievement. Still, in light of all he says about human desires, it is hard to know exactly what to make of comments like "The human mind is our embodied selves with consciousness and desires, as in the case of 'I desire humaneness'." What is the connection between the desires and the humaneness? Later thinkers like Dai Zhen will be able to say; Zhu, I think, ultimately cannot.

In any event, let us allow Zhu that the "human desires" of the "human mind" can be good. Much more frequently than Zhu makes this point, though, he emphasizes their problematic tendencies. Let us now examine these problematic tendencies more closely and see if we can discern whence they arise. The following passage can be read in two different ways:

> [A student asked] "In eating and drinking, where is heaven's pattern and where is human desire?" Zhu replied: "Eating and drinking are heaven's pattern, but demanding delicious flavors is human desire."
> [Zhu 1983, p. 224; Chan 1989, p. 200]

On first reading, the passage seems to lean toward the idea, familiar from the *Dao De Jing*, that connoisseur-like desires need to be removed entirely.[11] Another possibility, though, is that the problem lies not in one's

---

[11] See *Dao De Jing* 12.

desiring delicious flavors, but in one's demanding them. One puts improper weight on the food's taste, or in other words, one's desires are mis-ordered. That Zhu endorsed this latter interpretation of the passage can be seen from a second passage in which these matters are addressed more clearly:

> [Someone asked] "Were parents to feel boundless love for their children and to desire that the children be brilliant and become established, could that be called the sincere mind [of the Way]?" Zhu responded: "It is proper that parents love their children, but to love without limitation and thus to unquestioningly desire things on their behalf is improper. One must properly distinguish between heaven's pattern and human desires." [Zhu 1983, p. 232]

Part of loving is desiring things on behalf of one's loved ones. This can be proper, but when one comes to "unquestioningly desire things on their behalf," one has slipped over the line from heavenly pattern to "human desire." Zhu's emphasis makes it clear that the problem is not with the object of the desire, but with the amount of the desire – its being "without limitation." Unlimited desires would be impossible to put into any kind of harmonious ordering, since each would demand pride of place.

In a third passage, finally, Zhu is explicit about the cause of mis-ordering one's desires: It is our inevitable subjectivity that will, unless we have undergone exhaustive cultivation, lead to partial, selfish prioritizing:

> For each matter there are two possibilities: the correct one is the impartiality (*gong*) of heavenly pattern, the incorrect one is the self-regard (*si*) of human desire. One must exhaustively analyze every matter, expanding one's work at controlling and ordering [oneself] to apply at all times. However, humans' endowments of ether (*qi*)[12] all have biased tendencies, and thus what each of us sees is different. . . . We must make efforts to control and put in order our biased endowments of ether. [Zhu 1983, p. 225]

We all view things from our own perspectives. My mouth waters in anticipation when offered a delicious morsel in a way just not matched – at least for most of us – by my response to the prospect of someone else's

---

[12] "Ether (*qi*)" has been translated by others as "material force" and "psycho-physical stuff": It is the vital stuff that makes up the entire cosmos.

enjoying a gourmet treat. It is certainly worth asking how this fate might be overcome, and Zhu has much to say on the subject. This is not the place, though, to explore Zhu's view of self-cultivation.[13]

Instead, let me summarize what we have seen of Zhu's view of the desires. Many desires are clearly bad. If we read him sympathetically, though, we must conclude that it is not its object that makes a desire bad, but the strength of that desire at that time and place, in comparison with other desires one might have. Most desires can be acceptable, when felt to the proper degree. It is thus unjust to charge Zhu with advocating wholesale suppression of the desires. Still, despite oblique statements brought on by classical Confucian talk of "desiring humaneness," Zhu has little to teach us about the positive roles that desires can play in ethically proper motivation.

Before moving on to the thinkers who develop more positive accounts of desire, it would be well to note that these matters were not of merely academic interest. Emperors throughout the Ming and Qing dynasties heard, in neo-Confucian teachings about reducing or eliminating desires, a set of doctrines very congenial to their purposes. They did their best to see that these ideas, as they understood them, were taught throughout the land. Is it any wonder that the first emperor of the Ming should have been intrigued by the teachings of Song Lian (1310–81), a Confucian who believed that "the only material wealth a man might legitimately possess was the minimum needed for the continuance of life" [Dardess 1983, p. 165]? Zhou's no-desire dictum was featured prominently in an important Qing imperial compilation, and the civil service exams regularly contained questions about "controlling the self," with explicit reference expected to Zhu's interpretation of this idea in terms of self-regarding desires.[14] Even though we have seen that Zhu's views were not as extreme as Zhou's (or Song Lian's), the ways in which all of their ideas were used by power-holders led later critics to paint them all with a single brush.

4.2 EMBRACING DESIRES

Let us now look at the writings of four thinkers who helped define the strand of the Confucian tradition which embraced desires as

---

[13] See [Angle 1998].

[14] See Chen Keming's discussion of Kang Xi's *Xingli Jingyi* in [Zhou 1990] for the imperial collection, and [Elman 2000, ch. 8] for the exam questions.

fundamental to moral flourishing. By focusing on these four, I simplify reality in several ways, since I ignore their predecessors, their contemporary critics, and numerous others who put forward similar views.[15] I implied at the end of the previous section that one reason for pro-desire views was as a corrective to the extreme views of Song thinkers, especially as interpreted and promulgated by power-holders. A second and complementary factor is social change. Starting in the sixteenth century, China saw a dramatic acceleration in commercial activity, money economy, literacy, and participation in elite culture by merchants and others. Merchants' status improved, and their pursuits were valorized as many Confucian thinkers began to take more seriously claims about the importance of benefit (*li*) and desire-satisfaction.[16] I intend to offer no simple causal formula to explain the increasing prominence of pro-desire views, and a more complex and satisfactory explanation lies beyond the scope of my project. I have little doubt that the social changes I refer to here were intimately connected to the philosophical developments I am about to discuss, but I leave it to others to assess the precise relationship.

I turn now to the four protagonists of this section's narrative. Chen Que and Dai Zhen offer successively more sophisticated positive accounts of desire, while Huang Zongxi and Gu Yanwu put their recognitions of desire's positive role in the context of the important tradition of statecraft thought, which itself plays a part in the origins of nineteenth-century Chinese rights discourse. After considering their various views, I will conclude with some reflections on the similarities and differences between this strand of Confucianism and rights discourse in the West during the seventeenth and eighteenth centuries.

4.2.1 *Huang Zongxi*

I begin with Huang Zongxi (1610–95) for two reasons. First, he serves to remind us of the problems that neo-Confucians can have with the concept of desire, since he is far from an unambiguous proponent of satisfying one's desires. Second, his views were among those most cited by the

---

[15] Two of the most important predecessors of these four are Chen Liang (1143–94), on whom see [Tillman 1982] and [Tillman 1994], and Luo Qinshun (1465–1547), on whom see [Luo 1987]. Some representative critics are discussed in [Handlin 1983]; see especially the account of Feng Congwu (1566–1627).

[16] See [Yu 1987] for a groundbreaking account of these related processes; for related accounts in English, see [Brook 1998] and [Lufrano 1997]. A similar dynamic played out between Japanese merchants and Confucians at roughly the same time; see [Najita 1987].

later thinkers whom I identify as early participants in rights discourse. His treatise on statecraft, *Waiting for the Dawn*, was widely circulated at the end of the nineteenth century, and his history of Ming-dynasty Confucianism was reissued in 1905 with a new introduction by one of the day's leading reformers.[17]

Before looking at Huang's writings, I must make a brief digression to explain the term "statecraft (*jingshi*)." "Statecraft," or more literally "ordering the world," is the term used by neo-Confucians to denote a set of practical concerns with governance, geography, flood control, and other matters; it is contrasted to a variety of expressions which refer to more abstract teachings aimed primarily at personal moral improvement. Although statecraft thought flourished in the late Ming dynasty and throughout the Qing dynasty, it had antecedents at least as early as the Song dynasty.[18] Its hallmark is to think through Confucian values and concerns from the perspective of their actual, practical effects; thinkers who identify themselves as committed to its precepts tend to write more about government policies than about ontological or epistemic matters. Many of its adherents have been rather sanguine about the role that desires and self-regard can play in human society. In the next chapter, we will see that statecraft concerns led to, among other things, the first efforts to translate Western writings about rights. But that is getting ahead of myself.

Back to Huang. At the very beginning of *Waiting for the Dawn*, he writes:

> In the beginning of human life each man lived for himself (*zisi*) and looked to his own interests (*zili*). There was such a thing as the general benefit (*gongli*), yet no one seems to have promoted it; and there was general harm, yet no one seems to have eliminated it. Then someone came forth who did not think of benefit in terms of his own benefit but sought to benefit all-under-heaven. . . . Thus his labors were thousands of times greater than the labors of ordinary men. Now to work a thousand . . . times harder without enjoying the benefit oneself is certainly not what most people in the world desire. [Huang 1985 (1663), p. 2; translation from Huang 1993, p. 91, slightly altered]

---

[17] For more biographical information on Huang, see [Huang 1993].

[18] Ouyang Xiu and Chen Liang are among the most important earlier thinkers associated with statecraft ideas. See [Liu 1967], [Tillman 1982], and [Tillman 1994, esp. pp. 80–2]. More generally, see [Liu 1990].

Huang recognizes the importance of "benefit" quite explicitly: The problem prior to the rise of the first sage kings was not that people cared about benefit, but that "common benefit" was ignored. He also stresses that while living "for oneself" is a problem in one sense, it is nonetheless natural: Huang concludes this passage by reiterating that "to love ease and dislike strenuous labor has always been the natural inclination (*qing*) of man" [ibid.]. It is striking, in this regard, that Huang makes proper rulers out to be psychological oddities. Most people do not desire to put in extraordinary labors "without benefiting" themselves – and who can blame them? Huang even notes that of early worthies, some refused to become rulers, and others, including Yao and Shun, the most famous early sages of all, undertook ruling and then quit.

The rhetorical payoff of Huang's characterization of rulers comes in the subsequent paragraphs, wherein he shows that more recent rulers have greedily amassed all power and benefit to themselves while their people shouldered all the harm. What they have done is natural, perhaps, but it negates the role that rulers were set up to fulfill, which is to promote the general good rather than their own individual good. Still, one can't but wonder whether Huang's argument would have been more convincing if he had allowed that rulers can enjoy benefit for themselves, but only to a proper degree. Huang recognizes the ubiquity of self-regarding desires, but – perhaps influenced by earlier neo-Confucian writings – seeks to make an exception for rulers.

4.2.2 Chen Que

If we turn to Chen Que (1604–77), a contemporary of Huang and in fact his fellow student, we will find a much more plausible psychological picture of sagehood than that adumbrated by Huang.[19] A chief characteristic of Chen's thought is its ability to explain how the actions of our everyday lives can be morally praiseworthy. In his essay "Scholars Take the Ordering of Life as Fundamental," for instance, he analyzes the "ordering of life (*zhisheng*)" and explains its ethical significance. "The way of learning," he explains, "is nothing peculiar; it is simply for those who have countries to preserve their countries, for those who have families to preserve their families, and for gentry (*shi*) to preserve their

---

[19] Like Huang, Chen studied with the most famous Confucian of their day, Liu Zongzhou. For further biographical information and analysis of Chen's thought, see [Tao 1997, ch. 9] and [Chow 1994, ch. 2]. Chen is also discussed in [Yu 1987].

embodied selves *(shen).*" His explanation of "shen" shows why this should be so:

> "*Shen*" does not refer [only] to one's embodied self *(shen).* All the affairs of one's parents, siblings, spouse, and children are affairs internal to one's *shen.* They touch one's very skin, and so such obligations can never be passed on to others. Thus meticulously ordering one's life is the most fundamental concern of scholars. [Chen 1979a, p. 158]

Chen makes explicit what modern thinkers call the social dimension of the self. Preserving one's *shen* requires preserving all those with whom one has significant relationships, since part of how I am doing turns on how my parents, for example, are doing. This is an "internal" matter to me. It is crucial to keep in mind, at the same time, that one's most immediate affairs – one's own hungers and desires, for instance – are internal as well. Chen's understanding of our psyches embraces both our commitments to others and our most basic commitments to our physical selves.

We see this even more strikingly when we turn to Chen's essay "Discussion of Self-Regard (*Si Shuo*)." *Si*, whose primary meaning is personal or self-regard, is typically derogatory in Confucian writings. When Zhu Xi wants to emphasize that the desires he is talking about are problematic, for instance, he often calls them "*si* desires," which is usually, and appropriately, translated as "selfish desires." In Chen's essay, by contrast, *si* is interpreted as a good thing, and even as one of the most fundamental characteristics of a good person. First Chen emphasizes that the ethically superior person's concern for others is graded according to their relation to him: "There is no one whom the superior person (*junzi*) does not revere (*jing*), but there must be a difference between his reverence for his elder brother and his reverence for a fellow villager" [Chen 1979b, p. 257]. This means that the superior person loves his country, but loves his family more, and loves his family, but loves his *shen* more [ibid.].

Chen avoids descending into some sort of selfish parochialism through his analysis of that in which genuine love, and thus genuine self-regard, consists. He contrasts the means by which ignorant parents raise children to those of virtuous parents [ibid., p. 258]. The former seek to satiate all their children's desires, inevitably side with them when disputes arise with neighbors, love to hear their children praised, and become furious if their children are ever criticized. Chen says that these methods amount to cultivating haughtiness, hatred, and vice, while harming the child's spleen and lungs (due to excessive food and clothing). Can this be called having true self-regard for one's children?

Virtuous parents, on the other hand, keep their children from eating too much or dressing too warmly; Chen even says that such a parent will often, upon spying his child eating, snatch the food away. Parents should also make light of any praise their children receive, but take seriously all criticisms. The result will be children who will make daily strides toward virtue. "Can we deny," Chen concludes, "that this is to have self-regard for one's children?"

Chen's reasoning runs as follows. "Self-regard" does mean to love the embodied self (*shen*), just as everyone thinks. It is a good thing rather than bad, though, because (1) one's *shen* is, through one's relationships to others, broadly inclusive; and (2) a proper understanding of what is good for people leads to restraint and virtue, rather than excess and vice. Thus Chen is able to conclude that Shun – one of the sages whom Huang suggested had ruled despite its not being in his interest – "respected wealth and enjoyed protection such that none was without: this is the epitome of self-regard."

For what it is worth, I believe that Chen's understanding of Shun comes much closer to what a classical Confucian like Mencius would have said, as can be seen, for instance, in Mencius's repeated assertions that it is all right for kings to be "fond of musical entertainment" or "fond of money," so long as the king "shares [this] fondness with the people."[20] That is, the king's (natural) enjoyments are fine, so long as they are not indulged to the point that he devotes all the kingdom's resources to his own enjoyment, leaving the people with nothing. Instead, the king should recognize that the people have the same desires as he does, and see that they are able to fulfill their desires, albeit not in exactly the same ways, or to the same degree, as he can.

Accurately interpreting Mencius would certainly have mattered to Chen: He was deeply concerned with rooting out the pernicious influences – as he viewed them – of Buddhism and Daoism, which he saw as infecting all of Song- and Ming-dynasty Confucianism [Chow 1994, p. 54]. For our purposes, what matters still more is that the shape of Chen's rather plausible psychological account is mirrored in the works of some of his contemporaries and picked up by subsequent thinkers, all of which contribute to the strand of neo-Confucianism with which I am here con-

---

[20] *Mencius* 1B:1, 1B:6; [Lau 1970, pp. 60, 66].

cerned. Let us look now at how these ideas are developed in a somewhat less abstract context: the statecraft writings of Gu Yanwu.

4.2.3 Gu Yanwu

Gu Yanwu (1613–82) was one of the leading intellectuals of his day. Though his official career was truncated thanks to his resistance to serving the Manchus who conquered China in 1644, he traveled and wrote widely. He is remembered for his stress on the importance of evidence and practical results – abstruse metaphysics had not saved his beloved Ming dynasty from defeat – and thus figures importantly in both the "statecraft (*jingshi*)" and "evidential learning (*kaozhengxue*)" strands of Confucianism. The latter focused primarily on reinterpreting classical texts, and need not concern us here; as I have noted earlier, the former is quite important to the developments I am tracking in this and subsequent chapters.[21]

A pair of essays by Gu Yanwu nicely illustrates the tension between individual benefit and general good with which thinkers of his day were struggling. In "On Licentiates" he is harshly critical of the civil service examination system of his day, blaming many of China's ills on a system that fosters self-interested officials and seems to encourage corruption. In "On the Prefecture-County System," on the other hand, Gu argues that the chief faults of the current administrative system lie in not making adequate use of "self-regard (*si*)." On the surface the two essays seem to take diametrically opposed views on self-regard, the first blaming it and the second lamenting that it is not better used. Closer inspection will show that Gu is more consistent than this. The ultimate goal of the two essays – a world in which all flourish, free from abuses by superiors – is the same, and in each case, self-regard is seen as a crucial and legitimate means to that end.

The responsibilities that Gu believes licentiates (those who have passed local-level civil-service exams) should shoulder range from providing moral and intellectual education for the young to taking administrative posts and aiding the emperor in keeping the empire in order.

---

[21] The classic work in English on evidential learning is [Elman 1984]. For more on Gu's life and interests, see [Hummel 1970 (1943), pp. 421–6]. As I imply in the main text, evidential learning and statecraft are not unrelated; they share some concerns and methodology. I focus on the latter for simplicity's sake.

Unfortunately, Gu observes that the members of this key group fail miserably at these tasks. Only rare exceptions can actually understand the classics, and those able to put this knowledge to use in service of the emperor are rarer still. Instead, Gu says these largely dissolute licentiates spend much of their time in raising lawsuits and neglecting their duties [Gu 1959b, p. 22]. The result is that the group is more and more severely disciplined, but even so it seems that everyone seeks the status of licentiate.

The crux of Gu's analysis comes in explaining why the status is so sought-after. It is not that people aim to make a good name for themselves, which would be an appropriate motivation; rather, they wish to "preserve their selves and families (*bao shen jia*)" from abuse and indignity at the hands of local petty officials. Gu can understand this motivation, asking "Whose human feelings do not favor their selves and families?" The problem is that self-preservation was not the intended goal of the exam system, and when it is put to this purpose, it becomes perverted. Bribery and cheating are rampant, and the vast numbers of licentiates do no one any good.

Immediately after this discussion Gu again emphasizes that the problem is not with people's desires to preserve themselves, writing that not even the sagely "former kings" could do away with people's emotional commitment to their selves and family. Even if the legendary sages Yao and Shun were to rise again, they could not put an end to the bribery and cheating the present structure (*fa*) incites [1959b, p. 22]. Since seeking official status seems to be the only way to protect one's family, Gu cannot really blame people for seeking, and then abusing, that status. His solution is two-pronged: He believes that the institution for selection of officials must be changed so that the officials can serve their intended functions, and he hints that other structural changes are needed to remove the incentive to abuse government service. His primary concern in this article is the former, pursuant to which he proposes two reforms. The first is tightening the requirements for passing the exams, which should lead to a dramatic reduction in the number of successful candidates and to a concomitant improvement in their quality; the second is an increased use of personal recommendations, rather than exam success, as a means to official promotion. Neither of these is completely unproblematic. Reducing the number of successful candidates would put still further strain on a system in which the vast majority of exam-takers failed repeatedly, most never succeeding at all [Elman 2000]. It is true that recommendations allow judgments to be made about moral character in ways that anonymous exams do not. For this to work, rather than to provide even more opportunities for abuse, would require existing officials to be scrupulous in making recommendations. As we will see in a moment, Gu believes that there is more than one way to ensure such scrupulousness.

More important for our purposes than reforms to the exam system are larger changes Gu only hints at here but makes explicit in "On the Pre-fecture-County System," for unless the problems that motivated people to seek the licentiate's status are solved, any reform of the exam system alone is doomed to failure. If official status is the only way to preserve oneself, that is, such status will be sought by all. At the center of "On the Prefecture-County System" is the idea that unlike the situation under the ancient feudal system, in which local notables were responsible first to the people of their region and only secondarily to central authorities, in the current prefecture-county system local officials owe their alle-giance almost entirely to the central government. They are under con-stant supervision by superiors and must seek to ensure that the superiors' goals, chief among which is the collection of revenue for the central bureaucracy, are always met. The result, says Gu, is that local officials are forced to be cruel to their people, reaching the point that they are "unwilling to provide for their people a single day's worth of benefit (*li*)" [Gu 1959a, p. 12].

It is easy to see that Gu is coming at the same set of problems that he saw leading to the abuse of the exam system, but this time looking for a more fundamental solution. The theoretical basis for his analysis will sound familiar, since it, too, relies on accepting and affirming people's self-regarding emotions. Gu writes:

> The constant emotions of all people under heaven are to care for their families and have self-regard for their children. Even before the Three Dynasties it was known that the Son of Heaven's impulse on behalf of the people was not as strong as his desire to act on his own behalf. Sages make use of this, using the self-regard of all under heaven to bring about the impartiality (*gong*) of a single man, thus ensuring the orderly rule of the empire. [1959a, p. 15]

This passage bears comparison with Huang Zongxi's criticism of rulers that we examined earlier. Whereas Huang believed that early rulers – and all good ones – were able to suppress their self-regard on behalf of the whole country, Gu says that from the first, rulers were more concerned with their own well-being than with that of the people. His solution is to work with this reality, using everyone's self-regard in such a way that the actions of the "single man" (the emperor) come out impartially beneficial to all.

How is this to be achieved? In earlier sections of the essay, Gu urges that county magistrates be drawn from the local populace, rather than following the "rule of avoidance," according to which officials are required not to serve in their home counties. Rather than seeking to make officials distant from – and therefore impartial toward – the people they administer, Gu believes that the opposite policy will bring the best results. Immediately following the just-quoted passage about "using the self-regard of all under heaven," Gu explains:

> If county magistrates should come to have self-regard for one hundred *li* of land [i.e., for a county], then the people of the county will all be as his kin and the lands of the county will all be as his fields. . . . Since he treats the people as his kin, he will certainly care for them and never harm them; since he treats the county's lands as his fields, he will certainly order them and not allow them to be abandoned. . . . From the perspective of the magistrate, this is self-regard, but from the perspective of the son of heaven, who is concerned with the orderly rule of all under heaven, no more need be done than this. [1959a, p. 15]

In other words, if the emperor allows each region to be legitimately concerned with its own interests, the net result will be impartial concern for every region's interests, and thus for the interests of the whole empire. It is left to the emperor, presumably, to balance competing interests, though the implicit assumption seems to be that the legitimate interests do not, in fact, conflict – a premise we shall meet repeatedly, and examine carefully, in subsequent chapters.

In a study of Gu's view of self-interest, the contemporary scholar Cheng I-fan concludes that Gu has

> completely abandoned following the old, Song Confucian route of impartiality (*gong*) to an ideal state and, to the contrary, he is fundamentally indifferent to the self-regard in people's natures. He also does not worry about conflicts between the benefits of the world's people, so long as everyone's self-regard is utilized in a set, systematic fashion. If it is not wasted nor suppressed, the world will be ordered and peaceful. [Cheng 1984, p. 92]

This is a strong reading which immediately drew criticism.[22] I also believe that Cheng has somewhat overstated his case, but if we read Cheng's interpretation charitably, we should conclude that he does not miss the mark by much. It is clear, even from the sections of "On the Prefecture-County System" that I have quoted, that Gu's ultimate goal remains one in which the general good is well served and all people benefit, and that Gu sees this goal in terms of "impartiality (*gong*)." Still, in Cheng's defense, Gu does not primarily advocate impartiality as a route to that end; careful and systematic employment of people's feelings of self-regard is largely responsible for the ultimate achievement of impartiality. It is also true that while in "On Licentiates" Gu does say that self-regarding desires lead to the many problems he identifies with licentiates, we see that Gu does not condemn these desires themselves, but rather the social context in which they prompt so many people to seek to become licentiates. The doctrines of Gu's two essays, that is, are largely consistent with each other and with Cheng's characterization. The only qualification I would add is that in "On Licentiates" we do see hints of impartiality still being employed as a means, rather than simply as an end, in the ways that Gu characterizes the new licentiates that his reformed exam system will produce.

4.2.4 Dai Zhen

Dai Zhen (1723–77) was among the greatest philosophers of the Qing dynasty. He was one of the few thinkers of his time to combine the practical focus of the statecraft school with more abstract speculation about moral psychology and human nature. He was harshly critical of Song-dynasty thinkers like Zhu Xi, arguing that their teachings had been tainted by Buddhist and Daoist ideas, and had thus lost touch with the values of Confucianism's classical tradition. I believe that his criticisms are sometimes unfair or exaggerated, but at their core we see the finest expression of the new perspective on desires that this chapter has been following.

Dai succinctly expresses the core of his conception of desire when he writes, "whatever comes from desire is always for the sake of life and nurture."[23] Rhetorically, at least, this is a complete inversion of the Song

---

[22] See [Liu 1984], a comment on Cheng's original article.
[23] [Dai 1995, p. 160; cf. Dai 1990a, p. 149, and Dai 1990b, p. 83]

thinkers' tendency to see desires as first and foremost problematic. Dai certainly believes that desires can go too far, as we will see in a moment, but in their origins they are good, motivating us to seek things upon whose value all agree. Although Dai mainly uses "self-regard (*si*)" as a technical term for desiring too strongly, in some places he treats it similarly to "desire," giving it a less technical gloss and seeing it at the core of humaneness:

> Both self-regard for one's embodied self (*si yu shen*) and extending [this self-regard] to those close to oneself are aspects of humaneness. Self-regard for one's embodied self is to be humane towards oneself; to extend [this self-regard] to those close to oneself is to be humane towards those who are close to one. [Dai 1995, p. 181; cf. Dai 1990a, p. 241, and Dai 1990b, p. 116]

The basis of self-regard is having desires for oneself: caring for and seeking to nurture oneself throughout one's life. As is the case with desires themselves, that is, self-regard starts out aimed at universally valued ends. In this passage, in addition, Dai suggests that self-regard is actually an "aspect of humaneness." Precisely what this means is a bit obscure; I think the following passage, now put in terms of desires, makes the point clear:

> [Mencius understood that desires cannot be eliminated.] There can be no greater affliction in a human life than to lack the means to fulfill that life (*sui qi sheng*). If, desiring to fulfill one's own life, one also fulfills the lives of others, this is humaneness. If, desiring to fulfill one's own life, one reaches the point even of slaying others and paying no heed, this is inhumaneness. The inhumaneness actually begins with the desire to fulfill one's life, and if there were no such desire, necessarily there would be no inhumaneness. But if there were no such desire, then one would also regard the affliction and distress of others in the world with indifference. It is impossible for one to feel that one's own life need not be fulfilled and yet to fulfill the life of another. [Dai 1995, p. 159; cf. Dai 1990a, pp. 146–7, and Dai 1990b, p. 82]

The last two sentences make the crucial point: We must be motivated by our desires, else we will care neither about ourselves nor about others. Without desires – which is the same as saying without self-regard, in the sense of the prior passage – there can be no humaneness.

This is the clearest statement I have found in Dai's writings of the shift
that has occurred. We saw little in Zhu's writings to suggest that desires
were more than ineliminable: a part of our human nature, to be sure, but
not critical to the process of self-cultivation and world-ordering itself.
Perhaps under the influence of commercialization and the other trends
mentioned at the outset of this section, Dai seems to have rethought
what it means to "desire humaneness." He criticizes Song-dynasty Confucians as follows:

> [The Song masters said] "If it does not come from pattern then it
> comes from desire, and if it does not come from desire, then it comes
> from pattern." When they see others crying out from hunger and
> cold, or [feeling] the sorrow and resentment of an unfulfilled love,
> or hoping for life despite being close to death, it is all just "human
> desire"; they abstractly designate a sentiment devoid of feeling or
> desire as the "original suchness of heavenly pattern," and preserve
> it in their hearts. [Dai 1995, p. 211; cf. Dai 1990a, p. 387, and Dai
> 1990b, p. 165]

Given all the invective that Song thinkers launched at "human desire,"
Dai is wondering, What is left for "humaneness"? What, in particular, can
it mean to "desire humaneness"? Dai believes that the Song understanding of humaneness is "abstract" or "empty" (*kong*), divorced from
the flesh-and-blood desires about which we really care – and which alone
can serve to motivate us to do good for ourselves and others. At the heart
of ethical motivation, according to Dai, are our everyday desires. Desiring humaneness just is desiring food – or even, in the proper circumstances, desiring delicious food.

Particularly relevant both to Dai's interpretation of Song neo-
Confucianism and to my own larger purposes is the perspective that
rulers take away from the writings of Zhu and other Song thinkers. Dai
writes:

> The sages, in governing the empire, embodied the people's feelings,
> fulfilled the people's desires, and the Kingly Way was complete....
> Nowadays [however,] those who govern others regard the ancient
> worthies' and sages' embodying of the people's feelings and fulfill-
> ment of the people's desires as issuing mostly from baseness, trivi-
> ality, and tortured obscurity, and pay it no heed. As for censuring
> others [on the basis of] pattern (*li*), [modern rulers] find it easy to
> hold up the loftiest standard in the vast world, call it "righteousness,"
> and condemn people in its name.... When someone invokes

pattern to censure someone below him, the faults of the one below are [regarded by] everyone as too numerous to count. When a man dies by law, there are still some who pity him; but if he dies by pattern, who will pity him? [Dai 1995, p. 161; cf. Dai 1990a, p. 387, and Dai 1990b, p. 84]

The suggestion in this passage that people can "die by pattern" is one of Dai's most famous phrases, and it has been vehemently objected to by defenders of Zhu [Chan 1989, p. 207]. As I noted earlier, though, power-holders were able to stress the side of Zhu's teachings they found most useful in ways that did not redound to the benefit of the people. This would have been obvious to Dai. The interpretation of Zhu's ideas shared by Dai and the emperors was, admittedly, somewhat exaggerated and not wholly charitable. One reason that Zhu's text remained open to this kind of interpretation, though, was that Zhu did not provide a clear, positive role for desires to serve. Dai, like many seventeenth- and eighteenth-century Confucians, did.

I do not want to exaggerate the shift that Dai's view of desires represents. We find in his writings, after all, passages like the following:

Self-regard comes from feelings and desires, and becloudedness from the heart's discernment. To be without self-regard is humaneness, and to be without becloudedness is wisdom – but it is not by getting rid of feelings and desires that one becomes humane, or by getting rid of the heart's discernment that one becomes wise. [Dai 1995, p. 211; cf. Dai 1990a, p. 388, and Dai 1990b, p. 165]

"Self-regard (*si*)" is used in this passage as a technical term for errant desiring. This is even clearer elsewhere, when we read that "The two great afflictions of all men at all times, self-regard and becloudedness, are simply of two roots: self-regard arises from faults in desiring, and becloudedness from faults in knowing."[24] This technical use contrasts with the term's more general sense that we saw earlier, where self-regard was actually said to be "an aspect" of humaneness.

The difference between the two uses of "self-regard" arises from the fact that while we should care for ourselves, we must do so in a fashion consistent with the context in which we find ourselves and with our essentially social natures. We live in society, connected to others in many ways, fellow participants with others in groups of all sizes. Like all Con-

---

[24] [Dai 1995, p. 160; cf. Dai 1990a, p. 149, and Dai 1990b, p. 83]

fucians, Dai emphasizes the degree to which any assessment of whether our lives are going well must be relational: Whether we are doing well as parents depends on the lives of our children; whether we are doing well as sons and daughters, conversely, depends on the lives of our parents. Thus, in a passage quoted earlier, Dai writes: "If, desiring to fulfill one's own life, one also fulfills the lives of others, this is humaneness" [Dai 1995, p. 181]. This of course resonates with what we heard from Chen Que, who said of the sage Shun that he "respected wealth and enjoyed protection such that none was without: this is the epitome of self-regard."

As we have seen, Dai sometimes uses "self-regard" in just this same, broad way. In Dai's technical sense, on the other hand, "self-regard" means to desire things inconsistent with one's social nature. Like Chen, Dai believes that one person's life can be fully fulfilled if, and only if, everyone's lives are fulfilled. Suppose that one is given money and sent to buy food for the whole family. A desire to eat delicious food goes too far if one spends all the money in a teahouse on exquisite treats before one has even reached the market. The problem with such behavior can be seen in many ways, including long-term effects on what we might call one's individual well-being. The problem shows up more immediately in one's relational well-being: Thanks to such behavior, one is doing poorly as a son and as a brother. Depending both on how willing others are to sacrifice on one's behalf and on how obtuse one is, it may take some time before defects in one's relational well-being intrude on one's individual well-being. In the Confucian analysis, this does not alter the fact that our lives' fulfillment involves both these aspects. Improper desires are inconsistent with the overall well-being of our true – social – selves.

The simultaneous commitments to the possibility of a cosmos in which all flourish and to the necessity of such a cosmos if any are to flourish lie at the core of much of Confucianism. Unlike many of their predecessors, each of the four subjects of this section have insisted on understanding flourishing and fulfillment in terms of our actual, concrete desires. One way to highlight this is to emphasize that while our true selves are social, they are also embodied. To somewhat differing degrees, each of these thinkers believes that our everyday desires should neither be shunned nor merely tolerated, but embraced as essential to our well-being and to our ethical advancement. For Chen, Gu, and Dai, at least, desires are necessary for proper ethical motivation. Desiring humaneness comes directly from desiring to eat, sleep, and drink. In wanting things for ourselves, we want things for others. A society in which we are able to attain the things we properly desire is a society in which others attain what they properly desire, and so insofar as we hope to attain what we desire, we have a responsibility to see that others do so as well.

4.3 CONCLUSION

In sum, these Confucians believed both that we have legitimate desires and that we have responsibilities to see that others can fulfill their legitimate desires. This combination of ideas bears a striking similarity to the argument at the core of one of the founding texts of Western rights discourse, *On the Law of War and Peace* by Hugo Grotius (1583–1645). Grotius believed that the laws of nature were rooted in our sociability: We desire society, and thus we appropriately desire – as confirmed by our reason – to respect one another's rights, without which there would be no society.[25] Grotius combines these ideas, however, with the very un-Confucian idea that our rights can be exchanged via contract; even the right to self-defense can be transferred to the sovereign. Our Confucians have no concepts that can play this kind of role, and I suspect would reject such an idea if it were explained to them. They see our natures and our needs as uniform. How could one person's interest in his or her own self-defense become illegitimate through any kind of agreement – especially a merely hypothetical agreement, as was the case with Grotius and all subsequent social contract theory?

Western rights theories developed along a number of lines through the balance of the seventeenth and eighteenth centuries. John Selden (1584–1654) and Thomas Hobbes (1588–1679) minimized the role of natural laws or rights, seeing the rights we have in society as depending on the laws instituted by our sovereign; the sovereign's authority, in turn, derived from a hypothesized social contract that established society in the first place.[26] This formulation readily led to the idea, prominent in the writings of thinkers from Samuel von Pufendorf (1632–94) to Jeremy Bentham (1748–1832), that rights came only from corresponding obligations: Rights were passive, deriving from law rather than emerging directly from any natural or ethical conception of human well-being [Tuck 1979, p. 160]. There were also a great many differences between

[25] [Grotius 1990 (1625), pp. 91, 100]. See also [Tuck 1979, pp. 72–3].
[26] See [Tuck 1979, chs. 4, 6]. Tuck writes that Selden studied the historical changes in English law and concluded that "If human laws permitted a particular practice on a widespread scale, the presumption was that neither the natural nor the divine law forbade it" [ibid., p. 85].

Pufendorf and Bentham, chief among them the question of whether the laws from which our duties (and thus rights) derive could be natural or only man-made. Much of modern jurisprudence has followed Bentham on this latter point, believing only in man-made or "positive law." I will discuss one of the nineteenth century's leading proponents of such ideas in Chapter 5, when I compare Rudolf von Jhering's conception of rights with the way his ideas are interpreted by a leading Chinese theorist.

Pufendorf's alternative formulation, according to which rights derived from natural duties, which in turn derived from natural (or divine) laws, was nonetheless extremely important; it found its most famous expression in the writings of John Locke (1632–1704). The idea that certain rights could be inalienable, which derives in part from Locke, was gradually combined with certain other claims to form what scholars now call the "subjective theory of rights." Central to these developments is the idea that the moral world may not be well-ordered, even in principle; "clashes of rights [may] not be the result simply of human folly or blindness, but [may] be ultimate and unresolvable" [Haakonssen 1996, p. 312]. In subsequent chapters I will pay careful attention to Chinese correlates of this idea; we will see that even today, many Chinese rights theorists continue to see harmony, rather than conflict, at the root of their ideas of rights.

Embracing the value of desires is one way to defend the legitimacy of people's self-regarding interests; another way is to assert that people have rights to enjoy these same interests. In subsequent chapters I will explore some of the complications of taking the latter of these paths, as seen from the viewpoint of the Chinese thinkers concerned with rights. For now it might be most useful to reflect on some complications to which the approach of this chapter's four protagonists might give rise. One question is whether embracing desires is something that can be institutionalized so that people actually feel the results. This is particularly relevant given the seemingly straightforward ways in which rights can be institutionalized, thanks to their close connections to law. A second question for our Confucians concerns the possibility that embracing desires will lead to license: We saw both Chen and Dai say that selfishness is bad, but is this enough to restrain desires when necessary?

There is good evidence that all four thinkers studied here were aware of both these problems. Much of my discussion of Gu, in fact, concerned precisely the question of how to reform institutions so that people's self-regarding tendencies would mesh, rather than conflict. Huang also wrote about this issue extensively in *Waiting for the Dawn*, proposing among other things to make the various lower-level official positions – tax collectors, warrant-bearers, and so on – into rotating "draft" positions. One of his arguments is that if the occupants of such positions are in office for only short periods of time, they will not abuse their power, for they will know that others will soon take their places, and they could then be subject to the new officeholders' abuse in retaliation [Huang 1993, pp. 161–2]. Dai and particularly Chen emphasized a somewhat different approach to institutionalizing restraint: They stressed the importance of Confucian rituals. Chen instructed his son that "What distinguishes human beings from beasts is our capacity to devote ourselves to ritual practice. Human beings also set ourselves apart from beasts by practicing ritual in earnest."[27] This commitment to restraint through ritual has strong roots in classical Confucianism – especially in the writings of Xunzi (third century B.C.E.). This is an area where most Chinese rights theorists will part company with their Confucian forebears, however, even launching vehement attacks on Confucian ritual teachings. But I am getting ahead of myself. Our next task is to turn to the ways that existing Chinese concerns merge with interpretations of Western rights discourse in China's nineteenth century.

---

[27] Quoted from [Chow 1994, p. 48]. Chow also discusses Dai Zhen, though quite differently than I have, arguing that Dai's ethics "underscored extirpation of bad conduct and ideas rather than developing the good inherent in humans" [ibid., p. 190].

5

Nineteenth-Century Origins

IT IS OFTEN DIFFICULT to identify beginnings. Ask when rights discourse began in Europe, and you can receive answers that differ by centuries, depending on which stage of the ongoing evolution of concepts and practices related to "rights" – and to its correlates and predecessors in a half-dozen languages – one counts as the beginning. It might be thought that the beginning of rights discourse in China would be easier to locate: As there was no concept of rights in traditional thought, shouldn't we just look for the moment that the idea of rights was introduced to China from Europe? Unfortunately, this "moment" is rather difficult to identify precisely. To be sure, we must look carefully at early translations of European texts concerning rights into Chinese, but we will find that these translations seem to be part of an existing discourse almost as much as they begin a new one.

In addition, I need to be very careful when I say that the discussions initiated by these texts are about rights. Since my discussion of these matters will depend on some of the conclusions from Chapter 2, let me briefly review the relevant issues. I argued there that conceptual content depends on the inferential commitments we take on when we use language, and I further contended that the norms governing these inferences are instituted by the practices of the groups to which we belong. In other words, what someone means by his or her words depends on what the person and his or her community take to follow from what is said. Since the commitments of each of us differ in large or small ways from those of anyone else, our meanings will differ from one another. We regularly take one another to be talking about the same things, though, and seek to hold others to the propriety of certain inferences. If I say that autumn directly follows spring, it would be appropriate for you to correct me; if I insist, then you will conclude that I mean something different by "autumn" (or perhaps "spring," or even both) than you do. Another way to say this is that we have different concepts of autumn.

With this in mind, we can see that comparison of concepts across cultures will rarely be an all-or-nothing affair. Starting from the premise that there is no concept of rights in pre-nineteenth-century China, I will be looking for ways in which language comes to be used to express commitments similar to those I connect with "rights." No one in nineteenth-century China uses words that exactly entail what I believe to follow from "rights," but the same is true even of my contemporaries in the United States today. There is certainly a difference of degree, but more important is the difference of community. My fellow Americans and I take ourselves to be sharing a concept, and thus to be committed to the same norms for its use, even if our disparate commitments mean that some of the things which follow from these norms will differ.[1] When I interpret the language of a nineteenth-century Chinese thinker, on the other hand, I need to look at the commitments that he and his community will take to follow from what he has said. Some of the time we will find significant overlap with what I take to follow from "rights," but insofar as the norms guiding his discourse emerge from a context very different from mine, I am on shakier ground saying that he is using a concept of rights than when I say the same thing of someone today.

Let me try to flesh all this out with some examples. A contemporary scholar studying the nineteenth-century Japanese thinker Katō Hiroyuki – who will be an important figure later in this chapter – recognizes the danger of thinking that everyone shares a single stock of concepts. Despite a Confucian education, in the 1870s Katō adopted Western liberalism and constitutionalism. The scholar writes that

> At first glance, these Western ideas appear incompatible with Confucianism.... Yet the liberalism, natural rights, [and] constitutionalism ... that Katō adopted cannot be explained satisfactorily as ready made concepts, concepts that he imported from abroad and adopted or discarded as circumstances dictated.... Instead, I believe that these Western ideas, as construed by Katō, were consistent with cardinal Confucian presuppositions about man and society. [Wakabayashi 1984, p. 473]

---

[1] For instance, we might agree that it follows from a thing's being sentient that it has rights, but disagree on what is needed for sentience, and thus on what has rights.

Call this the danger of "ready-made concepts." Concepts do not fall from the sky – or from Europe – with their meanings already clear; they are what a community makes of them. Even if Katō and his colleagues used a word that we translate as "liberalism," the meaning of this word must come from the ways in which Katō and his community used it, or more accurately, from the ways in which Katō's community took it to be appropriately used.

I will try to avoid similar problems with thinking of "rights" as a ready-made concept, both for Chinese thinkers and for Japanese like Katō. This same scholar who rejects ready-made concepts, though, falls prey to a second danger. This comes out most clearly when he seeks to explain why Katō might have construed "liberalism" or "natural rights" differently from the European sources on which he drew. The scholar writes that

> When Katō and other mid-century Japanese thinkers translated Western philosophical concepts, they used character-compounds found in Chinese classical texts or else devised neologisms based on classical Chinese diction. In this way, Japanese thinkers might unwittingly carry over tacit assumptions and mental associations from the Confucian tradition. Then Japanese conceptions diverged from Western concept. [1984, p. 491]

The problem with this attitude is that it makes Japanese (and Chinese) speakers into passive victims of their language and their tradition. To the contrary, I believe they said what they wanted to say. In Lydia Liu's recent study of what she calls "translingual practice"[2] in nineteenth- and twentieth-century China, she talks of translation from a "guest language" into a "host language" – rather than the more conventional "source language" and "target language" – in order to stress the active role played by Chinese and Chinese speakers in the processes that she studies. She argues for the appropriateness of this terminology, which I endorse, since

> the translator or some other agent in the host language always initiates the linguistic transaction by inviting, selecting, combining, and reinventing words and texts from the guest language, and, moreover,

---

[2] She defines the study of translingual practice as examining "the processes by which new words, meanings, discourses, and modes of representation arise, circulate, and acquire legitimacy within the host language due to, or in spite of, the latter's contact/collision with the guest language" [Lydia Liu 1995, p. 26]. See the main text for "host language" and "guest language."

... the needs of the translator and his/her audience together determine and negotiate the meaning (i.e., usefulness) of the text taken from the guest language. [Lydia Liu 1995, p. 27]

We will see precisely these dynamics in the following pages. We will observe influences from various strands of the Chinese tradition, of course, but there will be no need to characterize these pejoratively as "unwittingly [carrying] tacit assumptions."

These various interactions between guest and host languages take place in a variety of contexts. Translations and religious writings of missionaries play a role, as do arguments by Chinese officials and others about how best to develop China's economy and reform its government. Chinese efforts to understand and then make use of international law are influential, as are Japanese political movements and theoretical tracts. The writings and translations done by Chinese who study for a time in Europe or in Japan, finally, also are important factors in the development of the discourse. My goal in this chapter is to look at what is said in each of these contexts, to see how something like rights begins to figure in each context, and to show how the overall discourse evolves from the middle to the end of the nineteenth century.

5.1 TRANSLATION OF INTERNATIONAL LAW

Translations do not come out of nowhere. Someone has to know a foreign work and want to translate it; someone has to want to publish it; language must exist or be manufactured into which to translate the work. These different factors shape what gets translated, how it is rendered, and who will read it. Early translations of "rights" are as much part of existing discourses as they are the inauguration of a new one. In this section I will illustrate these ideas by examining the earliest two translations of Western rights terminology into Chinese.

5.1.1 *The* Illustrated Compendium

Let us begin at the beginning: in the middle of increasing disputes between Chinese authorities and English merchants over trade in opium. The Chinese official who, drawing on centuries of statecraft thought, tries to deal with the aggressive foreigners is Lin Zexu (1785–1850).[3] He sup-

---

[3] Statecraft thought is discussed in the previous chapter; see especially the sections on Huang Zongxi and Gu Yanwu.

ports the efforts of the best-known statecraft thinker of the era, Wei Yuan (1794–1856), to study and advocate techniques and ideas known in the West. Wei Yuan, in turn, is able to draw on the talents of a small core of bilingual Chinese and foreigners. The result of these collaborations is the publication of the *Illustrated Compendium on Coastal Nations* in 1840. It contains a wide variety of material, ranging from maps to instructions for making cannons to discussions of diplomacy; buried among these, a scant eight pages among its more than three thousand, are translated selections from Emmerich de Vattel's *Le Droit des gens* (*The Law of Nations*), a textbook on international law published in France in 1758.

In all, the *Compendium* contains five selections from Vattel, all of them based on an 1833 English translation of Vattel's original [Svarverud 2000]. Two selections are translated by Peter Parker, an American missionary and physician living in Canton. The remaining three – of which two are based on the same sections as those Parker translated – are translated by Yuan Dehuai, a former imperial translator and a member of Lin's staff. A contemporary scholar has argued plausibly that Yuan used Parker's brief translations as bases for his longer versions [ibid.]. Parker's and Yuan's first selections are both drawn from a section on the prohibition of foreign merchandise. The paragraph begins, in an 1820 American translation, "Every state has, consequently, a right to prohibit the entrance of foreign merchandise, and the people who are interested in this prohibition have no right to complain of it, as if they had been refused an office of humanity" [Vattel 1820, p. 95]. We can well understand why Wei and his patron Lin would have been interested in the Western view of such prohibitions, for Lin wanted to impose just such a prohibition on Western merchants. In any event, Parker translates only the first of the two uses of "right," rendering it with "*li*," which can mean custom or rule. With regard to what might be distinctive about this type of rule, Parker's version follows the original rather closely, explaining that nations can prohibit trade out of a desire to avoid suffering losses at another's expense. Such prohibitions cannot be complained about on grounds of "humanity" – rendered "*renqing*" by Parker – because they are merely matters of profit [Wei 1840, p. 3031].

Parker next turns to the question of when war is justified. The sections of Vattel's work on which this selection is based are replete with the word "right(s)," but there is no term that seems to correspond with it in Parker's version. Parker writes that just wars "accord with heavenly pattern (*tianli*)" and with "righteousness (*yi*)," but we see nothing that corresponds to the twin uses of "right" in "In treating the law of safety, we have shewn that nature gives men a right to use force, when it is necessary for their defense, and the preservation of their rights" [Vattel 1820, p. 356]. Interestingly, Parker does use the word *"bingquan"* to render the power or authority to wage war; we will see later that *"quan"* comes to be used in the 1860s to mean rights [Wei 1840, p. 3032]. But that does not seem to be Parker's intention. Indeed, it may be an exaggeration to say that he intends *"li"* as a translation of rights at all. Only once of the eight times in which the sections he is translating use "rights" does Parker put *"li"* in a corresponding place in his Chinese text, leading a contemporary analyst to conclude that Parker was not "introducing *li* as a technical term for 'rights'" [Svarverud 2000, fn. 29].

Like Parker, Yuan translates only one use of "right" from the first sentence; unlike Parker, Yuan uses *"daoli,"* literally the "pattern of the way" and meaning something close to "moral principle," to render "right." Yuan's third selection is also the same as Parker's, but Yuan does translate several appearances of "right," again using *"daoli"* [Wei 1840, pp. 3034, 3036]. Yuan leaves his readers with the impression that these principles have the same status as any other moral principle; at one point he says that "this kind of moral pattern is eternally in people's hearts; this is something that all people know" [Wei 1840, p. 3036]. I noted in the last paragraph that Parker once uses *"quan"* to correspond with "authority." Yuan also does this once, though in a slightly different part of the section on war, and then uses *"quan"* twice in the next sentence, corresponding to places where the original has "rights" instead of "authority." Given his consistent use of *"daoli"* to translate "rights" and the contexts in which *"quan"* appears, the best interpretation of these uses of *"quan"* is that they all refer to the authority – the legitimate powers – of monarchs, rather than to any more general notion of rights.

Neither Parker's nor Yuan's rendering of "rights" had any noticeable impact on subsequent rights discourse. This is not the fault of the text in which they appeared; the *Illustrated Compendium* was widely read and influential [Masini 1993, p. 23]. Many terms still in use today, among them the Chinese words meaning "import" and "trade," originate in this work. That *"li"* and *"daoli"* fail to catch on as translations for "rights" seems nonetheless quite easy to explain. It is not that Parker's and Yuan's translations were bad, in the sense of failing to exactly capture the meaning of "rights"; that would not explain why Chinese who had no grounds for comparison failed to use them. The reason is rather that, in Parker's and Yuan's renderings, neither *"li"* nor *"daoli"* stands out as representing anything new or different. China had long had rules, customs, and principles grounded either in expediency or in morality; both "*li*" and "*daoli*" would continue to be used in their previous senses. It would take a more systematic presentation of a foreign rights theory, together with a more novel rendering of its terminology into Chinese, to make the distinctiveness of a new concept, however exactly related to rights, salient to Chinese readers.

5.1.2 *Martin's* General Laws of the Myriad Nations

More than twenty years passed after the publication of the *Illustrated Compendium* before another effort was made to translate a Western international law text into Chinese. In 1862, the American missionary W. A. P. Martin began work on a translation of Henry Wheaton's *Elements of International Law*, a standard text first published in 1836. A year later he offered his completed translation to the recently established Chinese diplomatic agency. Prince Gong, an uncle of the emperor and leader of the diplomatic agency, accepted Martin's draft, though he had members of his staff refine the text's style. It was published in 1864 as *General Laws of the Myriad Nations* (*Wanguo Gongfa*) and immediately proved useful. When a Prussian warship seized three Danish merchant vessels anchored in a Chinese port, Prince Gong was able to use definitions learned from Wheaton, together with the texts of Chinese treaties with Prussia, to force the Prussian minister to release the Dutch ships and to pay China $1,500 of compensation for having infringed on China's jurisdiction over its territorial waters. Prince Gong said about Wheaton's book that although "the said book on foreign law and regulations is not basically in agreement with the Chinese systems, it nevertheless contains sporadic useful points" [Hsu 1960, pp. 133–4].

Subsequent sections of this chapter will detail ways in which concepts and vocabulary introduced by the *General Laws* influenced both Chinese and Japanese rights discourses. In the balance of this section, I will look at these important formulations in their original contexts and ask, among other questions, why these translations succeeded in ways that Parker's and Yuan's renderings of "rights" did not.

The word most frequently used to translate "rights" is "*quan*." "Natural rights" is "*ziran zhi quan*," "personal rights" is "*siquan*," "rights of equality" is "*pingxing zhi quan*," "property rights" is "*zhangwu zhi quan*," and so on. "*Quan*" does not always correspond to "rights," however; in a number of places it is used to translate "authority" [Martin 1864, vol. 1, pp. 1b, 19b]. In addition, it appears as part of the compound "*zizhu zhi quan*," literally "the *quan* of self-mastery," which is used to translate "independence" [ibid., p. 16a].

The earliest meanings of "*quan*" are concerned with weighing, both literally and figuratively. In a famous passage from the *Mencius*, it is used to refer to the moral judgment of a virtuous person when deciding to bend a rule in order to achieve a greater good.[4] In many contexts, though, "*quan*" has no connection with morality, and often comes to mean simply power [Zhang et al. 1973, vol. 5, pp. 524–5]. A Chinese reader of the *General Laws* would immediately understand that there was something special about "*quan*." The *quan* of a state or individual are not simply the powers it happens to have; the text makes clear that *quan* is a normative notion, dependent on reason, justice, and agreements. That is, one can talk about the *quan* a state has to equality or independence whether or not it is equal or independent: These are things states ought to have. All this comes through in Martin's translation. Strikingly, at one point where Wheaton says that the two sources of the laws of nations are reason and usage, Martin renders this by "*li* 理" for "reason" and "*li* 例*" for "usage": almost the identical terms used in the *Illustrated Compendium* to correspond to "rights" itself.[5] Admittedly, since "rights" and "authority" are translated in the same way, it would be difficult for readers to see whatever differences Wheaton felt there to be between the two words, but in fact when one is speaking of a state's rights or authority, the two really come to much the same thing: legitimate powers.[6]

"*Quan*" continues its connection to "rights" on down to the present day. A more specific term, also introduced in *General Laws*, gradually comes to be even more important that "*quan*," however. This is the compound "*quanli*," accepted throughout the twentieth century as the standard translation of "rights." Like "*quan*" itself, "*quanli*" has a long history. The earliest use of the words "*quan li*" occurs in the Confucian classic *Xunzi* (c. 220 B.C.E.). The author says that when one has perfected one's learning and self-cultivation, "*quan li* cannot move one [to do wrong]."[7] Standard Chinese interpretations of this sentence seem to take it as a

---

[4] See *Mencius* 4A:17. Lau translates it in that context as "discretion" [Lau 1970, p. 124].
[5] [Wheaton 1878 (1836), pp. 8–9]; [Martin 1864, vol. 1, pp. 8–9]. Wheaton is here discussing the views of an earlier writer on international law, but the position is not too different from his own.
[6] For a helpful discussion of various interpretations of "authority," see [Wood 1995, pp. 4–8].
[7] [*Xunzi Index* 1986, 3/1/49]; see also [ibid., 47/12/76].

compound, rendering "*quanli*" as "power-and-profit."[8] For my purposes, nothing hangs on whether *quanli* is a single thing (and "*quanli*" a compound term) in this and other early uses. All that matters is that *quanli* (or *quan* and *li*) involves reference to personal profit or benefit, rather than to any more general notion of well-being, and that Xunzi believes we ought not be swayed by it. This negative connotation that Xunzi attaches to *quanli*, which is related to the repeated admonitions against *li* (profit) by other Confucians,[9] derives from Xunzi's belief that one should attend to ritual and ethical propriety rather than any sort of utility. "*Quanli*" is used repeatedly in subsequent texts, but I know of no uses of the term prior to the nineteenth century that give it a positive connotation.[10]

In the *General Laws*, the term "*quanli*" undergoes two kinds of transformations. First, it is regularly used in approximately its traditional sense, but with a positive connotation instead of its older negative connotation. In one case, for instance, Wheaton's original has a reference to certain "advantages of trade" that a British subject who has become an American citizen might have, in virtue of his new citizenship, when trading with England. Wheaton says that even if this person were to temporarily return to England, this "would not deprive him of those advantages" [Wheaton 1878 (1836), p. 118]. In the translation, "*quanli*" is used to render both "advantages of trade" and the subsequent "advantages" [Martin 1864, vol. 2, p. 24b]. "*Quanli*" is also used repeatedly to render the "privileges" that ambassadors have while on their foreign postings [ibid., vol. 1, pp. 4a, 4b, 5b]. In each of these cases, the "*quanli*" is used as a compound term expressing the combined powers and benefits that come with trade or with diplomatic status.

Unquestionably more important, at least in the long run, is the second change. "*Quanli*" is occasionally used as a direct translation for "rights." In Wheaton's text, we read: "A state is a very different subject from a human individual, from whence it results that obligations and rights, in the two cases, are very different" [Wheaton 1878 (1836), p. 12]. Martin's text puts the matter this way: "Now the various states and the multitudes of people (*shuren*) are widely different, and thus their obligations (*mingfen*) and rights (*quanli*) also have differences" [Martin 1864, vol. 1,

---

[8] E.g., [Li 1979, p. 20]; [Zhang et al. 1973, vol. 5, p. 525]. John Knoblock does not render it as a compound term, translating it as "the exigencies of time and place and considerations of profit" [Knoblock 1988, p. 142].

[9] See *Mencius* 1A:1, etc.

[10] For further discussion, see [Suzuki 1981, pp. 49–50], translated in [Suzuki 1997, pp. 45–6].

p. 7b]. Elsewhere, in a passage on the "conduct of foreign states towards another nation involved in civil war," Wheaton says that when such foreign states profess neutrality, they must "allow impartially to both belligerent parties the free exercise of those rights which war gives to public enemies against each other" [Wheaton 1878 (1836), p. 32]. In his translation, Martin refers to these as *"jiao zhan quanli"* [Martin 1864, vol. 1, p. 19b].

It is not clear that a reader of Martin's text would come away with a distinctive conception of *quanli* that would come anywhere close to Wheaton's understanding of rights. The several contexts in which it occurs muddle the question of whether *quanli* is a normative or merely empirical notion – that is, whether *quanli* are things we have through some kind of moral obligation, or simply through contingent circumstance. Are *quanli* just advantages, or are they something more significant? These ambiguities perhaps explain why, as we will see in the next section, it is *quan* rather than *quanli* that are discussed in China after the publication of the *General Laws*. In Japan, things are somewhat different; there, we will see that once the *General Laws* arrives from China in 1866, "*quanli*" is picked up very quickly as a translation for "rights."

Martin himself seemed to understand the difficulties that readers would have with *quan* and *quanli*, writing in a headnote to a slightly later translation which similarly dealt with international law:

> International law is a separate field of knowledge and requires a special terminology. There were times when we could not find a proper Chinese term to render the original expression, so our choice of words would seem less than satisfactory. Take the character *quan*, for example. In this book the word means not only the kind of power one has over others, but also the lot (*fen*) that moral pattern (*li*) prescribes to each person. Occasionally, we would add the word *li* 利 [to form a compound], as, for example, in the expression 'the original *quanli* of the common people,' and the like. At first encounter, these words may seem odd and unwieldy, but after seeing them repeatedly, you will come to realize that the translators have really made the best of necessity.[11]

We will have occasion to see what Martin's readers made of these concepts in the next two sections of the chapter.

---

[11] See [Martin 1878, translator's headnote]. This paragraph is translated in [Liu 1999, p. 149], though I have modified the translation somewhat.

5.2 THE SELF-STRENGTHENING MOVEMENT

Mid-nineteenth-century Chinese reformers recognized that more needed to be done than just translate Western legal texts. They felt that unless China was strong enough to negotiate as an equal with Western powers, it would continue to be exploited. Indeed, until China could successfully insist that existing treaties – to which China had been forced to accede at gunpoint – be revised, its interests could not be protected. This group of men has come to be called the "self-strengthening movement (*ziqiang yundong*)," and I now turn to the partial development of rights language within their writings. For simplicity's sake, I have chosen to focus on a single individual, Li Hongzhang. We will see that he pays considerable attention to the notion of "*liquan*," a traditional concept which in his hands begins to be transformed from "economic control" toward something rather close to "economic rights."[12]

Before I turn to Li, let me briefly note the general connection that existed between the self-strengtheners and statecraft thought. Readers will recall that thinkers sympathetic to statecraft ideals played important roles in the Confucian discourse about the fulfillment of individual desires that I discussed in the last chapter. Statecraft thinkers were also direct sources of inspiration to all those committed to China's self-strengthening. Given the manifest technological advantages enjoyed by Western powers, one of the central tenets of self-strengthening was promoting practical, technological development. Such matters had long been advocated by statecraft thinkers, who justified these pragmatic pursuits through the ways they fulfilled the people's (legitimate) desires. Under the influence of texts like the *General Laws*, certain of the self-strengtheners started to talk about the reasons for their policies in new ways, but these changes represent only incremental steps from their starting point.[13]

Li Hongzhang (1823–1901) rose to prominence during the massive Taiping Rebellion, which lasted from 1850 to 1864 and which at its height threatened to topple the Qing dynasty. Li distinguished himself as both administrator and general and was appointed governor-general of the

---

[12] Li is not the only possible representative of the changes I describe here; another relevant figure is Xue Fucheng (1838–94), an official and diplomat who also wrote about *liquan* in ways that stretched traditional boundaries. See his four essays on *liquan*, which both mention the need for "*quan* of self-mastery (*zizhu zhi quan*)" and invoke the *General Laws*: [Xue n.d., p. 383].

[13] For more on the relation between statecraft and self-strengthening, see [Liu 1994a].

province of Jiangsu in 1862. At that time he moved to Shanghai, from where he directed the province's defense against the rebels and where he encountered the technology and power of Western nations for the first time. Li sought to learn all he could about the sources of Western power and the intentions of Western nations. Throughout the twenty-five years that Li subsequently served as imperial commissioner of trade and foreign relations for North China, he was a leader of the self-strengthening movement.[14]

In 1867, proponents of self-strengthening held a series of discussions in preparation for negotiations with Western powers that aimed at revising current treaties. David Pong writes that

> Of the seventeen officials involved in the deliberations, five used the term *quan*, and of [this] group, three did so to mean preserving China's authority or control over specific matters, while Chonghou and Li Hongzhang used it to convey the notion of inherent rights as well. . . . Thus from its original meaning of China having the ultimate say in protecting its traditional socio-political order from foreign encroachment – a defensive position – the concept of *quan*, and especially its derivation, *liquan*, had come to connote as well China's right to pursue its own course of development. [Pong 1985, pp. 34–5]

In short, Pong argues that in these discussions, we can see two meanings of "*quan*," one more traditional and one the new idea of "inherent rights."

In the last section I spent some time reviewing the history of the terms "*quan*" and "*quanli*"; before I move on, I want to do the same for "*liquan*," which Pong rightly identifies as at the core of the self-strengtheners' concerns. As I said earlier, "*li*" means benefit or profit, while the basic meaning of "*quan*" is power. The words "*li*" and "*quan*" occur together in classical-era texts, though as we saw earlier with "*quanli*," it is often difficult to say whether they are intended as a compound term or as two separate terms.[15] Post-classical texts, however, clearly use "*liquan*" as a compound term, meaning something like "economic control." To cite just one example, the seventeenth-century

---

[14] See [Liu 1994b (1970)] and [Liu 1994c (1967)].

[15] See the classical-era text *Zuo Zhuan*, "*ji you li quan, you zhi min bing*," which Legge translates as "Since you have such advantages and the power, and moreover the handles of the people . . ." [Duke Xiang 23; trans. in Legge 1985 (1872), p. 501].

official and scholar Han Tan (1637–1704) made the following comment about monetary policy: "The less money coined by the government, the more the people will use their own counterfeit money to benefit themselves. Economic control (*liquan*) will be dispersed among the masses."[16]

Han's statement is interesting because it makes clear that *liquan* is a matter of control or power rather than genuine authority. The government's loss of control over the money supply does not mean that counterfeiters are somehow legitimate. There is no temptation, therefore, to see Han's comment as about rights: In particular, he is not asserting that through government inaction, the people have gained economic rights. If Li Hongzhang comes to use "*liquan*" to mean economic rights, as Pong believes, then this is indeed a significant conceptual evolution.

Let us look at two examples of Li's use of "*quan*" and "*liquan*." First, discussing a variety of demands made by Western powers, he says:

> In addition to these, there are still other demands. Above, none fail to invade our nation's *liquan*; below, they inevitably seek to wrest away our merchants' livelihoods. These can all be denounced on the basis of the upright words of the *General Laws of the Myriad Nations*: "All nations have the *quan* of protecting their people and administering their financial affairs." [Li et al. 1930, vol. 55, p. 9a (consecutive p. 5149)]

If taken out of context, the reference here to *liquan* could easily be interpreted as referring to mere economic control. When coupled with the citation from *General Laws*, though, it sounds like Li is claiming that all nations have inherent rights to economic sovereignty. The *quan* to which the *General Laws* refers, after all, are not powers that nations just happen to have, as a matter of contingent reality; they are powers that morally must accrue to all nations.

It is even clearer that Li understands *quan* in this way in a second passage. Here Li complains that foreign merchants heed only the requirements of the Customs Office – which was overseen by foreign officials – and ignore the Chinese commissioners (*jiandu*), whose responsibilities included the collection of internal duties on trade (the *lijin tax*):

> The Customs Office appropriates *quan* that ought to be China's (*zhongguo yingyou zhi quan*). Those who understand [moral] patterns are content with the natural lot (*benfen*) of things; those who

---

[16] [Han 1827]. For Han's biography, see [Hummel 1970 (1943), p. 275].

rely on force take whatever they like. In this period of treaty revision, they hope to monopolize everything . . . , steal the *quan* of China, and find ways for their merchants to profit. In the course of the treaty revisions, no matter what the cost, we cannot include words authorizing the Customs Office. Then the coastal *liquan* will no longer go to the foreign countries, and foreign merchants will know that the Customs Office is without genuine (*zhen*) *quan*. [Li et al. 1930, vol. 54, p. 22b (consecutive p. 5108)]

This passage makes two crucial points. First, reinforcing the conclusion to which we came after the first passage, *quan* can be subject to moral norms (the *quan* that ought to be China's) rather than merely matters of actual control. Second, we see here that Li recognizes this very distinction. His goal in the treaty revision process is to make clear that the Customs Office lacks "genuine *quan*," which I take to mean something like rights, as opposed to mere power.

Let me sum up. At least partly under the influence of the *General Laws*, Li began to talk about *quan* in ways that departed from the value-neutral notions of power and control found in traditional discussions of the term. Li's uses are clearly marked as different from the earlier ways in which *liquan* had been discussed; his listeners and readers can attribute commitments to him accurately, seeing him as having opted out of their way of talking about *liquan*. They might resist using his new concept, referring derisively to "Li's so-called '*liquan*.'" Or they might think through the commitments entailed by the old concept and the new one and then decide in favor of the new: Seeing China for the first time as a nation among nations, it might now seem important to talk about China's morally legitimate powers – and about the foreigner's lack of this legitimacy. This process of reflecting on one's concepts and their attendant commitments is the exercise of "expressive rationality," as we saw in Chapter 2.

It is important to note that through Li's writings, and throughout the reflections they may have prompted – for others did come to use "*quan*" in the way that Li did – there were no hints that "*quan*" could be applied to individuals, or even to the people as a collective. These were ideas applicable to states. This is not at all surprising, given the context in which the terms were discussed. It suggests, though, that it might be premature for me to translate "*quan*" as "rights." By doing so I would assert that "*quan*" carries with it much the same set of inferential commitments that "rights" does, but a central aspect of all familiar, contemporary versions of that concept is their applicability to individuals. "Authority" may therefore do a better job of capturing what "*quan*" means at this moment to Li and his community.

5.3 JAPAN

Rights discourse began in Japan at about the same time it did in China, but followed a quite different early course. We have just seen that early rights discourse in China focuses on the state as subject for rights; people, either individually or collectively, are not yet part of the picture except insofar as they are part of a state. In Japan, people quickly come to be at the center of rights claims, in part because of the importance that was placed on fulfilling people's desires. This connection between rights and desires anticipates a similar dynamic that plays out in China slightly later. For the purposes of this book, I am interested in Japanese rights discourse not so much for its own sake – though a comprehensive treatment of the discourse remains to be written – as for the ways in which it intersects with and influences Chinese rights discourse. A number of the key Chinese texts on rights from the early twentieth century were written in Japan, where numerous critics of the Qing dynasty traveled, both for study and for freedom to write what they liked without fear of imprisonment. These Chinese thinkers were variously influenced by the Japanese intellectual climate, even including the words they chose to express new ideas. I pursue Japanese notions of rights as background to understanding these Chinese thinkers' ideas.

5.3.1 Translations

As early as 1862, two Japanese had been sent by their government to study law in the Netherlands; from their notes, we can see that they translated the Dutch term "*regt*" with "*honbun*," which literally means something like one's original lot or natural station in life [Yanabu 1994, pp. 2–3].[17] In 1868, after returning to Japan, one of these two students wrote a work on international law in which he rendered rights/*regt* as "*ken* (C: *quan*)."[18] He states that he consulted the Chinese *General Laws*, which had been brought to Japan in 1866, in arriving at this translation of "*regt*"

---

[17] The two students were Nishi Amane (1829–97) and Tsuda Shinichiro (1829–1903).

[18] That is, the character which he used is prononuced "*ken*" in Japanese and "*quan*" in Chinese. This is the same character that earlier we saw used in China.

[Yanabu 1997, pp. 162–3]. It is safe to conclude, therefore, that *"ken"* was first used as a translation of "rights" under the influence of Martin's earlier Chinese translation.[19]

Another text produced in 1868 used *"kenri* (C: *quanli)"* for "rights." In his essay *On Constitutional Government,* Katō Hiroyuki (1836–1916) wrote that in regimes in which monarchs monopolize power, the people are treated like servants, and "it goes without saying that they cannot enjoy a single right (*kenri*)."[20] Since this text also came after the introduction of *General Laws* in Japan, it is exceedingly likely that Katō borrowed *"kenri"* from Martin.

I will discuss the development of Katō's ideas extensively later, since he will be among the figures most influential on the views of Chinese students in Japan. First, though, I want to note that in the 1870s, *"kenri"* had a serious rival for translating "rights." In several articles that appeared in the important journal *Meiji Six* (*Meiroku Zasshi*), authors use another word that is also pronounced "kenri," but written slightly differently. The first character in this rival compound, *"ken* 權*,"* is the same in each word, but the rival term adds *"ri* 理*"* instead of *"ri* 利*."* The latter, recall, has a basic meaning of benefit or profit. The former means pattern, order, or principle. So far as I know, no one commented on the differences between the two words, and at least one author used them both in the same paragraph with no distinction that I can detect.[21] As we will see later, these authors associated with *Meiji Six* tended to view rights as a matter of either positive or natural law; it perhaps made sense for them to prefer a translation that stresses the role of rights in an orderly system, rather than a word that stresses the benefits that come from enjoying the right. And perhaps it is the decline of natural-law explanations of rights, also detailed later, that accounts for the failure of the rival *"kenri"* to take hold.[22] In any event, the rival will make virtually no mark on the twentieth century.[23]

---

[19] The *Wanguo Gongfa* was translated into Japanese a few years later, in 1871. See [Chang 1991].

[20] [Suzuki 1981, pp. 45–6]; translation from [Suzuki 1997, p. 41].

[21] For uses of the rival *"kenri,"* see articles by Nishimura Shigeki (1828–1902), Nishi Amane, and Mori Arinori (1847–89) in *Meiroku Zasshi,* translated in [Braisted 1976, pp. 510–13, 40–3, and 78–86, respectively]. See also discussion in [Suzuki 1981, pp. 51–3].

[22] The same can probably be said for some of the other translations of "rights" that were tried out in the 1860s and 1870s. See, for example, the discussion below of Fukuzawa Yukichi.

[23] In at least one essay from 1901, Liang Qichao (on whom see the next chapter) uses the rival *"kenri,"* pronounced *"quanli"* in Chinese; see [Liang 1989c (1901), p. 106].

5.3.2 *Confucians, Liberals, Radicals, and Bureaucrats*

If the words used in Japan to translate "rights" (and related words in other European languages) were diverse, the social and political commitments of the people using these different words were still more so. The title I have given to this section makes it sound like they can be easily separated into convenient groups, but that was far from the case. Confucian values and terminology loom large in the writings of many figures, even those most explicitly antagonistic to Confucianism. Similarly, even those who identify themselves as Confucian draw on ideas or words that are the results of Japan's ongoing encounter with Western nations. A complete account of these dizzying complexities is not my objective here, yet I do need to summarize the context in which rights are discussed, even if in fairly simplistic fashion. The following paragraphs are offered in that spirit.

I think the best way to understand the 1870s and 1880s is by identifying three rough groupings: the bureaucrats in power and their conservative supporters, the radicals seeking political participation, and the initially apolitical liberals associated with *Meiji Six*. It is the latter two groups who write most about rights, in the varying formulations discussed earlier. To the extent the conservatives were concerned with notions of rights and independence, it was – like the Chinese officials discussed earlier – on the rights and independence of the state that they focused.[24]

The radicals were relentlessly political and practical. Their touchstones were political participation and popular sovereignty; they used their famous slogan "*jiyū minken*," or "freedom and popular authority," to call for the people to receive their rightful voice in governance. These demands went along with, and were partly justified by, advocation of liberating desires from the restrictions of feudal society. In "The Passions Must Prevail," one champion of popular authority wrote that the object of human life "is for the self to gratify its desires, to rejoice in the extreme, nothing else. . . . Heaven put [things in the world] for the people to enjoy, and those who use them are to have their own way, free and unrestrained."[25] This embracing of the passions was often seen as

---

[24] See, e.g., the concern of Torio Koyata (1847–1905): "Using the two characters '*min*' and '*ken*' ['people' and 'authority' or 'rights'], [the radicals] want to destroy the country's order, violate political laws, and form parties and classes. . . . Racing blindly after one another, they will only make the country lose its independence and bring on disaster." Cited in [Motoyama 1997, p. 249].

[25] Seki Shingo (1854?–1915), quoted in [Motoyama 1997, p. 240]. For further evidence of these concerns, see the "Dialogue on People's Power," discussed in [Tucker 1996, pp. 15–16].

originating in Western ideas, and was often practiced partly through the ostentatious adoption of Western-style luxuries [Motoyama 1997, p. 241]. We will see in a moment, though, that the roots of an affirmative attitude toward desires run deep in Japanese thought, just as they do in China.

Readers will have noticed that I translated "*ken* (C: *quan*)" as "authority" in the phrase "freedom and popular authority." It is more common to translate the phrase as "freedom and popular rights," but given the collectivist focus of the movement, "authority" seems to capture the idea's commitments better than "rights," as I have also argued earlier for Li Hongzhang's use of "*quan.*"[26] The same will be true of the Chinese movement for "*minquan* (J: *minken*)" in the 1890s, which we will explore in a few moments.

If we turn to the liberals, we will see that rights and desires are again prominent themes in their writings. These writings are more sophisticated than are those of the radicals, and often show subtler signs of connection to the Japanese tradition.[27] For the sake of simplicity I will focus on two figures, both of whom will exert considerable influence on subsequent Chinese rights discourse, Katō Hiroyuki and Fukuzawa Yukichi.

5.3.2.1 Katō Hiroyuki. I have already mentioned Katō as the man who introduced "kenri" into Japan. Not only did he use the word; he also discussed rights more extensively than anyone had in China. The passage from *On Constitutional Government* that I quoted briefly continues as follows:

> A realm which is not the private property of the sovereign and aristocracy is a "realm of rights." For this reason, those who are subjects possess rights. There are two sorts of rights: private rights (*shiken*) and public rights (*kōken*). Private rights are rights involving one's own person, called by some the right to freedom. Public rights are rights involving national affairs.[28]

Katō then enumerates eight private rights, including "the right to life," "the right to independence," and "the right to freedom of thought,

---

[26] Yanabu is similarly resistant to interpreting "*ken*" in this context as "rights": He prefers "power" or "authority" (using the English words in his article) [Yanabu 1997, pp. 168–70].

[27] For one analysis of a radical essay that reveals subtle connections with Confucianism, see [Crawford 1997].

[28] [Suzuki 1981, p. 46]; translation from [Suzuki 1997, p. 41].

speech, and writing." In each of these cases, the word I am translating as "right" is "*kenri*."

In order to be sure what to make of Katō's advocacy of *kenri*, we need to understand why he thought people had *kenri*. This will also help us deal with an otherwise puzzling aspect of Katō's intellectual development: In the 1880s he would publicly reject his earlier work on rights, take some of his previous work out of print, and throw his support behind a unified state and its pursuit of Darwinian success in a competitive international arena. It was this later Katō whom young Chinese intellectuals would encounter when they came to Japan in the late 1890s, so we would do well to understand how the later Katō emerged from the earlier.

The key to Katō turns out to be his relation to Confucianism. This may seem surprising, since the puzzle looked to involve a change from rights to Darwinism. Closer inspection reveals that Confucian commitments and vocabulary permeated Katō's writings and point to continuities underlying his dramatic change. This is not to say that Katō was a Confucian; I am more comfortable allowing people to decide their identities for themselves, and he did not call himself a Confucian. He studied and reacted to Confucian texts, both of classical Chinese and more recent Japanese vintage, and we can see important roles that ideas and words from these texts play in his thought. Still, he – like many of his generation, and like many Chinese whom we will look at subsequently – was interested in articulating a new politics and a new ethics that departed in many ways from the tenets and practices of Confucianism.

Katō's earliest writings were set in the context of the challenges Western nations posed to China (and, implicitly, to Japan). He argued that the mere adoption of Western technology by Eastern nations was inadequate; the latter needed to cultivate the proper spirit as well, which, borrowing a term from the Confucian classic *Mencius*, he identified as "*jinwa* (C: *renhe*)."[29] "*Jinwa*" means harmony among men; in the *Mencius*, it is identified as the critical factor for military success. Katō believed that this harmony, in turn, grew out of an even more venerable Confucian notion, "humane government (*jinsei*; C: *renzheng*)."[30] The basic meaning of "humane government" within Confucianism is rule by the virtuous, in which the responsibilities of the rulers to love and care for their subjects are fulfilled. For Katō, however, this was not enough. He believed that humane government could only be successful, and *jinwa*

---

[29] [Wakabayashi 1984, p. 471]. See *Mencius* 4:1.
[30] [Wakabayashi 1984, p. 474]. See *Mencius* 1:5.

achieved, if Western forms of constitutional government and rights were instituted. He wrote:

> By no means do I imply that the political system of the ancient sage kings was not fair and equitable and based on humaneness. I simply believe that the way they instituted their system of government was not without imperfections. For the very reason that they were sage kings, such imperfections did not develop into evils during their own reigns. But in later eras, when foolish rulers assumed the throne, evils tended to surface.[31]

Katō here echoes the reformist themes of statecraft Confucianism, though his connection of these problems with Western political models is new.

There is a second reason that Katō found it necessary to promote constitutional government and subjects' rights: He believed rights to be the natural possessions of all people. Once again, though, his commitment to what he called "heaven-endowed rights (*tempu jinken*; C: *tianfu renquan*)" was strongly influenced by Confucianism.[32] He wrote that "it is man's nature to possess various desires, the strongest of which is for unrestricted independence to achieve personal happiness. . . . No man, whether high or low, rich or poor, intelligent or ignorant, may be restricted by others. Each may follow his own desires in his private affairs. Hence, various rights have come into existence through civil society" [Wakabayashi 1984, p. 481].[33] By now the connection between affirming desires and Confucianism should not be surprising, though Katō does put it in stronger terms than any Confucians had. Katō and his contemporaries drew on the progressive attitude toward desires adopted within the "Ancient Learning" school of Japanese Confucianism, which both was influenced by similar trends in China and made further developments of its own. The interaction among merchant culture and values, economic and social changes, and Tokugawa (1568–1868) Confucianism was even more explicit in Japan than was the case in China.[34]

---

[31] [Wakabayashi 1984, p. 474], slightly altered.

[32] On the earlier Japanese Confucian conception of heaven, and its relation to early rights discourse, see [Matsumoto 1978] and [Tucker 1996].

[33] For further examples of liberals like Katō basing their rights theories on desires, see [Matsumoto 1978, p. 184].

[34] See [Wakabayashi 1984, pp. 482–3], [Matsumoto 1978], [Najita 1987], and [de Bary 1979].

It remains only to explore Katō's reaction against natural rights and his turn to Darwinism. I might summarize his notion of heaven-endowed rights as follows:

1. People all have desires which they can legitimately pursue, insofar as they do not interfere with the desires of others.
2. The state's goal is to cultivate a spirit of unity and harmony within the country, on the strength of which its people can further pursue their desires.
3. Since the goodness and humaneness of rulers cannot be relied on, the institutions of constitutional power-sharing and rights are needed to protect the people's interests.

Notice how central the people (or citizenry) are to this reasoning: It is within the context of the group that legitimate desires are adjudicated, since desires are legitimate only insofar as they can be pursued without hindering someone else in the group. What Katō realized very early on was that if the state's interests suffered, so too would those of its citizens.[35] Already in 1872 he tutored the emperor using his own translation of Johann Bluntschli's *Allgemeines Staatsrecht* – a work that would later be influential on Chinese thinkers – which viewed the state as an organism that had its own rights, superior in many ways to those of individual citizens [Motoyama 1997, p. 260]. As he put it in the 1882 work that supposedly represents his conversion from natural rights to Darwinism, "Wars inevitably break out. Once war breaks out, the rights of the vanquished nation suffer irreparable damage. This holds not only for the government in question, but also for its citizens. Therefore, whether or not a people possess rights depends on [their nation's] victory or defeat" [Wakabayashi 1984, p. 490].

In the context of Katō's thought, it makes sense to translate "*kenri*" as "rights," not least because he sees them as applicable to individuals. Still, especially in his later writings, we can see that these rights are held only in the context of a flourishing collective, and thus the rights of the collective take on considerable importance. The important issue here is not to quibble over when "rights" is the best translation and when it is not, but to try to get a clear view of the content of the rights-related concepts that thinkers like Katō and Fukuzawa use by understanding the commitments that the concepts entail.

---

[35] Katō's terminology does not distinguish between "state" and "nation," nor between "citizen" and "member of a nation." For present purposes, we can ignore these differences.

5.3.2.2 Fukuzawa Yukichi. Fukuzawa Yukichi (1835–1901) was a leading liberal theorist and populist who wrote extensively on rights. He used a variety of terms to correspond to "rights": He employed both *"tsūgi"* and *"ken"* in his 1866 *Conditions in the West*; *"kenri tsūgi"* – abbreviated to *"kengi"* – in his 1876 *An Encouragement of Learning*; and *"kenri* 權理*"* in his 1878 "People's Rights: A Plain Account."[36] Despite these terminological differences between Fukuzawa and Katō, and notwithstanding some other important differences between the two, to which I will come in a moment, the two men's views of rights shared two very significant features. First, Fukuzawa also saw the origin of rights in "heaven." As he put it in an 1876 work, "When men are born from heaven, they are all equal," and equality, in turn, "means equality in essential human rights" [Fukuzawa 1969, pp. 1, 10]. Second, Fukuzawa saw both heaven-endowed nature, and rights, as bound up with desires: "It is a basic human right for man to be able to attain what he wants, as long as he does not infringe on the rights of others" [ibid., p. 11].

Fukuzawa did not derive his understanding of rights from Confucianism any more than Katō did. Fukuzawa was significantly influenced by his reading of Blackstone's *Laws of England*, among other sources [Tucker 1996, p. 1]. Still, in both the precise shape that his conceptualization of rights took (e.g., in its connection to heaven) and his willingness to endorse the value of human desires (even extending to the love for money [Tucker 1996, pp. 19–20]), Fukuzawa was a child of his age. Both he and his audience were prepared to consider and endorse the inferences entailed by his concepts in significant part because of the previous movement within Japanese Confucianism to valorize desires. Since I have already developed these themes extensively, I will not dwell on them further here.

I do not want to leave the impression that Katō and Fukuzawa were alike in every way. Both cared about the well-being and strength of the nation, but to a greater extent than Katō, Fukuzawa throughout his life saw independent individuals as central to national independence.[37] Be this as it may, the central themes relevant to Japanese rights discourse are already clear. Rights were attributed to individuals by some thinkers, in large part based on an understanding of people's needs that rested on a positive account of human desire. In various ways, though, these needs and desires were understood to be essentially connected to the needs

[36] See the excellent discussion in [Tucker 1996], as well as [Fukuzawa 1969].
[37] See [Fukuzawa 1969, pp. 16–20].

and well-being of larger groups, most important of which was the nation. Although Fukuzawa and Katō went out of fashion for a few years, by the end of the 1890s when Chinese thinkers like Liang Qichao and Liu Shipei – the subjects of the next chapter – were in Japan, Fukuzawa and Katō had been rediscovered and their ideas once again promoted.[38] Their ideas would mesh with and supplement similar ideas within the Chinese tradition to help spark a flowering of rights discourse. But first let us return to China, and see what develops there in the years before Chinese intellectuals begin their pilgrimages to Japan.

5.4 REFORMERS IN THE 1890s

In each of the preceding sections, we have seen how internal trends and concerns mixed with external texts and traditions to produce early discussions of rights or related notions. It is already difficult to cleanly distinguish "internal" from "external," since the ideas and vocabulary of foreigners undergo change as they live in China, and those of Chinese (and Japanese) change after living or studying abroad.[39] As we move into the 1890s, clear distinctions between internal and external become still harder to make. This will continue to be a feature of Chinese rights discourse down to the present day; it is never a discourse of pure, traditional ideas, but neither is it ever solely a matter of imported concepts and concerns. In the 1890s each of the contexts in which I have identified rights discourse as emerging – international law, self-strengthening, missionaries, and Japan – will play a role, merging with old and new concerns and entering new arenas of debate. The 1890s are distinctive in part for the broadened range of participants in rights discourse: journalists, publicists, and reformers outside of government all add their voices to the conversation. The result is more complex and contested than anything we saw in previous decades, though these complexities are only a hint of what we will find when we enter the twentieth century.

Much of my analysis in this section will revolve around the term "*minquan*," of which "people's authority" is a good first approximation. I will begin by looking at some strands within Confucian tradition that have been identified by other scholars as contributing to the emergence of concern with *minquan*. Next I will strive to make connections between

---

[38] [Tam 1991, p. 7].

[39] For a particularly striking example, see Lionel Jensen's discussion of the ways that early Jesuit missionaries to China evolved into a "Sino-Jesuit community" [Jensen 1997].

these native strands and what is explicitly said about *minquan* prior to 1898. After a brief excursion into another important rights-related concept, *zizhu zhi quan*, I will look at the critique of *minquan* written in 1898 by Zhang Zhidong, a powerful government official and proponent of moderate reform. The section will conclude with an examination of the reaction to Zhang by two proponents of *minquan* living in Hong Kong.

5.4.1 Traditions of Reform

Much has been made of the role of Western imperialism in stimulating a recognition by Chinese that some manner of reform was needed, and many have emphasized that Western ideas helped to shape the ways in which the needed reforms came to be understood. We saw earlier that both Chinese and Manchu officials associated with the "self-strengthening" movement were certainly reacting, in no small part, to military defeats and unequal treaties; we also saw the degree to which their responses came to be couched in terms that evolved out of the inter-pretation of Western texts. At the same time, we also saw that preexisting concerns and intellectual tendencies played important roles in motivating these individuals to engage with Western ideas and texts in the ways they did; we noted in particular the commitment of Wei Yuan, Li Hongzhang, and the others to "statecraft" thinking. In this section, I will sketch three other strands within the evolving Chinese tradition that clearly influence how rights discourse is articulated in the 1890s – and by whom.

The first is an aspect of Confucianism that has come to be called *minben sixiang*, which means "people-as-root thought." It holds that only when the people flourish will a state be strong; the well-being of both rulers and officials is decidedly less important than the well-being of the people. One classical Confucian work puts it this way: "When Heaven gave birth to the people, it was not for the sake of a ruler. When Heaven established a ruler, it was for the sake of the people."[40] It is often claimed, in fact, that classical Confucian political theory includes a "right to rebel" against a tyrannical ruler. This notion is based primarily on a passage in the *Mencius* in which it is made clear that rulers who "mutilate humane-ness" and "cripple rightness" no longer count as true rulers; to kill such a person is to punish an outcast rather than to commit regicide.[41] This

---

[40] See [Knoblock 1994, vol. 3, p. 224]; quoted in [Mizoguchi 1991, p. 10].
[41] *Mencius* 1B:8; cf. [Lau 1970, p. 68].

passage clearly supports the idea that the people's well-being is of paramount importance, to which any ruler must be committed in order to merit his position. Other passages in the *Mencius* lead me to reject the idea that the text treats rebellion as a people's right, however. For one thing, a later passage says explicitly that while ministers lacking royal blood should remonstrate with a misguided ruler, they cannot depose him; only ministers with royal blood can depose a ruler who ignores their repeated advice.[42] In addition, the *Mencius* also indicates that while people who act against a bad ruler cannot be blamed for what they do, they still do not act rightly. The following passage, which criticizes those rulers who hoard all "enjoyments" for themselves, seems quite explicit:

> Should there be a man ... who is not given a share in [the realm's] enjoyments, he would speak ill of those in authority. To speak ill of those in authority because one is not given a share in such enjoyment is, of course, wrong. But for one in authority over the people not to share his enjoyment with the people is equally wrong.[43]

Another passage makes the related point that for a ruler to fail to provide properly for his people, and then to punish them when they "fall into excesses" seeking what they need, is to "trap" the people.[44] The stress throughout is on the ruler's responsibility to the people, rather than on any correlative right that the people might have. The fact that speaking ill of a bad ruler is still wrong seems to make clear that no general right to speak out is intended – even though speaking out cannot be avoided.[45]

Even if "people-as-root" did not mean that the people had a right to rebel, it did lay the foundation for critiquing rulers. The most famous such critique was that of Huang Zongxi, whose *Waiting for the Dawn* we began to examine in the last chapter. Huang argues that emperors routinely assumed that the wealth of the nation was intended for their personal benefit, and so passed strict laws which tried to ensure that "[nothing] beneficial should be left to those below, but rather that all blessings be gathered up for those on high."[46] Huang urged a number of institutional changes that he felt would lessen the ability of rulers (and other power-holders) to take advantage of the people. Huang certainly

---

[42] *Mencius* 5B:9; cf. [Lau 1970, p. 159].
[43] *Mencius* 1B:4; cf. [Lau 1970, p. 63].
[44] *Mencius* 1A:7; cf. [Lau 1970, p. 58].
[45] For an interesting discussion of whether some sort of right to speak should be endorsed by early Confucians, see [Wong in press].
[46] [Huang 1985, p. 2]; translation from [Huang 1993, p. 98].

did not go as far as would the reformers of the 1890s, but his ideas were not lost on them; in fact, one leader of the reform movement had several thousand copies of *Waiting for the Dawn* secretly printed and distributed in the late 1890s.[47]

One more aspect of the people-as-root idea bears emphasizing before we move on: The interests and powers of the people are conceptualized collectively. Huang thought that the people as a whole – whom he referred to as "all-under-heaven (*tian xia*)" – should benefit, but he never put this in terms of protecting the interests of every individual. We will see that 1890s reformers, too, tended to think collectively. When they talk of *minquan*, for the most part they have in mind the authority of the people as a group. We will see a few hints of a more individualized conception of *quan*, but these are rare exceptions to the general trend.[48]

Another large trend that fed into the 1890s reform movement was the ever-increasing economic and social power of local landlords, gentry, and merchants, and the related arguments that came to be made in favor of local self-government. We saw earlier that Gu Yanwu argued strenuously against the central government's "rule of avoidance" – which mandated that officials not serve in their home counties – and term limits, in part because he sought to increase the ability of local elites to influence policy related to them. Although, in the face of opposition from the central court, progress toward local self-rule was slow, institutions serving local needs did continue to be created.[49] Virtually all of the proposals put forward by *minquan* advocates in the 1890s bear some relation to these earlier trends. For one thing, the proposals tended to serve the same local elites, since they, rather than the entire populace, were the "people" envisioned in at least the first stages of power-sharing and representative assemblies. We can also find explicit evidence that reformers saw their visions as promoting local self-rule and decentralization.[50]

---

[47] [Huang 1993, pp. 71–2]. For more evidence that reformers of the 1890s and early 1900s saw themselves as building on the ideas of Huang and others, see [Mizoguchi 1991, p. 10].

[48] For more on this collective conception of *quan*, see [Mizoguchi 1991, p. 10], as well as the examples cited therein.

[49] This trend began at least as early as the start of the Southern Song dynasty (1127–1278); see [Hymes 1986]. [Chow 1994, ch. 3] discusses related trends in the early Qing dynasty, which may have accelerated in the latter half of the nineteenth century, on which see [Mizoguchi 1991, p. 6] and [Rankin 1986].

[50] See [Mizoguchi 1991, p. 7]. See also [Lee 1998], which discusses several aspects of the connection between local self-rule and reform in more detail.

A final traditional contribution to 1890s reform thought is the so-called New Text school of thought. "New Text" refers to specific versions of the Confucian classics and to certain commentaries on those classics. The New Text interpretation of the classics was one which emphasized the ethical and political lessons that could be read out of the classics, whereas the competing Old Text interpretation tended to look for historical information. According to the New Text view, Confucius used words that carried subtle messages of praise or blame when he edited the classics; bases could therefore be found in the classics for criticism of a wide variety of improper government practices.[51]

A number of the figures treated in this chapter were advocates of New Text readings of the classics – from Wei Yuan, who commissioned the very first international law translation, to Kang Youwei and Liang Qichao, who were central participants in the reforms of the 1890s, as we will soon see. In addition to finding grounds for criticism of the ruler, men like these also found support for the very ideas of reform and progress in the New Text tenet that human history would pass from an era of "disorder" to one of "approaching peace" and finally to one of "universal peace." Kang Youwei, in particular, viewed Confucius as a full-fledged prophet who foresaw the need for fundamental reforms.[52]

New Text ideas were not as closely related to the specifics of *minquan* as either of the other strands of thought that I have canvassed in this section, nor did they continue to exert their influence for as long as some of these other ideas. I suspect that two reasons lie behind this. First, the very idea of a New Text school depends on a considerable familiarity with, and concern for, difficult and often obscure texts from the classical tradition. Such familiarity is possible only in certain social and cultural circumstances. These circumstances began to break down after the end of the nineteenth century.[53] Second, the principal purpose served by the New Text ideas was the justification of reform, progress, and so on. These ideas paved the way for Chinese interpretation and adaptation of similar Western ideas, but in so doing the New Text ideas also led to their own irrelevance: Chinese became content with the justifications for reform –

---

[51] [Wood 1995] is a careful study of the use of such interpretations of one text, the *Spring and Autumn Annals*, to ground political theory in the Song dynasty. [Elman 1990] studies the revival of New Text interpretations in the mid-Qing dynasty.

[52] See [Chang 1971, p. 50 and *passim*] and [Cheng 1997] for discussion.

[53] For the background to this thought, notice what underlay the healthy New Text school in the eighteenth and nineteenth centuries; see [Elman 1990].

and even revolution – that they built on newer foundations, and thus could leave behind the "three eras" and Confucian code words for praise and blame.

5.4.2 Minquan *to 1898*

The year 1898 is the pivot around which the balance of this section will revolve. 1898 is famous for the "Hundred Days" reform effort, in which the youthful Guangxu emperor threw his support behind reform, issuing a series of wide-ranging edicts. After slightly more than one hundred days, a palace coup led by the empress dowager ended the reforms and resulted in the execution of several reform advocates, and the flight to Japan of a number of others. In addition to this abortive attempt to institutionalize reform, 1898 also saw some very important writings in favor of *minquan*, as well as the most famous argument against *minquan*, *Exhortation to Learning* by the moderate reformer Zhang Zhidong. I turn first to the advocates of *minquan*.

Coined in Japan sometime in the late 1870s, the word "*minquan* (J: *minken*)" was first used in Chinese soon thereafter by two diplomats familiar both with the Japanese usage and with political institutions in various Western countries.[54] It was not widely adopted in China until fairly late in the 1890s, when reformers in Hunan, Hubei, and Shanghai began to invoke it as one of the goals of their proposed institutional changes.[55] What did it mean? "People's authority" may be the best translation one can find, but let me note one respect in which it may be misleading. *Minquan* was not about complete popular sovereignty. No one in China in the 1890s advocated full-scale democracy – nor, of course, did very many people in the West at this time. The goal of *minquan* advocates was instead an institutionalized, consultative role in a constitutional monarchy. They saw participation in national and provincial assemblies as means to strengthen the nation. One Hunanese reformer put it this way:

---

[54] See Section 5.3 for the Japanese term "*minken*." Guo Songtao, minister to France and England in 1876–7, used the term in the May 19, 1878 entry in his diary [Judge 1997]. Huang Zunxian, attaché in Japan and Britain and consul in San Francisco, used it in his 1879 *Annals of Japan*. See [ibid.], [Masini 1993, p. 189], and especially [Ng 1995]. Huang was an official in Hunan beginning in 1897, and had a role in the term's popularization among Hunanese reformers. See [Min 1985, p. 200] and [Kamachi 1981].

[55] A thorough exploration of the background to these various reform movements is beyond my scope. [Min 1985, p. 200] explains that New Text ideas were among the earliest stimuli to the reformers. See also [Lewis 1976] and [Rankin 1986].

If we do not establish a national assembly there will be no uniting the citizen's voices. . . . When asked "What would it be like to establish a national assembly now?" we answer "the national assembly represents the people's public duty (*gongyi*)." "But is the national assembly not then a representation of the people's authority (*minquan*)?" We say that the [imperial] order we have now received, the instructions we have taken, of the public duty to enlighten each other and revive learning is a public undertaking of the people. Considering the public duty to be a public undertaking, and the public undertaking to be a public assembly, what else can we call it but the people's authority? It precisely means the people's authority! Besides, people's authority is people's duty. "People" cannot be separated from "authority." The people devote themselves to their duty and the people engage in their own undertakings, while the ruler's authority draws together these myriad undertakings. "People's authority" is to manage one's own undertakings. If the people lack authority, they cannot devote themselves to their duties. If they do manage their own undertakings, then the sovereign's authority will also reach its utmost.[56]

In other words, responsibility for the fate of the nation rests not only on the shoulders of the ruler, but also on those of the "people," by which the author clearly meant elite members of the society, since they are charged with reviving learning. These "people" have a part in the shared "public duty" which can only be carried out if they are able to contribute their "undertakings" to the public good, which in turn requires that they have a forum for so contributing: thus the national assembly and the people's (limited) authority, or *minquan*.

In Shanghai, another prominent advocate of reform wrote about *minquan* in a very similar vein. He explicitly rejects the Western model of "democracy (*minzhu*)," preferring joint governance between ruler and people [Wang 1953 (1896), p. 147]. He demonstrates that the notion of a ruler consulting with his people has ample precedent in the Confucian classics, and urges that a recognition of people's authority, institutionalized in a parliament, will support the state by solidifying the power of the ruler, increasing the identification of the people with the interests

---

[56] [Anonymous 1966 (1897), p. 821]. Translation based on [Wakeman 1972, p. 65], though Wakeman confusingly translates "*minquan*" as "people's rights" while rendering "*junquan*" as "ruler's authority." For more analysis of this passage, see also [Ng 1998, ch. 6].

and needs of the state, and increasing the ability of the state to fend off external enemies [ibid., pp. 147–8]. To those who fear that *minquan* means that authority will simply devolve onto the people, he replies that such people "do not know that in a nation governed jointly by the ruler and the people, when there is an important national issue, it is sent to the parliament for discussion and decision, which is then executed by the ruler. . . . The highest authority is still held by the ruler" [ibid., p. 147].

We will see later that there were indeed people who feared what *minquan* might mean for the ruler's authority. First, though, I want to turn to what is probably the most radical pre-twentieth-century Chinese statement relating to rights, and to explore the degree to which this doctrine, which puts greater weight on the individual than anything we have seen so far, derives indirectly from the writings of Protestant missionaries.

5.4.3 Individual Rights?

Virtually all of the thinkers we have looked at so far in this chapter view the subjects of *quan* – the ones who have rights or authority – as collectivities. For a range of reasons, as Chinese rights discourse develops in the twentieth century it will continue to posit a closer, more harmonious relationship between individual and collectivity than is found in at least some versions of Western rights theorizing. One strand of the nineteenth-century Chinese discourse, though, does highlight the *quan* of individuals: These are the writings that place at their center the claim that "every person has the *quan* of self-mastery (*ren ren you zizhu zhi quan*)."

We have already seen that Protestant missionaries played roles in stimulating Chinese rights discourse. Through their translations of international law texts, Parker, Martin, and others all contributed to the development of terminology and concepts related to rights. In this section, the role of more purely religious writings becomes important. The source in which I am particularly interested is the *Globe Magazine* (*Wanguo Gongbao*), which was published in Chinese during 1874–83 and 1889–1907.[57] It began as a successor to the *Church News* (*Jiaohui Xinbao*), but went through a series of format and content changes, each time growing more secular in orientation. It was among the most widely read periodicals in China prior to 1896 [Shek 1976, p. 196].

---

[57] The magazine was edited by the Rev. Young J. Allen, and its name was subsequently changed to *Review of the Times*. See [Shek 1976, p. 196].

We saw earlier that "*zizhu zhi quan*" was used in the *General Laws* as a translation for "independence." It works quite well as a gloss on independence: Literally meaning "the power to rule oneself," it readily conveys the idea of being independent from the control or authority of another. In the writings of Alexander Williamson in the *Globe Magazine*, this term, and variations on it, come to be used to express the idea of free will.[58] For instance:

> The source of [man's] ability to distinguish between good and evil lies entirely in his having self-mastery (*zizhu*) over his opinions. If he lacked mastery over his opinions, he could act neither for good nor for evil.... It is like when God created the archangels: he had to endow them with the power to be masters of themselves (*zineng zuozhu zhi quan*). As a result when these angels did good, it was certainly through self-mastery; when they did evil, this was also through self-mastery. [quoted in Liu 1994d, p. 6]

One scholar comments on this passage that "this kind of moral right of self-determination is a central topic in Christian theology" [ibid., p. 6]. A second scholar translates as "the right of personal autonomy" the term I rendered as "the power to be master of themselves," and concludes that this missionary had introduced "the concept of basic human rights" [Shek 1976, pp. 198–9].

I believe that it is anachronistic to read "rights" into Williamson's language. The idea behind the Christian doctrine of free will, after all, is that one can choose to do good or do evil: One has this ability or power. As Williamson puts it elsewhere: "The capacity to make free, independent choices without interference from outside is the basis of man's humanity" [ibid., p. 197]. Here the Chinese original does not allow the translator to substitute "rights" for "capacity." There is no reason to conclude that when Williamson expresses this same idea with "*quan*," he is using it in any sense other than its traditional meaning of "power." Not only that, but whatever Williamson may have taken to follow from his assertion, it seems clear that no Chinese reader needs to have attributed to him any distinctive concept of rights. Williamson's discussion of free will made adequate sense without conceptual innovation.

---

[58] Williamson was not the only one to use terminology close to "*zizhu zhi quan*" in the pages of the *Globe Magazine*, but he will suffice for my purposes. For further discussion, see [Liu 1994d].

This is not to say, however, that scholars who see Williamson playing a role in the development of Chinese rights discourse are all wrong. In light of what we have seen earlier, it is a striking feature of the "powers" Williamson discusses that they belong to individuals. If someone already committed to the inference from *quan* to legitimacy were to interpret Williamson's writings, then they might well come to use the term to express a new set of commitments, namely to the legitimacy of individual powers.

The earliest example of something like this process of adapting Protestant claims about free will can be found in a remarkable essay called the *Complete Book of Substantial Principles and General Laws*, written by Kang Youwei (1858–1927) from 1885 to 1887. Kang was one of the intellectual leaders of the reform movement, both through his direct participation in reform agitation and through his teaching: Several other prominent thinkers studied with him, including both Tan Sitong and Liang Qichao, the latter a subject of this book's next chapter.[59] Kang drew on many aspects of the Chinese tradition; he was a chief proponent of the New Text ideas about reform and development mentioned earlier. He also strove to learn everything he could about Western science, religion, and philosophy, and incorporated many of these ideas into his wide-ranging writings. One of his main sources for things Western was the *Globe Magazine*, whence he probably derived the term "*zizhu zhi quan.*"

The *Complete Book of Substantial Principles and General Laws* has an unusual organization which Kang based on his understanding of Western mathematics. Each section begins with one or more "substantial principles." These are general truths which the following analysis will take as axioms. Based on these axioms, he then derives several "general laws," each of which is contrasted to various "lesser alternatives" which do not follow from the axioms. Contemporary Chinese practices are inevitably to be found among these lesser alternatives, which makes the text into a wholesale critique of Chinese customs, values, and institutions.

At the center of the whole structure is the notion of *zizhu zhi quan*. This is introduced in the "General Discussion on Humankind," an excerpted version of which runs as follows:

Substantial Principles. . . . [1] Human beings are formed by taking their respective share of the primordial substance of heaven and

---

[59] See [Liang 1989a (1896), p. 99] for Liang's own 1896 discussion of *zizhu zhi quan*. He defines it as "each person doing all he ought to do, and receiving all the benefits he ought to receive."

earth. [2] Every individual possesses a soul and hence possesses reason. . . .

Universal Laws. . . . [1] People have the *quan* of self-mastery. *Note*: This is a law derived from geometrical axioms and is wholly in accordance with the substantial principles that human beings are formed by taking their respective share of the primordial substance and that every individual possesses a soul. . . . [Kang 1978, p. 699]

The next section of the text discusses "Husband and Wife," and Kang continues on to examine other categories of human relationship (ruler-subject, teacher-disciple, and so on), in every case arguing for equal relationships based on equal *quan* of self-mastery.

It is quite clear, I think, that Kang is here influenced by the Protestant teachings we looked at earlier, but in the context of Kang's writings, I find myself more tempted to read *"quan"* as entailing commitments similar to those entailed by "rights." In particular, Kang links *quan* very closely to equality. His argument is not that we in fact have free will, since God made us that way, but rather that since we are all equal, we ought to be masters of ourselves. Another way of saying that is that we have a right to self-mastery. Some years later, a student of Kang's wrote the following: "When Christianity was first founded . . . it established [the concept of] the Heavenly Kingdom which gives each person the right of autonomy (*zizhu zhi quan*) and abolished all inequalities to restore equality."[60] This once again conflates Christian doctrine with developing ideas about rights, but since it recognizes the normative character of *quan* in the tie it makes to equality, and since it explicitly applies *quan* to individuals, "rights" may not be a bad translation for this instance of *"quan."*

5.4.4 Zhang Zhidong

Like the self-strengthener Li Hongzhang, Zhang Zhidong (1837–1909) was an official who, while firmly grounded in Confucian values, recognized the need for reform. Among his many progressive activities was his patronage of the pioneering literati newspaper, the *Chinese Progress* (*Shiwu Bao*), which was published in Shanghai from mid-1896 to mid-1898, when it was closed down after the failure of the Hundred Days reform. Zhang had envisioned the *Chinese Progress* as a means to gather

---

[60] The student is Tan Sitong (1865–98). The quotation is from [Shek 1976, p. 198].

and publicize information on foreign relations and other topics; certain sensitive areas of domestic affairs were to be taboo [Yoon 2000, p. 12]. As it turned out, though, the men whom Zhang employed to run the newspaper had a more radical agenda which very much included advocating *minquan*.[61] Despite Zhang's repeated attempts to control what was published, editorial after editorial appeared in the *Chinese Progress* extolling *minquan*, including some of the very articles I examined a few paragraphs ago.[62] In an effort to clarify his own position, Zhang wrote an extended essay entitled *Exhortation to Learning (Quanxue Pian)* in which he supported a variety of reform efforts but criticized the notion of *minquan*. Zhang's essay was submitted to the court, and as the Hundred Days reform crumbled, an imperial edict was issued requiring officials in all provinces to publish *Exhortation to Learning*.

In the sixth chapter of *Exhortation to Learning*, entitled "Rectifying *Quan*," Zhang argues that "the doctrine of *minquan* brings no benefits and a hundred harms" [Zhang 1970 (1898), vol. 1, p. 23a]. In the next several pages, he outlines a series of reasons why giving the people *quan* would lead to these harms. Two of the more interesting reasons make it clear that he sees *minquan* as demanding power or authority for the people at the expense of the power of the government. He writes, for instance, that people with capital can already open business enterprises, and those with skills can already invent things, even without *quan*; if officials lost their *quan*, though, criminal activity could not be restrained and the people would suffer. Officials have to have the authority, that is, to distinguish between legitimate and illegitimate businesses and to suppress the latter. *Minquan*, in Zhang's eyes, would strip officials of this authority. Similarly, Zhang says that people can already open their own schools, even without *quan*; if officials were to lose *quan*, though, then the route to official status through education would lose its appeal and people's motivation for study would lapse [ibid., pp. 23b–24a]. Zhang clearly sees *quan* as something that is desirable, and if officials no longer have it, there is less reason to work to become an official.

We saw earlier that advocates of *minquan* explicitly claimed that *minquan* did not imply a usurpation of the ruler's authority by the people: It meant a sharing of authority, based in part on consultation

---

[61] Yoon adds that the "literati-journalists," who were not officials, saw the magazine as a means to influence the government [Yoon 2000, p. 2].

[62] Zhang was particularly incensed by the pro-*minquan* editorials of Wang Kangnian, Zhang's hand-picked director-general of the newspaper. Wang is the "prominent advocate of reform" writing in Shanghai whom I discussed earlier.

in a national assembly. Zhang does not believe that authority can be shared; if the people have *quan*, then officials do not. After outlining the various problems he sees with *minquan*, Zhang adds that he believes that "*minquan*" is a poor term for capturing the foreign ideas that inspired it:

> An investigation of the origin of the doctrine of *minquan* in foreign countries reveals the idea that a state should have a parliament where the people can express their public opinion and communicate their group feelings. It is only desired that people should be able to explain their feelings; it is not desired that they should wield any power. Translators have altered the wording to call it "*minquan*," which is a mistake. [1970 (1898), vol. 1, p. 24b; translation adapted from Teng & Fairbank 1954, p. 168]

Transmitting the feelings of the people to their leaders is legitimate, but should not be confused with matters of *quan*. At the end of this chapter, Zhang says that once the people's level of education has risen sufficiently, he would support a purely consultative parliament, but not the idea of *minquan*.

By "*quan*," Zhang means legitimate power or authority. He understands and endorses the norms that limit and legitimize state power. Reading between the lines, we can see that he fears *minquan* both because there are no norms constraining it – it would become naked power, benefiting criminals more than anyone else – and because he sees no means to adjudicate the sharing of legitimate authority.[63] On the former question, I believe Zhang is very astute. What might the basis for people's *quan* be? There are certainly classical precedents for a ruler's having responsibility to the people, and even for a ruler's obligation to consult, in some limited fashion, with the people. I argued earlier, though, that people-as-root does not include people's political rights, nor any other basis for people having legitimate political power. On the latter issue, we should remember that the most common reason given by *minquan* advocates for needing a ruler was that the people were not yet ready to govern themselves. In their eyes, the monarchy is justified by its unique ability to carry out what the Hunanese writer we examined earlier called "public undertakings": to keep the state in harmony and order, strong enough to sustain itself in a hostile international arena. If

---

[63] He writes, for instance, that so long as China recognizes the Confucian "bond between ruler and subject, *minquan* cannot be implemented" [Zhang 1970 (1898), vol. 1, p. 13a].

the people knew enough and were organized enough to do this themselves, then perhaps the monarch would no longer be necessary.[64]

After discussing *minquan*, Zhang takes up the related claim, discussed earlier in the context of Kang Youwei's writings, that all people have the *quan* of self-mastery (*zizhu zhi quan*). Zhang thinks that this is even worse than *minquan*. Zhang's arguments against the *quan* of self-mastery take similar form to the considerations he adduces against *minquan*. First, he says that "*zizhu zhi quan*" is a bad translation of the Christian idea of free will, which is not actually about any sort of authority [Zhang 1970 (1898), vol. 1, p. 24b]. I think that Zhang is basically right: He has correctly identified the source of this phrase, as we saw earlier, and insightfully notices its lack of any connection, in its original context, with authority. He apparently has no problem with the commitments entailed by the Christian concept of free will, but he rejects the innovation entailed by Kang's use of the phrase. He rejects the conceptual innovation because he feels that if each person had his or her own power of self-mastery, the result would be selfish chaos. Zhang adds that in all Western nations, no matter whether they are monarchies, democracies, or constitutional monarchies, there are laws and other legitimate means of checking individual power: This, he says, is equivalent to people not having the *quan* of self-mastery [ibid., pp. 24b–25a]. Once again it is clear that what Zhang is worried about is power unchecked by any norms or institutions. He understands how state *quan* can be subject to norms (like the "Three Bonds") and thus rendered legitimate; he does not see the grounds for a comparable process for people's *quan*. He thus can see the former as authority, while the latter is mere power.

5.4.5 *Voices from Hong Kong*

Although the failure of the Hundred Days brought to a halt discussion of *minquan* in venues like the *Chinese Progress*, the most thorough and sophisticated treatment of *minquan* – including an answer to Zhang's implied challenge to find grounds for people's authority – came in late 1898 from Hong Kong. Protected from the Chinese government by their residence in the British colony, He Qi (1859–1914) and Hu Liyuan (1847–1916) collaborated on "A Postscript to *Exhortation to Learning*," subsequently published in 1901 as part of their *Real Interpretation of the*

---

[64] Tu-ki Min's reflections on what he calls the "reluctant inevitability" of the monarch, as seen in reformist writings, are quite insightful. See [Min 1985, pp. 207–8].

New Policies. He Qi had spent a decade in England, earning degrees in both medicine and law, before returning to Hong Kong in 1882. He had an active career in Hong Kong as a public servant, declining an invitation in the late 1890s to serve as a diplomat for the Qing court [Xu 1992, pp. 3–5]. Hu Liyuan was educated solely in Hong Kong. Starting in 1887, when he translated one of He Qi's English essays into Chinese, Hu and He worked together to publish a whole series of reform proposals. He Qi would write in English, then Hu Liyuan would translate into Chinese.[65]

As early as 1887 He Qi wrote – in English – about foreign nations' violations of China's "sovereign right." He continues: "If China wishes to have diplomatic relations with other countries on an equal footing and desires foreign powers to respect her sovereignty and rights, she must do more than simply get strong" [He 1992 (1887), pp. 137–8]. He Qi explains that China needs more than military strengthening: It needs to reform its corrupt legal system so that foreigners will be willing to submit to it, and more generally to improve "her loose morality and evil habits, both social and political" [ibid., p. 138]. When Hu Liyuan translates this material into Chinese, he uses "*quan*" to translate "rights" [He & Hu 1994 (1901), p. 86]. Together they produce a series of institutional proposals over the next decade. They seek a parliament, a cabinet system, and the *quan* for members of the press to speak and write freely. With the exception of what sounds like a right to free speech, most of their ideas are quite similar to proposals made by advocates of *minquan* within China.[66]

The biggest departure from previous writing and thinking about *minquan* comes in the essay that He and Hu compose to rebut Zhang Zhidong's indictment of *minquan*. They write that

> As for "*quan*," it is not [a word for] military power, nor for bureaucratic influence. *Quan* is that with which one pursues the great norms and laws under heaven, and that with which one establishes the greatest justice and fairness under heaven. There must be something with which one accomplishes these things, and lacking any other name for it, we can simply call it "*quan*." Given that we are

---

[65] A contemporary scholar writes that in so doing, Hu would "insert some of his own ideas" [Xu 1992, p. 7], but gives no specific examples. So far as I know, no one has yet studied the differences that may exist between the English and Chinese versions of the writings of He and Hu.

[66] For their views on the parliament and related reforms, see [Xu 1992, pp. 48–9]. The *quan* to free expression they champion is, in Chinese, "*you fangyan zhi quan*" [ibid., p. 58].

speaking of the great norms and laws, the greatest justice and fair-
ness, thus *quan* must be given by heaven, rather than being established by people. Heaven gives people their lives, thus it must also
given them the *quan* with which to attend to their lives. [He & Hu
1994 (1901), p. 397]

The role attributed here to heaven recalls the similar claims made in
Japan a number of years earlier, but it is quite unlike anything that we
have heretofore seen in China. In fact, the logic resembles that of John
Locke more than that of the earlier mainland *minquan* advocates we
examined earlier. Locke believed that there are natural laws defining our
moral duties, and that there must be natural rights, corresponding to
these duties, which enable us to fulfill the duties and laws. *Quan*, according to He and Hu, comes about in just such a way: It is the means by
which one realizes heavenly morality.

Other aspects of the Hong Kong thinkers' views are more similar to
those of their counterparts on the mainland. They believe, for instance,
that *minquan* will unify a collection of dispersed individuals: "*Minquan*
is that through which the rulers and people . . . of a nation can be combined into a single mind."[67] In fact they maintain that the *quan* of
self-mastery, which we saw Zhang attack precisely for its centrifugal tendencies, also serves to unify rather than disperse. Their reasoning to these
conclusions is fascinating. They assert that only in society do we ever
have *quan*, because only when we are part of a group is there a moral
standard relevant to us. Alone, we simply choose to do that which benefits us; *quan* is neither needed nor relevant. In society, we are given the
quan to do that which benefits us and our group, or at the very least to
do that which does not harm the group [ibid., pp. 416–17]. *Minquan* is
the *quan* of the collective. With it, people can do that which heaven
intends for them, and their group can flourish. Without it, the state will
descend into chaos and the people will suffer.

5.5 CONCLUSION

Two of the last three subjects of this chapter – Kang's focus on individuals, and He Qi's Lockean natural-rights doctrine – suggest that Chinese
rights discourse may be moving, at the end of the nineteenth century,
closer to what many in the West now take to be the mainstream of inter-

---

[67] [He & Hu 1994 (1901), p. 397; see also pp. 403–4].

national ideas of human rights. For better or for worse, things do not develop this neatly. In fact, things do not develop this neatly in Western nations, either; in the next three chapters I will draw repeated connections between Chinese and Western discussions of rights, as the two (or more) discourses increasingly interact with one another.

The idea of assigning rights to individuals certainly does pick up steam in twentieth-century China, though virtually all theorists will continue to maintain that groups have rights as well. Locating rights solely in collectivities, or perhaps more accurately solely in the members of certain collectivities, is nonetheless an idea that does not go away. For related reasons, it will be endorsed by supporters of both of twentieth-century China's revolutionary political parties, the Nationalists and the Communists.

Conceptual changes thus continue in the new century, but terminological development starts to settle down. Yan Fu's influential 1898 translation into Chinese of Huxley's account of social Darwinism, *Tian Yan Lun*, uses "*quanli*" to translate "rights."[68] In a letter Yan wrote to Liang Qichao – on whom see the next chapter – several years later, Yan expressed reservations about "*quanli*" as an adequate translation for "rights," and considered a variety of alternatives.[69] By 1904, Yan returned to "*quanli*" in his translation of Edward Jenks's *A History of Politics* [Liu 1994d, pp. 20–1]. I will not dwell on the concepts Yan expressed through these different uses of "*quanli*"; in the next chapter I look instead at two of Yan's contemporaries who wrote more extensively about *quanli*.[70] In their hands we will see important innovations coupled with striking and explicit connections not just to ideas discussed in this chapter, but also to the Confucians we met earlier. Chinese rights discourse is dynamic, while remaining, at least thus far in my story, distinctively Chinese.

---

[68] [Yan Fu 1986, vol. 5, p. 1396], published in 1898, though available in manuscript form as early as 1895.

[69] This letter is cited in [Liu 1994d].

[70] For two different discussions of what Yan meant, see [Liu 1994d] and [Suzuki 1997, p. 50].

6

Dynamism in the Early
Twentieth Century

THE TWENTIETH CENTURY brought with it the beginnings of
sustained engagement between Western and Chinese rights discourses. This chapter focuses on the works of the two Chinese intellectuals who best exemplified this trend at the turn of their century. The first
is Liang Qichao (1873–1929), who was a student of Kang Youwei, a
sometime employee of Zhang Zhidong, and a participant in the failed
Hundred Days reform movement, after which he fled to Japan and wrote
the essay we will examine here. My second subject is Liu Shipei
(1884–1919). After a classical education, Liu found himself drawn to
revolutionary activities in Shanghai, where he wrote the texts with
which I am here concerned. For a time Liu became increasingly radical,
even founding an anarchist journal in Tokyo, but after 1908 he left
politics and returned to his first (and abiding) passion, namely classical
scholarship.

Choosing to focus on Liang and Liu also means choosing to leave out
a host of interesting texts and authors; justifying my choice of subject
matter thus has two dimensions. On the positive side, I include Liang and
Liu because they are the most sophisticated advocates of a "new morality" in their day. Their grasp of foreign ideas far exceeds that of most of
their contemporaries; their knowledge of and engagement with their own
traditions are similarly broad and deep. Their writings on *quanli* are fascinating and, given the intellectual standing of each, also influential. As
far as the negative side – why I left out so many others – goes, I reason
as follows. First, I need to consider my subjects carefully and in depth,
since it is only from inferential connections among people's commitments that we determine the contents of their concepts. Second, the early
twentieth century, while vitally important, is only one part of a longer
narrative; my ultimate concern is with the shape of a larger discourse.

Finally, I know that the ideas and, in many cases, texts of those whom I omit are accessible for those interested in pursuing this period's rights discourse in greater depth.[1]

The central theme of this chapter is that if we read texts carefully, mindful of how they were read by their intended audiences, we can recover connections between the concepts in these texts and elements of their authors' traditions – connections that are lost if we presume that all instances of "*quanli*" simply mean rights, and that all instances of "rights" mean the same thing. I explore the complex relations between the texts and ideas of Liang and Liu, on the one hand, and foreign texts and authors with which they explicitly engage, on the other. The interactions we see with German and French ideas of rights are rich and fascinating; they contribute to the significant dynamism that Chinese rights discourse enjoys in the first decades of the century. These interactions do not negate, on the other hand, the connections to tradition that I have already noted. Chinese rights discourse appears to develop in its own, distinctive fashion.

6.1 LIANG AND JHERING

6.1.1 An Appeal to "History"?

Rudolf von Jhering (1818–92) wrote *Der Kampf ums Recht* (*The Struggle for Law*) in 1872. He was already regarded as one of Germany's most important legal philosophers, and *Der Kampf* helped to ensure a worldwide reputation. It was translated into Chinese between 1900 and 1901 [Jhering 1900–1]. Jhering's doctrines stimulated Liang Qichao to publish *Lun Quanli Sixiang* (On Rights Consciousness) in 1902 as part of his manifesto *On the New People*. Liang tells us that the "essential points" of his essay, which is among the earliest and most sustained treatments of a concept of rights to appear in Chinese, are mostly taken from *Der Kampf* [Liang 1989d, p. 32]. We will see that there are indeed certain similarities that make Liang's "*quanli*" resonate with Jhering's notion of "*Recht*," and these similarities – chief among which is a kind of individual assertiveness – help to explain Liang's interest in Jhering. My discussion of the two thinkers, in fact, will offer at least the beginnings of an explanation of why German conceptions of law and rights were so attractive to Chinese intellectuals.

---

[1] I refer here in particular to [Svensson 1996] and [Angle & Svensson 2001].

As is often the case with cross-cultural comparisons, though, we will also see that these similarities mask some less obvious but very important differences. For Jhering, the relation between following the procedures of the law and exercising one's *Recht* is crucial; for Liang, in contrast, *quanli* are deeply related to ethical concerns. This difference, in turn, colors their respective notions of assertiveness, which thus turn out not to resemble one another as closely as first appeared. When we see *Recht* and *quanli* as separate concepts emerging from separate discourse contexts, these differences will make sense.

My goal here goes beyond simply interpreting Liang and Jhering: I demonstrate that significant and important conceptual differences can exist even when one person takes himself or herself to be explicating and in fact translating the ideas of another. To make clear what is at stake, consider the following passage:

> In ancient times, Lin Xiangru scolded the King of Qin saying: "Smash both my head and the jade disk!"[2] Now given the size of the state of Zhao, how could such love be expressed for a tiny thing like a jade disk? He was saying that Qin could smash the disk, kill him, invade his territory, endanger his state, and still he would not surrender. Ah! This was nothing other than "*quanli*"! [Liang 1989d, p. 33]

In a later passage, Liang amplifies the idea that ancient China can teach us about *quanli*. He is impressed by the classical Daoist Yang Zhu's teaching that "no one [should] give up a hair" on his head, which strikes him as exemplifying the idea that we should not allow even minor invasions of our legitimate benefits. While Liang adds that Yang's other famous doctrine of "no one benefiting the world" (on which see later) was mistaken, Liang concludes that "Yang Zhu was in fact a philosopher who advocated *quanli*, and provides a good method with which to save China in its hour of need" [ibid.].

Taken together, the claims we've just examined lead to a puzzle. On one hand, Liang clearly identifies his talk of *quanli* with Jhering's talk of Recht. On the other hand, Liang asserts that ancient Chinese both theorized about and acted on this same idea of *quanli*. This leaves us with

---

[2] According to the *Shi Ji*, in 283 B.C.E., Lin was dispatched by the king of Zhao to take the priceless jade of the He clan to the state of Qin. The king of Qin had offered to exchange twelve cities for the jade. When Lin realized that the king of Qin planned to keep the jade without relinquishing the cities, he took back the jade disk, backed against a pillar, and made the declaration Liang cites. See [Ch'ien 1994, pp. 263–4].

at least three possibilities: (1) Liang is right on both counts. Jhering and Yang Zhu were discussing the same concept. (2) Liang is right to see a connection between himself and Jhering, but anachronistically reads *quanli* into the ancient Chinese figures' concerns. (3) Liang is right that his concerns are similar to those discussed by Yang and exemplified by Lin, but wrong to think that there is more than a superficial resemblance with Jhering's ideas.

Joseph Levenson has famously argued that choice (2) is one of the keys to understanding not only Liang, but also "the mind of modern China." Levenson wrote that "Every man has an emotional commitment to history and an intellectual commitment to value, and he tries to make these two commitments coincide. . . . [As Liang began his career, he was] straining against his tradition intellectually, seeing value elsewhere, but still emotionally tied to it, held by his history" [Levenson 1967, p. 1]. The attempt to live up to both commitments led him to try to "smuggle Western values into Chinese history" [ibid., p. 4].

My focus here is not on Levenson's argument, which has been amply discussed elsewhere.[3] Levenson does clearly articulate one position against which I will be arguing, though, because I believe that when we take seriously all that Liang says about *quanli*, we do not find a tension between "value" (that is, Jhering's ideas) and "history" (face-saving references to the Chinese tradition). Instead, we will uncover a largely consistent and coherent doctrine which builds on orientations found in the Confucian tradition. Liang's understanding of *the abilities and interests that one should legitimately be able to enjoy*, which is how I will suggest we gloss his "*quanli*," has a deep basis in the Confucian idea of an ethical, and not merely legal, ordering of the world. To see this contrast between Jhering and Liang, we will have to look at both Jhering and Liang in their respective contexts, and it is to the first of these tasks that I now turn.

6.1.2 Jhering's Struggle for Rights and Law

"The life of the law," writes Jhering, "is a struggle – a struggle of nations, of the state power, of classes, of individuals" [Jhering 1915, p. 1]. Here we find the two terms that are highlighted in the title of Jhering's *Der Kampf ums Recht*: "*Kampf*" is "struggle" and "*Recht*" can be either "law" or "right." As we will see, it is through struggle for individual rights that

[3] See, e.g., [Schwartz 1976].

Jhering believes we struggle for law. This tight relationship has deep roots in Jhering's understanding of what *Recht* is. He says that

> The term *Recht* is, it is well known, used in our language in a twofold sense – in an objective sense and in a subjective sense. This *Recht*, in the objective sense of the word, embraces all the principles of law enforced by the state; it is the legal ordering of life. But *Recht*, in the subjective sense of the word is, so to speak, the precipitate of the abstract rule into the concrete legal right[4] of the person. [1915, p. 6]

In his 1877 philosophical treatise *Purpose in Law*,[5] Jhering explains the relationship between the two senses of "*Recht*" in a similar fashion.[6] He writes that "without law there is no securing life and property," and

> The form by which law, or right regarded objectively, affords its protection to both interests is, as is well known, by right in the subjective sense. To have a right means there is something *for us*, and the power of the State recognizes this and protects us. [Jhering 1913, pp. 49–50]

He puts this last thought in even more pithy form when he defines a subjective right as "an interest protected by law (*Rechtlich geschütztes Interesse*)" [Jhering 1915, p. 58; Jhering 1872, p. 44].

To have a right one must meet two criteria. First, one must have some kind of *interest*: there must be something *for one*, something that matters to one. Second, this interest must be recognized and protected by the state. Law, or *Recht* in the objective sense, is the systematic institutionalization of these protections: the "legal ordering of life." This latter doctrine has come to be known as "legal positivism": the insistence that there are neither natural laws nor natural rights, but only those laws that are enforced by some authority.[7]

---

[4] Jhering's translator often renders "*Recht*" as "legal right." I will leave this unamended except when it is misleading.

[5] The English title given by Huski to his translation of *Der Zweck im Recht* is *Law as a Means to an End*, which trivializes "*Recht*" inappropriately. I therefore use *Purpose in Law*, which is more common in the secondary literature; see, e.g., Weir's translation in [Wieacker 1995, p. 355].

[6] Scholars have noted some significant shifts in Jhering's ideas between *Der Kampf* and *Der Zweck* [conversation with James Whitman]; see also [Fikentscher 1977]. Without wanting to deny that differences do exist, I believe that Jhering was quite consistent in his understanding of the idea of *Recht* itself.

[7] "Positivism" has meant different things to different people. German legal positivism, also called "pandectism," started with Savigny in the early nineteenth century, and was

A crucial move in Jhering's argument comes when he explains how it is that those of us who are conscious of our rights think about our "interests." The following passage – which Liang, as we will see, paraphrases in his essay – is revealing:

> In those suits at law in which [there is a] disproportion . . . between the value of the object in controversy and the prospective cost [to the litigant] . . . , the question is not of the insignificant object in controversy, but of an ideal end: the person's assertion of himself and of his feeling of right. . . . It is not a mere money-interest which urges the person whose rights have been infringed to institute legal proceedings, but moral pain at the wrong which has been endured. He is not concerned simply with recovering the object . . . but with forcing a recognition of his rights. An inner voice tells him he should not retreat, that it is not the worthless object that is at stake but his own personality, his feeling of legal right, his self-respect – in short, the suit at law ceases to appear to him in the guise of a mere question of interest and becomes a question of character. [Jhering 1915, pp. 28–9]

In this passage Jhering tells us that disputes over rights can cease to appear "in the guise of a mere question of interest." This might sound surprising, given that we have just seen that he defines rights as interests protected by law. The problem is that Jhering uses "interests" in two senses. The "interests" mentioned in the passage now under consideration are of a limited type, with "money-interest" as their paradigm. Both in *Der Kampf* and in *Purpose in Law*, Jhering also develops a second, broader notion of what it is for something to be in our interest. This does include concrete things, like the "object in controversy" from the foregoing passage, but also encompasses the ways in which other people can be "for us" – as for instance in the reciprocal relationships of the family – and most importantly the ways in which we can be for ourselves

developed by Puchta, Jhering (in his early days), and Laband, among others. Their central premise was that law as a "positive science in which the rules of law and how to apply them were drawn exclusively from the system, concepts, and doctrinal principles: extralegal values or aims, whether religious, social, or scientific, were denied any title to create or alter the law" [Wieacker 1995, p. 341]. As such, pandectism is clearly a species of the broader notion of positivism mentioned in my main text, but one can reject natural law without being a pandectist. This was Jhering in the latter part of his career (with whom we are now concerned), after he renounced the conceptual method of pandectism: He came to believe that all manner of human purposes were relevant to understanding what laws there were.

[Jhering 1913, p. 50]. He says that "the legal expression for [this last kind of interest] is the right of *personality*" [ibid.]. Note that when he described what was really at stake in the lawsuit, Jhering put it first of all in terms of one's "personality." There is a sense, in short, in which the maintenance and development of one's personality or character is an important interest we each have, and one of the most fundamental roles that rights play is to provide protection for this type of interest. As Jhering puts it, "Man is not concerned only with his physical life but [also] with his moral existence. The condition of this moral existence is right, in the law" [Jhering 1915, p. 31].[8]

The scope of this "moral existence," extends beyond one's immediate "personality," since one's will and one's labor can establish a bond between oneself and anything at all. Any object can become

> part of my own strength and my own past, or the strength and past of another, which I possess and assert in it. In making it my own, I stamped it with the mark of my own person; whoever attacks it, attacks me; the blow dealt it strikes me, for I am present in it. Property is but the periphery of my person extended to things. This connection of the law with the person invests all rights, no matter what their nature, with that incommensurable value which, in opposition to their purely material value, I call *ideal value*. [Jhering 1915, p. 59]

Jhering takes the imagery of this passage very seriously. We feel – or at any rate, should feel – pain when our rights are violated. We do so because of our "feeling of right [*Rechtsgefühl*]." Jhering says that the "feeling of right" is the key to

> the whole secret of the law. The pain which a person experiences when his legal rights are violated is the spontaneous, instinctive admission, wrung from him by force, of what the law is to him as an individual, and then of what it is to human society. . . . Not the intellect, but the feeling, is able to [say what law is]; and hence language has rightly designated the psychological source of all law as the *feeling of right*. The consciousness of right (*Rechtsbewusstsein*), legal conviction, are scientific abstractions with which the people

---

[8] The translator uses "right, in the law" to make explicit the connection between objective and subjective *Recht*; Jhering's original only has the single word "*Recht*" [Jhering 1872, p. 27].

are not acquainted. The power of the law lies in feeling. . . . [1915, p. 61]

Anyone who has not experienced or at least observed the pain that should come when one's rights are violated has no real knowledge of the law.

I will deal with the connection Jhering mentions between the individual and "human society" in a few moments. First let me take stock. Jhering is concerned to show why rights and law are things for which we should struggle rather than take for granted. The last two paragraphs have articulated a pair of ideas which suggest that we ought to look to Darwin and to Hegel in order to understand Jhering's ultimate commitment to the struggle for law. One of Jhering's greatest contributions to German jurisprudence was his insistence that conceptual analysis alone was insufficient: He argued that we also need to pay attention to actual human drives and purposes.[9] The idea that the "psychological source of all law is the feeling of right" aims to give jurisprudence a naturalistic footing: Individuals or groups struggling for legal recognition and protection are analogous to individuals and groups competing in a Darwinian competition for survival. Indeed, the title of *Der Kampf* was modeled on Haeckel's Darwinian "*Kampf ums Dasein* (the struggle for existence)."[10] Struggle directed by the feeling of right, Jhering came to believe, could explain the genealogy of law far better than abstract conceptual analysis.

Whatever we today make of the implication that the "feeling of right" is tantamount to a biological faculty, Jhering's account of the development of law as a struggle of interests certainly has some pull on us. Be this as it may, however, we will likely see little in the Darwinian side of Jhering's account to explain the normative aspect of law: In what direction *ought* law to develop? It is here that Jhering draws on Hegel, when he asserts that a crucial function of rights and law is to protect our developing personalities. In particular, Jhering's claim that "property is but the periphery of my person extended to things" recalls Hegel's even stronger claim that property is the concrete "existence of personality" itself [Hegel 1991, p. 81]. Jhering comes close to this idea when he writes that, for an individual in a lawsuit, "it is not the worthless object that is at stake but his own personality." Taken together, these ideas lay at least

---

[9] See note 7 and [Wieacker 1995, p. 357].
[10] [Conversation with James Whitman]; see also [Wieacker 1995, p. 357].

the foundation for a less genealogical and more prescriptive account of *Recht*, according to which we ought to develop laws and rights that protect people's personalities.[11] As we will see later, this stress on the normative import of personality is one of the many features of Jhering's view that Liang finds attractive.

To sum up, the positivist insight – that there are no laws or rights other than those enforced by some authority – should not lead to passivity, for two reasons. First, as we will see in more detail later, if rights recognized by the state are not actively claimed, the laws on which they are based will lose their concrete reality. The "legal ordering of life" itself, that is, depends on people's active assertion of their rights. Second, since laws by their very nature defend only those interests already recognized by the state, the only way that new rights can come to be realized is through struggling against the status quo. Jhering's contention is that the psychological mechanism that stands behind both motives to struggle is the feeling of right, and it is this idea that Liang will discuss in terms of "*quanli* consciousness."

We have already seen that Jhering believes our rights, which is to say our subjective *Recht*, to be dependent on the law, or *Recht* considered objectively. Only those interests publicly recognized as *Recht* count as individual, subjective *Recht*. One of Jhering's most striking doctrines is his claim that there is also a dependence in the other direction. He writes:

> Concrete law not only receives life and strength from abstract law, but gives it back, in turn, the life it has received. It is the nature of the law to be realized in practice. A principle of law never applied in practice, or which has lost its force, no longer deserves the name; it is a worn-out spring in the machinery of the law, which performs no service and which may be removed without changing its action in the least. [Jhering 1915, p. 70]

Although this principle applies to all parts of the law equally, the realization in practice of public and criminal laws is virtually guaranteed, since these are explicit duties imposed on public officials. The realization in practice of private law, in contrast, depends on individuals' taking action. Jhering is not saying that criminal law is always perfectly carried out, but he does believe that those who violate the criminal laws tend to be prosecuted, since there are officials whose job this is. There is no explicit requirement, though, that individuals claim what is their due.

[11] For more discussion, see [Pleister 1982].

One might have some interest that is protected by law – that is, have a right – and yet not insist on redress when that right is violated. If individuals, therefore, "for any reason neglect to assert their rights, permanently and generally, be it from ignorance, love of ease, or fear, the consequence is that the principles of right lose their vigor" [ibid., p. 71]. It then follows, given the essential role noted in the previous passage that is played by the "force" of *Recht*, that such neglected rights "no longer deserve the name" of rights. Jhering concludes that the very existence of "the principles of private law" depends on "the power of the motives which induce the person whose rights have been violated to defend them: his interest and his sentiment of legal right" [ibid., p. 72].

Again: According to Jhering, if we fail to exercise our subjective *Recht*, then the objective *Recht* on which the former depends will be vitiated to the point of non-existence. This argument depends on a concrete understanding of law (that is, objective *Recht*) that was quite distinctive of Jhering. Not only are laws not, in Jhering's eyes, "natural laws" identifiable through reason; neither are they mere abstractions of any kind. Laws are those things that in practice protect people's interests, and anything that fails to serve this function – even if it is because the people fail to ask for protection – is not a law.

The final move in the argument of *Der Kampf* follows immediately from this intimate interrelationship between subjective, individual right and objective, inter-personal law. Jhering tells us that

> in defending his legal rights [an individual] asserts and defends the whole body of law, within the narrow space which his own legal rights occupy. Hence his interest, and this, his mode of action, extend far beyond his own person. The general good which results therefrom is not only the ideal interest, that the authority and majesty of the law are protected, but this other very real and eminently practical good which every one feels and understands . . . : that the established order of social relations is defended and assured. [1915, p. 74]

Both an individual's and his group's interests suffer, that is, when he fails to assert his rights. This imposes on us, says Jhering, duties both to ourselves and to society to defend our rights.[12] In the same way that it is a

---

[12] These duties may be complicated, of course, if defending one's rights actually undermines things like trust or loving relationships; for two different suggestions that rights might have such deleterious effects, see Joseph Chan's contemporary Confucian argument [Chan 1999, pp. 221–2], and my discussion of Marx in the next chapter.

citizen's duty to defend his state by opposing a foreign invader, so it is his duty to defend internal threats to the public order by claiming his rights. The struggle for our rights just is the struggle for law: thus the purposeful ambiguity in the book's title, *The Struggle for Recht*.

These doctrines found audiences around the world. By 1915 *Der Kampf* had been translated into nearly thirty languages [Jhering 1915, p. xii]. Jhering's ideas, especially as interpreted and popularized by Liang's "On *Quanli* Consciousness," exerted a significant influence in China: Numerous essays insisted on the need to resist attempts to deprive one of *quanli* lest one be guilty of having thrown *quanli* away, as well as on others of Jhering's doctrines. Rather than focus on these downstream effects of Jhering in China, though, I will now turn to his immediate interpreter, Liang Qichao, and assess the relation between Liang's ideas and Jhering's.

6.1.3 *Liang and* Quanli

Liang was a central participant in some of the rights-related trends of the 1890s discussed in the previous chapter. In 1896 he briefly discussed the "power (or right) of self-mastery (*zizhu zhi quan*)," which I treated earlier in the context of Liang's teacher, Kang Youwei. Liang defined *zizhu zhi quan* as "each person doing all he ought to do, and receiving all the benefits he ought to receive" [Liang 1989a, p. 99]. We will see similar ideas expressed when he begins to explicate *quanli*. In 1898, Liang actively promoted "people's authority (*minquan*)," expressing views similar to those of the reformers I discussed earlier [Yoon 2000].

Liang's first uses of "*quanli*" come in 1899, in essays written in Tokyo after Liang fled China. In a piece called "The *Quan* of Strength," for instance, he contrasts two terms, both of which are romanized "*quanli*": "權力" and "權利." The former adds a second character meaning "strength" to "*quan*," producing a compound that unequivocally refers to power. The latter is the term that has come to be translated as "rights." Liang's thesis in "The *Quan* of Strength" reflects the powerful influence that social Darwinism had on him at this point, particularly as interpreted and taught by Katō Hiroyuki (on whom see the previous chapter). Liang writes that the meaning of "the *quan* of strength" is the "*quanli* 權利 of those who are strong," which he says is the same as the English phrase "the right of the strongest" [Liang 1989b, p. 29]. Liang's basic line is that no one is born with *quanli* 權利 as the idealists believe; all that really matters is who is stronger. We should focus, therefore, on the *quanli* 權力 that simply and uncontroversially means "power."

In addition to finding Katō's Darwinist ideas attractive, Liang was also influenced while in Japan by Tokutomi Sohō (1863–1957). Among other things, Liang was very taken with Tokutomi's defense of "human desire as a natural thing and a positive driving force behind one's success" [Tam 1991, p. 18]. As we saw earlier, a revaluation of the importance and validity of desire, growing out of both Confucian and Western sources, played a significant role in nineteenth-century Japanese rights discourse. Some of Liang's writings make clear that he knew and approved of the related views of Chinese Confucians discussed earlier in Chapter 3 [Liang 1959 (1905)], and we just saw that in 1896 Liang connected *zizhu zhi quan* with "receiving benefits." Tokutomi's views provided Liang with a more immediate stimulus to think in this same direction. Let us now look at how these different ideas came together in Liang's most sustained treatment of the subject, "On *Quanli* Consciousness" of 1902.

In an early passage of "On *Quanli* Consciousness," Liang sounds very like his social Darwinist "The *Quan* of Strength" of a few years earlier. He writes that *quanli*

> is born from strength. Lions and tigers always have first-class, absolute *quanli* with respect to the myriad animals, as do chieftains and kings with respect to the common people, aristocrats with respect to commoners, men with respect to women, large groups with respect to small, and aggressive states with respect to weak ones. This is not due to the violent evil of the lions, tigers, chieftains, and so on! It is natural that all people desire to extend their own *quanli* and never are satisfied with what they have attained. Thus it is the nature of *quanli* that A must first lose it before B can invade and gain it. [Liang 1989d, pp. 31–2]

If we were to go only on the basis of this passage, the obvious conclusion would be that Liang means by "*quanli*" exactly what Xunzi meant two millennia earlier: power and profit. The idea that it is natural for people to seek to increase their share of power and profit calls to mind Xunzi's statement, at the beginning of his "Essay on Rites," that "men are born with desires" [Knoblock 1994, p. 55]. It is true that Liang immediately turns to invoking Jhering, but the passage he alludes to does little to lessen the impression that "*quanli*" is simply power and profit. Liang tells us that "Jhering writes that the goal of *quanli* is peace, but the means to this end is none other than war and struggle. When there are mutual invasions, there is mutual resistance, and so long as the invasions do not cease, the resistance will also not end. The essence is simply that *quanli* is born from competition" [Liang 1989d, p. 32].

As soon as we look further into Liang's essay, however, we learn that "*quanli*" cannot simply mean power and profit. For one thing, Liang tells us that "the strength of *quanli* consciousness truly depends on a person's character" [ibid.]. Character (*pin'ge*) is something that "noble warriors" and "pure businessmen" have, and that "slaves" and "thieves" lack. Liang adds that "others have misunderstood the true characteristics of *quanli*, believing that it involved nothing more than continuous calculation of physical, material benefit. Ah! Is that not despicable?" [ibid., p. 33]. He gives an example, drawn from Jhering's text [Jhering 1915, pp. 28–9], of a lawsuit:

> Suppose that I have an item that I took from another by force. The one whose item was taken will angrily resist [my appropriation] in court, wherein his goal is not [regaining] the thing itself, but [attaining] sovereignty over the thing. Thus it often happens that before a suit begins, people will announce that in previous suits all the benefit that they attained was subsequently used to perform charitable deeds. If the person had been bent on profit, why was this done? This kind of suit can be called an ethical question, not a mathematical one. [Liang 1989d, p. 33]

Liang concludes that "the natures of *quanli* and benefit are precisely opposed."

Liang relies on a distinction between "physical (*xing er xia*)" and "metaphysical (*xing er shang*)" in order to develop the idea that *quanli* is concerned with things like character, nobility, and ethics. He writes:

> The reason for which humans are greater than the other myriad things is that they not only have a physical existence, but also a metaphysical existence. There are numerous aspects to metaphysical existence, but the most important of them is *quanli*. Thus animals have no responsibility toward themselves other than preserving their lives, while in order for those who are called "human" to completely fulfill our self-responsibilities, we must preserve both our lives and our *quanli*, which mutually rely on one another. If we do not do this, then we will immediately lose our qualifications to be human and stand in the same position as animals. Thus the Roman

law's seeing slaves as equivalent to animals was, logically, truly appropriate. [1989d, p. 31]

This passage is a paraphrase of a similar passage in *Der Kampf*, wherein Jhering contrasts concern with physical existence with concern for "moral existence *(moralische Existenz)*" [Jhering 1915, p. 31]. Readers not familiar with Jhering's work may well have thought of another possible source for Liang's comparison between humans and animals: Mencius's statement that a man lacking in moral inclinations "is not far removed from an animal."[13] While the close similarities between Liang's and Jhering's texts make me confident that Liang was paraphrasing Jhering, the connection to Mencius was not lost on him. Later in this essay, Liang says that, "Mencius said that '[if the people] are allowed to lead idle lives, without education and discipline, they will degenerate back to the level of animals.' If we consider the legal principles of the Roman law, . . . isn't this close to this idea [of Mencius]?" [Liang 1989d, p. 39][14]

When Liang comes to explaining where *quanli* consciousness comes from, we find an important further tie to Mencius. Liang writes that

In general, that when people are born they are possessed of *quanli* consciousness is due to innate good knowing and good ability.[15] And why is it that there are great inequalities – some are strong while others are weak, some lie low while others are destroyed? It always follows the history of a nation and the gradual influence of government [in making the nation inferior]. Mencius said it before I: "It is not that there were never sprouts [on the mountainside], but cattle and sheep continuously graze there, so that it becomes barren." [*Mencius* 6A:8] If one observes the histories of nations that have been destroyed – whether East or West, ancient or contemporary – one sees that in the beginning, there have always been a few resisting tyrannical rule and seeking *quanli*. Again and again the government seeks to weed out [those resisting its tyrannical rule], and gradually those resisting get weaker, more despondent, have [their resolve] melt away, until eventually that violent, intoxicating *quanli* consciousness comes increasingly under control, is ever more

---

[13] *Mencius* 6A:8; translation from [Lau 1970, p. 165].
[14] *Mencius* 3A:4; translation from [Lau 1970, p. 102].
[15] *Liangzhi* and *liangneng*, both originally from *Mencius* 7A:15. *Liangzhi* became a central theoretical term for Wang Yangming. Good knowing is the inborn faculty we all have to know (and feel) what is good and what is bad.

diluted and thin, to the point that any possibility of a return to its former strength is forgotten and it is permanently under control. A few decades or centuries of this situation continuing, and *quanli* consciousness will have completely disappeared. [1989d, p. 38]

The connection Liang draws between *quanli* and "innate good knowing (*liangzhi*)" is striking. Unlike many in Liang's essay, this passage has no correlate in *Der Kampf*. Liang is telling us that *quanli* consciousness is an innate characteristic of humans, albeit one that can be gradually diluted and even destroyed by a tyrannical government. Both in this passage and in the previously cited one we have seen that *quanli* consciousness is connected with our ethical sensibilities far more than with any concern for law. We thus begin to see that "*quanli*" may have less to do with Jhering's "*Recht*" than had originally appeared.

But I am getting ahead of myself. So far we have seen that despite an initial suggestion that the struggle for *quanli* is tied to unending desires for material improvement, Liang's view of our motivation and justification for demanding *quanli* is considerably more complex. Echoing to one degree or another both Jhering and Mencius, Liang explains that human existence has a "metaphysical," ethical dimension that distinguishes us from animals. Based on what we have seen thus far, let me hypothesize that having *quanli* represents being able to exercise abilities and enjoy interests crucial to being a whole person, where the understanding of what is necessary for a person to be "whole" rests ultimately on ethical norms. *Quanli* consciousness is our awareness or feeling of the importance of these abilities and interests; it is this consciousness that should, if appropriately developed, make us feel pain when the abilities and interests are curtailed.

This talk of "whole" persons calls to mind Jhering's emphasis, echoing Hegel, on the "personality." In *On the New People* Liang also puts stress on personality (*renge*), though the term is mentioned only twice in "On *Quanli* Consciousness" itself. He argues in "On Civic Virtue," for instance, that one's personal virtue can be irreproachable and yet, if one is without civic virtue (i.e., if one does not feel the pull of responsibilities to one's group), one can fail to have full-fledged *renge*. For Liang, in other words, "personality" is linked to identification with a group. Like many thinkers who will follow him, Liang views personality as depending both on individual well-being and moral development and on an individual's constructive contributions to the various groups with which he or she identifies.

Thus far I have concentrated on sections of "On *Quanli* Consciousness" in which Liang cites, paraphrases, or even quotes Jhering. There are several other important sections in which Liang sets Jhering's text aside and discusses *quanli* in contexts that will be more familiar to his readers. One theme that comes out in these sections is the importance of actively struggling for one's own, ethically legitimate, interests – of looking forward, to the future and to the betterment of one's lot – rather than relying on others to provide them. Consider, for instance, Liang's rejection of the central Confucian value of humaneness (*ren*). He writes that

> In general, Chinese excel at talk of humaneness, while the Westerners excel at talk of righteousness (*yi*). Humaneness is concerned with others. If I benefit others, they will benefit me: the emphasis is always on the other. Righteousness, on the other hand, is concerned with oneself. I don't harm others, and they are not allowed to harm me: the emphasis is always on me. Of these two ethics, which is, in the end, correct? As for what's correct in the great utopian world of one or ten thousand years hence, I don't dare say. As for today's world, though, I want to say that the world-saving great ethic is truly that of righteousness. [1989d, p. 35]

He goes on to apply this idea as follows:

> If we apply this to humane government,[16] we can see that it is not the best form of government. Chinese people simply hope for humane government from their lord. Thus when they run into humaneness, they are treated as infants; when they meet inhumanity, they are treated as meat on a chopping block. In all times humane rulers are few and cruel ones common, and so our people, from the time thousands of years ago when our ancestors taught this doctrine down to the present, have taken being cruelly treated like meat as heavenly scripture and earthly precept. It has been long since the consciousness (*shixiang*) expressed by the two characters "*quanli*" was cut off from our brains. [1989d, pp. 35–6]

The upshot seems to be that he connects humaneness with the passive expectation that others will provide for one, while in fact the "best policy is to make people each able to stand on his or her own, not having to rely on others" [ibid.]. One's sense of righteousness, which he implies

---

[16] That is, the kind of government advocated by Mencius.

comes close to consciousness of *quanli*, is what informs one's judgments of what we should stand up for – or in Jhering's terms, that for which we should struggle.

We have to do more than just defend our own interests, however. I have already mentioned Liang's endorsement of the ancient philosopher Yang Zhu's teaching that we should "not give up a hair on our head." Liang is less enthusiastic about another of Yang's slogans, though; to Yang's claim that the world will be well-ordered only if "no one [tries] to benefit the world," Liang responds:

> Yang Zhu did not fully understand the true character of *quanli*. He knew that *quanli* should be preserved and never forfeited, but he didn't know that it is only through aggressiveness that *quanli* is born. Idleness, play, leaving things to fate, hating worldly affairs – these are all executioners that kill *quanli*, and yet Yang Zhu promoted them every day. To use such a method to seek *quanli* – isn't this like drinking poisoned wine in a search for longevity? [1989d, p. 36]

"Aggressiveness (*Jinqu*)" is a major topic in *On the New People*, meriting a chapter all its own, entitled "On the Aggressive and Adventurous Spirit (*Lun Jinqu Maoxian*)." Now "aggressiveness" might well be thought not to have any close relation to the "ethical legitimacy" of the interests for which we struggle. Close reading of this chapter of *On the New People*, however, shows this thought to be mistaken.[17] Early in the chapter Liang identifies the "aggressive and adventurous spirit" with Mencius's "flood-like energy (*haoran zhi qi*)."[18] In the original passage, Mencius begins by discussing two famous exemplars of courage approvingly. Mencius goes on, though, to stress the connection between righteousness and the best sort of courage (namely that exhibited by someone with flood-like energy). Indirectly quoting Confucius, Mencius writes that "If, on looking within, one finds oneself to be in the wrong, then even though one's adversary be only a common fellow coarsely clad, one is bound to tremble in fear" [Lau 1970, p. 77]. The point of the original passage, in short, is that while raw courage is admirable, it is best if it is combined with ethical purpose.

---

[17] My analysis here stands in marked contrast to Hao Chang's otherwise excellent treatment of *On the New People*. Chang argues that Liang was consciously rejecting an ethical outlook, advocating instead a Machiavellian, merely "political" virtue. See [Chang 1971]. I subject this claim – including the comparison to Machiavelli – to sustained criticism in [Angle 1994].

[18] See *Mencius* 2A:2; translated in [Lau 1970, pp. 76–8].

Liang's analysis in the balance of the chapter suggests that he drew the connection to Mencius in full knowledge of this ethical side to flood-like energy. In his discussion of hope, which Liang identifies as one of the chief features of an aggressive and adventurous spirit, Liang quotes a poem by the famous Ming-dynasty Confucian Wang Yangming (1472–1529) which says in essence that anyone can achieve his ideals if only he keeps looking forward. Liang admires Wang's poem because of its talk of striving to realize ideals. Most of Liang's praise in this section, in fact, is aimed at those who are not simply concerned with fulfilling today's desires, but sacrifice for "tomorrow" [Liang 1989d, p. 24]. It would be twisting the meaning of this passage to suggest that it is ethically neutral. If Liang had wanted to praise someone who had achieved extraordinary things by ignoring ethics, the Chinese tradition offers him many choices: Qin Shi Huang, Ming Taizu, and so on. Instead, Liang chose Wang Yangming, well known as a champion of personal discipline and ethics.

The section on zeal, another aspect of the "aggressive and adventurous spirit," provides still clearer evidence of Liang's continued concern with ethics. He lists various types of people who are motivated by zeal, and includes "hero (*yingxiong*)," "filial son (*xiaozi*)," and "loyal minister (*zhongchen*)." All three, and especially the last two, are paradigmatic ethical categories. Liang gives a variety of specific examples drawn from both China and the West; the Chinese examples he chooses are all famous ethical exemplars.

I believe it is crucial to pay particular attention to Liang's Chinese examples, who are very familiar to him and his audience, and to be cautious about the conclusions we draw from the Western examples Liang cites. For example, Liang quotes Napoleon's slogan "The word 'difficult' is only found in a fool's dictionary." It cannot be denied that this sounds like an instance of the sort of courage that Mencius found to be inferior to full-fledged flood-like energy. From the little context Liang gives us, though, it is hard to tell what he really makes of Napoleon. It is different with Chinese examples. Liang goes on to cite the case of Zeng Guofan, a nineteenth-century general, scholar, and reformer known for his stress on personal ethics. Zeng also, according to Liang, believed that with the proper spirit anything could be accomplished, and is grouped together with Napoleon as "heroes of aggressiveness and adventurousness and models for future generations" [Liang 1989d, p. 29]. Liang could have chosen any one of a wide range of Chinese figures whose courage led them to great achievements, including numerous conquerors of questionable ethics like Napoleon. I think his having chosen Zeng speaks volumes.

Returning to "On *Quanli* Consciousness," we are now in a position to understand the lesson that Liang draws from Yang Zhu. We have to do more than sit back and defend our integrity. Yang Zhu was convinced that such a policy would allow one to live out one's allotted span free from the dangers that came with political involvement.[19] The underlying problem with such an attitude is that it ignores the degree to which an individual's flourishing depends on his group's doing well; and for the group to do well, we have to act on our ethical responsibilities to the group. This is in fact the master concept of the whole *On the New People*: the importance of one's relation with and ethical responsibilities to one's group, which in the modern world is paradigmatically one's nation.

Jhering's views on this subject are close enough, at least on the surface, to Liang's for Liang to carry right on from his criticism of Yang Zhu to a paraphrase of a passage from the chapter of *Der Kampf* entitled "The Assertion of One's *Recht* Is a Duty to Society." Jhering illustrates the relation between individual and society by considering what will happen to an army under attack if individual soldiers flee in order to protect their lives: If only a few flee, then their lives will indeed be preserved, but only because of the efforts of the rest of the army; if, on the other hand, many flee, then the day will be lost to the enemy and all will be slain. "What difference would it make," Liang comments, "if the fleeing soldiers were to personally stab the resolute ones with their swords?" [Liang 1989d, pp. 36–7].

6.1.4 Quanli *and Law*

There is little doubt that both Liang and Jhering believe that individuals have responsibilities to their nations. I have suggested several times that the similarities between Liang and Jhering mask an important difference over the sources and justification of *quanli* and *Recht*. The best way to bring this out is to ask about the relation of each to law. For Jhering, as we have seen, this is an intimate relationship: The two are as closely related as "subjective *Recht*" to "objective *Recht*." It is part of the very meaning of *Recht* that rights are tied to law. In my discussion of Liang to this point, in marked contrast, we have heard virtually no mention of law (*falü*). There is in fact one passage in "On *Quanli* Con-

---

[19] See [Graham 1989, pp. 53–64].

sciousness" that deals with law, which we will examine shortly, but I have not distorted Liang's text.[20] The relationship between *quanli* and law is simply not a crucial issue as far as he is concerned. The context in which Liang comes to his discussion of *quanli* is very different from that in which Jhering writes about *Recht*. Jhering is working within a positivist tradition of jurisprudence, even if he is striving to stretch the boundaries of that tradition by recognizing ways in which motivations from outside law can prompt our concern for objective and subjective *Recht*. Liang, in contrast, is pushing at the boundaries of a very different tradition, one which sees ethical concerns as central and definitive of our proper concerns.

The strongest argument that Liang bases *quanli* on ethics, rather than law, comes from looking at what he says about law itself. The only passage in Liang's essay on *quanli* that significantly concerns law runs as follows:

> Being untiring in one's competition for *quanli*, and *quanli's* [eventual] establishment and protection, all rely on the law. Thus those who have *quanli* consciousness must take struggling for legislative *quan* as their most important principle. Whenever a group has law, no matter whether they do good or bad, they all follow that which has been determined by he who has legislative *quan* in order to protect their *quanli*. The law of citizenries who are strong in *quanli* consciousness will be ever improving, each day getting closer to perfection.... As *quanli* consciousness gets increasingly developed, people's duties become increasingly strong. Strength meets strength, *quan* is weighed against *quan*, and thus an equal, excellent new law is created. In the period when both new and old laws are transmitted there is often the most intense and cruel competition. When a new law appears, those who had previously relied on the old law to enjoy special *quanli* must necessarily be particularly harmed. Thus those who promulgate a new law are as good as issuing a declaration of war against those people who previously had power. Thus out of the wrangling between progressive power and reactionary power, a great struggle arises! [Liang 1989d, p. 37]

In the context of Jhering's claim that rights are legally protected interests, Liang's statement that the "establishment and protection" of *quanli*

---

[20] There is in addition the passage, quoted earlier, dealing with a lawsuit. The connection to law in that case is largely incidental.

relies on the law deserves careful scrutiny. Also worth our attention is an important tension between distinguishing laws as good or bad, on the one hand, and as old or new, on the other. Are new laws better? Or are they only better for some, worse for others?

We have seen that for Jhering, the idea that the protection of rights relies on the law is true by definition: Rights just are those interests protected by law. If we look at the role of law in the whole of *On the New People*, I believe we come to a different conclusion. While "law (*falü*)" appears hardly at all in "On *Quanli* Consciousness," it occurs fairly often in other sections of *On the New People*, a total of 63 times in the complete text. Liang regularly emphasizes the connection between law or rule of law and civilization. Rule by law is that which allows people to join together to determine their own futures. Every bit as important as law, in fact, are the institutions on which it rests. In one passage, for instance, Liang argues that in order to develop a nation's level of commerce, its commercial *quanli* must be protected. To do this, commercial law must be established. To accomplish this, the powers and responsibilities of judges and courts must be laid down, which in turn requires that a legislature be empowered, which requires a responsible government, and so on [Liang 1989d, p. 64]. Liang certainly believes that new laws and institutions are needed for the protection of *quanli* in China. As this passage illustrates, though, he does not believe that *quanli* are defined by such a relation to law.

Suppose, then, that there is nothing in "On *Quanli* Consciousness" nor in the rest of *On the New People* that suggests a tighter relation between *quanli* and law than the latter's tending, in practice, to reinforce or protect the former. What of the tension I noted between good laws and merely new laws? To put this question slightly differently, what is the distinction that he makes between good laws and bad ones? Do good laws just serve the interests of the strongest parties more efficiently, or are they somehow ethically superior? If I can show that the latter is the case, then my argument that ethics rather than law lies at the heart of *quanli* will be further strengthened, since the law itself will be seen to depend on ethics.

Much of the passage cited earlier suggests that so-called good laws are simply those that serve the stronger party, but "and thus an equal, excellent new law is created" seems to cry out for an ethical interpretation. On balance, I believe that the evidence suggests that Liang understood good laws as not just efficacious, but also ethically praiseworthy. In the section of *On the New People* entitled "On Self-Rule," Liang invokes the classical Confucian sage Xunzi's idea that people need artificial restraints if they are to live ordered and harmonious lives, for if left to themselves, people's desires will overcome them and inevitably lead to strife [Liang 1989d, p. 51]. While Xunzi believed that codes of ritual propriety could serve this restraining role, Liang looks to law. He goes on to emphasize, however, that while laws are instituted by people, they are not "smelted onto us from the outside. It is not the case that one leader invents them in order to restrain the people. Instead, they come from the innate good knowing (*liangzhi*) common to all people's hearts" [ibid., pp. 51–2]. All laws, that is – or at least all proper, good laws – express and mandate ways of ordering society that are implicit in our innate feelings for one another. These rules need to be made explicit and taught, for the feelings on which they are based, we can assume, are fragile. We need the "artificial" laws, since human nature alone will not do. But there is an implicit ethical ordering to life. Whether new or old, for laws to be good, they must meet this standard.

Quite obviously, talk of ethically good and bad law fits uncomfortably alongside the suggestions we saw earlier that laws come into being simply due to the triumph of one group's strength over another's. The best explanation for Liang's talking in both ways is his commitment to the importance and even inevitability of progress. The imposition of strong, despotic laws onto an earlier, less organized society might be thought to be "good" at least from the perspective of its eventually allowing for further stages of (moral) development.[21] Still, I cannot conclude that Liang is completely unambiguous in his linking of law with ethics. If we had strong evidence that he believed *quanli* to be derived from law, we might be tempted to conclude that Liang looks a lot more like Jhering than I have been insisting. It is clear, though, that Liang has little to say about the relationship between law and *quanli*. Thus for all the similarities Liang himself obviously saw between his ideas and Jhering's, I conclude that *quanli* and *Recht* are importantly different.

What Liang is applauding is ethical aggressiveness: struggling to exercise those abilities and receive those benefits that properly belong to one. As I hope I have shown, the *quanli* for which we should struggle may turn out to be protected by laws, but they are not defined by laws. They are defined by ethical norms, by our place in the ethical order of the world. The idea of *quanli* that Liang develops in "On *Quanli*

---

[21] I thank Peter Zarrow for this suggestion.

Consciousness," like many of the central concepts of *On the New People*, shows clear connections to enduring Confucian themes.

Insisting on understanding Liang's *quanli* as rooted in aspects of the Chinese tradition, rather than simply borrowed from abroad, is not to deny that there are deep and important resonances between Liang's writings and Jhering's. Many Chinese thinkers who discuss *quanli* after Liang continue to see a socially located "personality *(renge)*" as the subject of *quanli*. The close tie that Jhering asserts between individuals' assertion of rights and the maintenance of social – and legal – order is similarly echoed by later authors. Before we look at these later developments, it will be well to consider a second instance of rights discourse from Liang's decade. As compared with Liang, Liu Shipei draws on different foreign sources and is somewhat more explicit about his working from native starting points. That he ends up conceptualizing *quanli* in much the same way as Liang can teach us a good deal about the dynamics of the Chinese rights tradition during this period.

6.2 LIU SHIPEI'S CONCEPT OF *QUANLI*

Liu Shipei (1884–1919) was born into a leading Yangzhou scholarly family in 1884.[22] In 1902, at the age of 18, he obtained the *juren* degree in the civil service examinations. He failed the metropolitan exam in Beijing the following year – only two years before the exam system was abolished – and made his way to Shanghai. There he would live for the next two years, write the texts with which I am here concerned, and engage in revolutionary political activities. He fled Shanghai to avoid arrest in 1905, returned home and was married, then traveled to Japan in 1907 on the invitation of Zhang Binglin, a leading revolutionary and editor of the radical flagship *People's Journal*. For a time Liu became increasingly radical, publishing and coediting (with his wife, He Zhen) the anarchist journal *Tian Yee*, as well as participating in the founding of the Institute for the Study of Socialism. Liu and his fellow anarchists' ideas helped to set the stage for the growth of a Chinese interpretation of Marxism, but Liu himself soon abandoned radical politics, returning to China in 1908 and informing on some of his erstwhile companions in the revolutionary movement. He focused primarily on scholarly pursuits in the following decade, though he did participate in the ill-fated effort

---

[22] This summary of Liu's life is drawn from [Chang 1987], [Zarrow 1990], [Bernal 1976], and [Onogawa 1967].

to make Yuan Shikai emperor. He became a professor at Beijing University in 1917, only to die of tuberculosis two years later.

Beyond a certain point, we can only speculate about the passions and personalities that shaped Liu's erratic public life.[23] Two things help to provide some unity behind his strange journey from aspiring exam-taker to revolutionary to reactionary: scholarship informed by a deep knowledge of the Chinese philosophical tradition, and a penetrating, iconoclastic intelligence. Liu helped to found the *National Essence Journal* in 1905, and remained committed to its mission of keeping Chinese philosophy and culture alive for the rest of his life.

A word on Liu's audience and influence may be in order. Like Liang Qichao, he was concerned with rethinking Confucian ethics in the light of new ideas and new realities. In some of his writings, Liang did this more in the mode of journalist than scholar, while Liu was first and foremost a scholar and thinker. Liang's writings were thus more accessible and certainly more widely published. There seems little question, though, that among progressive intellectuals both in China and Japan, Liu represented a powerful intellectual force. As Hao Chang concludes in his study of Liu, "the only person among the revolutionary intelligentsia to rival Zhang Binglin's intellectual prestige was Liu Shipei" [Chang 1987, p. 146].

Prior to Liu's temporary conversion to anarchism in 1907, he authored four major works. In this chapter, I focus on two of them: the 1903 *Zhongguo Minyue Jingyi* or *Essentials of the Chinese Social Contract* (hereafter *Essentials* [Liu 1936a]), which Liu coauthored with Lin Xie,[24] and the 1905 *Lunli Jiaokeshu*, which I will translate as *Textbook on Ethics* (or simply *Textbook* [Liu 1936b]). Liu's other two significant pre-1907 works are the *Rang Shu* (*Book of Expulsion*) published in 1903, and the *Lixue Ziyi Tongshi* (*General Explanations of Neo-Confucian Terminology*) of 1905. The former, largely concerned with promoting ethnic nationalism, does not touch on *quanli*. The latter does deal with *quanli* to some extent, particularly in Liu's discussion of "righteousness (*yi*)"

---

[23] [Zarrow 1990, p. 35] canvasses a few possible explanations for Liu's repudiation of the revolutionaries.

[24] Lin was a revolutionary educator and propagandist. Martin Bernal concludes that Liu was the major author of this joint work since Liu's name appeared first, despite the fact that Lin was older [Bernal 1976, p. 92]. While this is far from definitive evidence, the overwhelming similarities between the views expressed in the *Essentials* and in the *Textbook* render moot questions of whose views are dominant in the *Essentials*. I will use it, therefore, simply as another source for Liu's ideas.

[Liu 1936c, pp. 19b, 20b, 21a]. However, since the material on *quanli* in *General Explanations* is very similar to the more lengthy treatment in the *Textbook*, I will generally cite only the *Textbook*.[25]

The *Essentials* is a fascinating selection of and commentary on ethical and political writings from the whole range of Chinese philosophy. Liu and Lin develop their own views through comparisons of Chinese authors with Rousseau (as Liu and Lin understand him). Each section begins with representative quotes from classical to early-modern sources. Liu and Lin then add extensive commentaries, usually much longer than the original quotations. They often make direct comparisons to passages from Rousseau's *Social Contract* (in Chinese translation), so by reading between the lines one can construct a picture of Rousseau's ideas, but their main point is to explore the Chinese sources for evidence of concern with the *min yue*, or social contract. Full treatment of this text would take me too far afield; suffice it to say that I do not believe that Liu and Lin are anachronistically reading Western ethico-political doctrines back into Chinese history in order to assuage their wounded cultural pride. Liu and Lin are engaged in a legitimate exploration of and reflection on their tradition from the vantage point of concepts like *min yue* – concepts related to Western notions, but in many cases not identical with them.[26] Since my interpretation of Liu's understanding of *quanli* precisely illustrates this point, I will set this theme aside for the moment.

6.2.1 Personal Interests

Evidence for Liu's understanding of *quanli* is scattered throughout his ethical writings. A good place to begin is with the connection that he draws between *quanli* and a general notion of interest. Lesson Six of Liu's *Textbook on Ethics* is devoted to the definitions of *quanli* and *yiwu* – the latter a term used to translate "duty," about which I will say more later. Liu notes that the legalist text *Han Fei Zi* (c. 200 B.C.E.) records definitions for "personal (*si*)" and "general (*gong*)."[27] "Personal," the text

---

[25] See [Chang 1987, pp. 150–6] for discussion of the *General Explanations*.

[26] See also Hao Chang's excellent analysis of this text in [Chang 1987].

[27] The terms "*si*" and "*gong*" are more commonly rendered in English as "private" and "public," respectively. One reason for dissatisfaction with these conventional translations is that private implies hidden, while *si* does not. Confucian writers have long made clear that personal feelings are public, since they are open to and exert influence upon others. See, for example, *Mencius* 7A:21.

says, means to "seek oneself (*ziying*)" and "general" means to "turn one's back on the personal (*beisi*)." Liu then connects these ideas to *quanli*, writing that "the doctrine of 'seeking oneself' comes close to the Western idea of *quanli*" [1936b, I, 6b]. This is, at least on the surface, a surprising connection for Liu to make. Throughout Chinese history *si* almost always has been derided as an obstacle to morality. Mencius, for example, said that one of the types of unfilial behavior was to neglect one's parents by focusing too narrowly on personal concern for one's wife [*Mencius* 4B:30]. By linking *quanli* and *si*, therefore, it would appear that Liu is either bucking the Confucian tradition by elevating the value of *si*, or else indirectly breaking with the high esteem in which the Western tradition has held rights, for which *quanli* is supposedly a translation.

We saw earlier that in fact for a classical Confucian like Xunzi, *quan* and *li* – like *si* – represented personal considerations that one ought to ignore. Just following the passage with which I began, though, Liu says that a problem with all traditional Chinese ethical theories is that they neglect *quanli* [1936b, II, 6b]. It is clear from this and others of Liu's comments in the *Textbook* and in the *Essentials* that Liu believes *quanli*, and implicitly *si* as well, to be good things – aspects of our lives that need to be valued. Looking further into Liu's understanding of human nature will help us to comprehend his motivations for viewing *quanli* and *si* positively.

In the *Essentials* Liu discusses the *Lectures on the Four Books* by the Confucian official and thinker Lü Liuliang (1629–83). Lü believed that the origins of his country's troubles lay in improperly cultivated minds, and he condemned his age as a "utilitarian world" [Liu 1936a, III, 16a]. Lü wrote that the solution to these problems was to unify the ruler and the ruled – to insist that the ruler look only to the general good and suppress any selfish, personal desires. Liu's reaction to all this is twofold. He applauds Lü's criticism of rulers for following only their personal interests, adding that this idea of the unity of the interests of ruler and ruled is echoed in Rousseau's *Social Contract*. At the same time, however, Liu believes that Lü's proposal that rulers (and the ruled) need to do away with personal desires – to "eliminate the distinction between general and personal," as Liu puts it – is misguided. "From the first moments of life," Liu writes, "there is not a person but that has thoughts of seeking their personal interests" [1936a, III, 17b]. It is impossible to wipe out this basic feature of human nature. The good news is that we have no need to eliminate personal interests. "If you want to control the pursuit of personal profit on the parts of both the people and the prince, there is nothing better than drawing a line between the realms of general and personal" [ibid., 17b]. I will explain later how Liu sees this drawing of lines as helpful, when I discuss "extension."

For the moment, note that Liu makes a similar point when discussing the ancient utopianism of the "*Li Yun*" chapter of the *Book of Rites*. In "*Li Yun*," we are told of a wonderful time in which the "Great Way" was practiced, leading all in the cosmos to think only of the general good. There were no robbers; no one locked their doors [Liu 1936a, I, 8b]. Liu thinks that while these are beautiful images, the understanding of human motivation upon which they rest is badly mistaken. He cites Rousseau as maintaining that "having a mind to seek the good of the masses comes from the concatenation of many people's having minds to benefit themselves" [ibid., 9a].[28] This is the same idea, Liu continues, as Mencius's claim that the extension of kindness from those close to us – including, at least for Liu, kindness to ourselves – to those more distant from us gives rise to humaneness (*ren*).[29]

The problem that Liu has identified with the idealism of Lü and the "*Li Yun*" passage needs to be carefully stated. His point is not that people are motivated only by things that directly benefit them, but rather that personal interests are a basic, natural part of our motivational systems that cannot be ignored. Liu's resistance to the idealism of the "*Li Yun*" chapter springs from its failure to validate personal desires as an individual's first concern. A humane ethical system must be built on the foundation of humans' actual motivational systems.

Liu is well aware that this idea had been developed by Confucians before him. Liu's remark about people having "thoughts of seeking their personal interests" from the moment they are born echoes the famous first line of *Waiting for the Dawn* by Huang Zongxi: "In the beginning of human life each man lived for himself (*zisi*) and looked to his own interests (*zili*)" [Huang 1985, p. 2; translation from Huang 1993, p. 91]. As we saw earlier in Chapter 3, Huang's attitude toward personal interests is actually somewhat complex, since he believes that sages must ignore

---

[28] Liu cites this idea as coming from Book III, Chapter 3, of the *Social Contract*. While Liu is usually quite reliable in his citations of Rousseau, this one is somewhat mysterious, since the chapter in question is wholly concerned with different kinds of governments. The sentiment Liu expresses here is not at all foreign to Rousseau's work, though; in Book II, Chapter 4, Rousseau writes that "This proves that the quality of right and the notion of justice it produces are derived from the preferences each person gives himself, and thus from the nature of man" [Rousseau 1987, p. 157].

[29] See, e.g., *Mencius* 1A:7. I expand on this theme later.

these considerations in order to rule well. Liu's ideas come closer to Confucians like Chen Que and Dai Zhen who take desires and personal benefit to be even less problematic than does Huang. One of my goals in the remainder of this chapter will be to highlight the connection between this strand of the neo-Confucian tradition and Liu's view of *quanli*.

6.2.2 Legitimate Abilities

A second theme in Liu's discussion of *quanli* is the positive ethical role that Liu seems to assign to *quanli* when he says, for instance, that *quanli* is essentially like Wang Yangming's (1472–1529) notion of innate "good knowing (*liangzhi*)."[30] In the *Textbook*, in the course of praising Wang's idea of good knowing for the way in which it "forces the manifestation of people's committed spirits (*zhiqi*)" [Liu, 1936b, I, 24b], Liu writes that

> Chinese people all believe that sagehood is something imparted by heaven (*tian*), not something that one can stand up and grab for. Since the doctrine of good knowing was first proposed, [though, they] have believed that the good knowing of everyone is the same, and that that which a person receives from heaven is always the same. That which people receive from heaven is that referred to in "Yao and Shun are the same as all people." Thus lowly and poor people can look within and seek to enter the Way. . . . The Westerner Rousseau invented the doctrine of "heaven-endowed people's *quan*," according to which goodness is the root nature of all people. [He] hopes that all people will willingly desire the general [good] and all things will return to equality (*pingdeng*). Although Wang Yangming did not say [precisely] this, in practice the doctrine of "good knowing" and that of "heaven-endowed people's *quan*" are mutually the same. That which people receive from heaven is the same, and thus that which [their] *quanli* attains ought to be without any differentiation. [1936b, I, 25a]

Liu makes some very similar points during his discussion of Wang in the *Essentials*. He says that Wang's "good knowing" doctrine originates in Mencius's teaching that human nature is good, and that Rousseau similarly believed human nature to be good in Mencius's sense. There is

---

[30] See note 15.

indeed at least a surface similarity between Rousseau and Mencius on this point. The difficulty, of course, is reading "good knowing" into Rousseau. Liu attempts to do this by emphasizing that good knowing is the same for everyone, regardless of intelligence, position, and so on. Similarly, says Liu, Rousseau stresses that in the state of nature, everyone has the same ability to act freely (*ziyou quan*) [Rousseau 1987, p. 142 (I.2)]. After the social contract has been established, the law makes no distinctions based on intelligence or power. Thus, Liu concludes, Wang and Rousseau "emerge from the same track" [1936a, III, 3a].

Since my purpose here is not to compare Wang and Rousseau, I will not pursue Liu's suggestions along these lines. The importance I see in the passages I have just been citing is rather in the ways that they shed light on what Liu means by "*quanli*." In both passages Liu emphasizes that since we all have the capacity for good knowing, according to Wang, therefore we all can act morally. There is no division into people good from birth and people bad from birth; even "lowly and poor people can look within," see what their good knowing directs them to do, "and seek to enter the Way." In identifying this with "heaven-endowed people's *quan*," Liu seems to be saying that our *quanli* are our abilities to act morally.

The last sentence I quoted from Liu's *Textbook* is particularly important in this regard. Since our moral potentials, our moral abilities, are all the same, "thus that which [our] *quanli* attains ought to be without any differentiation." Recalling that a basic meaning of "*quan*" is power, we see here that in the context of Liu's discussion of "that which [our] *quanli* attains," the stress seems to be on this idea of "power" or "ability." We all have the power to achieve morally worthy ends. We all have the ability to contribute positively to the moral betterment of ourselves and our societies.

This fact about our moral capabilities has two complementary implications. First, it suggests a rejection of any paternalistic division between moral superiors and moral inferiors, the former guiding the latter. Whatever we ultimately conclude about the relation between Liu and "Confucianism," we can see that he had no sympathy for the strand of that tradition exemplified by Confucius's claim that "the people can be made to follow [our path], but cannot be made to understand it" [*Analects* VIII:8].

Second, it makes clear that Liu will tolerate no excuses for failure to be politically and morally involved in the future of Chinese (and human, for that matter) society. If what one person's *quanli* is able to attain is less than another's, Liu is saying, the fault may very well lie in the agent's lack of effort. He concludes this section of the *Essentials* by summarizing these twin benefits of both Wang's advocacy of "good knowing" and Rousseau's notion of *quanli*: "this doctrine of good knowing not only accelerates the manifestation of an active spirit by the benighted masses, but also is enough to accelerate [the appearance of] the common people's disposition to compete for *quanli*" [1936b, I, p. 25b]. The syndrome that Liu hopes doctrines like Wang's and Rousseau's will spark has two halves: People come to realize that they have legitimate interests and strive to fulfill them, while at the same time recognizing that with these interests come responsibilities. People's active energies need to be both aroused and harnessed.

6.2.3 Extension

Liu certainly cares about more than just our personal interests. If we turn to his comments on the *Analects*, for instance, we will begin to see the connection he draws between personal and general concerns. He stresses the reciprocal nature of the relationships discussed by Confucius and uses this to explicate the distinctive conception of the "general" that he finds in the *Analects*. "Although the way of the Confucians lies in valuing the general," Liu writes, "the essence of valuing the general lies in doing-one's-best-for-others (*zhong*) and using-oneself-as-a-measure (*shu*)" [1936a, I, p. 11b].[31] Liu then cites several passages from the *Analects*, all of which insist that to cultivate oneself and to reach one's own goals, one has to help others do the same. Like the neo-Confucians we saw earlier in Chapter 4, Liu is drawing on the "social conception of the self" which lies at the heart of Confucianism. We are more than atomistic individuals: We are partly constituted by, and our well-being is dependent upon, our relationships with others. We have to extend what we care about, therefore, to include others.

Liu believes that reflection on our own lives, selves, and interests should make evident to us how important *quanli* is to our self-worth and to our ability to play positive roles in our larger community. If we take ourselves as models for the others with whom we interact, we will recognize that the same kinds of personal interests that are important to us

---

[31] "*Zhong*" and "*shu*" are often translated as "loyalty" and "reciprocity," respectively, but in the Confucian context the translations I have used here, adapted from D. C. Lau's translation of *Analects* IV:15, are more perspicuous. See [Lau 1979, p. 74].

will be important to them. Extending our care to others, therefore, involves doing our best to see that they attain the same sorts of personal satisfactions as we do. This is surely a familiar idea to any parent (or spouse or sibling). Part of what makes our lives go well is for the lives of our children (or spouses or siblings) to go well – for them to attain the kinds of *quanli* that we value. Liu's point, in other words, is that Confucius did not advocate valuing the general at the expense of the personal, but instead taught that the general would grow out of the personal. *Quanli* seems to represent precisely the kind of personal benefit from which an ethical system must begin.

Extension is not the only metaphor that Liu uses when talking about the need to heed others' interests as well as one's own. He also talks of limitation. He writes, for instance, that "freedom (*ziyou*) of ideology; freedom of action; these are definitely an individual's *quanli*. Freedom is what Zhuangzi meant by 'let it be, leave it alone'.[32] But freedom cannot be without limits. Thus Chinese ancients always talked of humaneness (*ren*) and righteousness (*yi*) together" [1936b, I, 27b]. Liu subsequently defines righteousness as "affairs attaining appropriateness," and connects this to "restraining one's freedom" so that one does not "lower another's welfare" [ibid., p. 28a]. Later, he adds "that which makes righteousness a virtue is its [ability] to limit an individual's freedom and make it not invade another's freedom" [ibid., p. 28b].

In the *Textbook*, Liu writes that "All actions in which one fails to use-oneself-as-a-model (*shu*) are instances of going beyond the limits of one's legitimate personal interests and abilities (*quanxian*)" [1936b, II, p. 31b]. This sort of transgression can come about in either of two ways: (1) We "invade others' *quan* by doing things that negate proper distinctions" or (2) we "invade others' *li* by coveting improper goods" [ibid.]. Notice that Liu has analyzed *quanli* into two spheres corresponding to the two terms out of which it is compounded. *Quan* seems here to refer to the abstract side of one's interests: the "space" in which one expects to be able to operate, the realm over which one expects to have control. *Li*, on the other hand, comprises material benefits and interests. We will see later that some Chinese theorists in the 1990s make the same analysis.

---

[32] "Let it be, leave it alone" is Watson's translation of "*zai you*" from Zhuangzi [Watson 1968, p. 114]. I am endorsing this as what I think Liu thought that Zhuangzi meant – since this is a traditional interpretation of "*zai you*," and fits the context well – and not as the correct interpretation of Zhuangzi, on which see [Lau 1991].

On the surface, all this talk of limiting and restraining might sound diametrically opposed to the image of extension that we just examined. Where the previous metaphor encourages us to expand our concerns and even to impose our values on the world around us, this new metaphor speaks of holding ourselves back, of not invading the ability of another person to determine his or her own way.

The key to seeing that the two images are not – at least in Liu's eyes – in tension, but are actually complementary, lies in Liu's very traditional definition of righteousness: "affairs attaining appropriateness." Expansion and restraint need not be in conflict. The basic idea is quite intuitive: We want people to care for others, to try to do for others what they (the carers) think right – but only to a point. In some relationships, we normally welcome a good deal of expansive caring. We accept quite a bit of shaping and guidance from our parents, for instance. Even here, though, there are limits which, if transgressed, make us feel "invaded." In other types of relationships we may be more likely to feel an elder sibling's (or a spouse's) caring as invasive, depending on how strongly she or he tries to persuade us to value things in her or his way.

Still, there are obvious problems. Where does one draw the line between extending oneself to care for others and restraining oneself from invading them? How does one know how much caring is appropriate? Liu's answer to these questions draws on a central theme of Confucian thought that he sees echoed and confirmed in the writings of Rousseau. There is a pattern of human interrelationship, Liu believes, that makes for a harmonious, happy society of self-motivated people. Confucians referred to this pattern as *li*; Rousseau called it the general will. In both cases there is assumed to be a way that, given (or despite) the actual natures of people, society can work.

It is particularly interesting that Liu does not make the identification between *li* and general will in the context of discussing the thinkers best known for advocating *li*, like the Song-dynasty philosopher Zhu Xi, but instead draws on the writings of the Ming-dynasty official Lü Kun (1536–1618). Lü's biographer, Joanna Handlin, describes Lü as pessimistically "capitulating to the 'selfishness that naturally accompanies human desires'," and

> remind[ing] his fellow officials of their responsibility "to see that the things of the world attain their due." "If the ignorant men and women ... do not fulfill their allotted desires," Lü elsewhere warned, "the world will not be peaceful." Aware that "those who do

not have enough will die chasing after their shares," Lü called for a balanced and equitable distribution of goods. [Handlin 1983, p. 134]

What is most important here for our purposes is not Lü's pessimism but his recognition – however reluctant – of the importance of affirming people's desires. We can see in Liu's remarks on Lü the feeling that here Liu has found something of a kindred spirit, especially in the link that Lü suggests between *li* and *shi*, which means force, power, or effectiveness. As Liu reads him, Lü argues that reliable, effective political action comes from heeding the proper patterns of human "role-responsibilities" (the *li*) – which very much include the legitimate desires, interests, and sphere of activity of the common people [Liu 1936a, III, p. 1b].[33]

This way of understanding the relation between extension and restraint – that there is an ideal pattern of activities according to which restraint and extension will be in harmony with one another – also brings us back to Wang Yangming's notion of good knowing. Our faculty of good knowing, according to Wang, is precisely our means for determining our proper place in the overall pattern of human, and even cosmic, activities. Liu's invocation of good knowing as support for his understanding of our *quanli* and our responsibilities, therefore, provides further evidence that Liu has just this image of an ideal pattern in mind.

6.2.4 Quanli *and Responsibility*

The relation between one's *quanli* and one's ability to play a positive role in the community is a theme on which Liu places considerable importance. There is a reciprocal relation, he believes, between one's *quanli* and one's ethical responsibilities (*yiwu*). This is most clearly illustrated in his discussion of rulers. "Ancient sages," he writes,

> spoke vigorously about the difficulty of being a ruler. Since the people were to be given leisure and joy while the ruler assumed all worries and effort, thus humans' natural desires (*renqing*) are such that no one would want to occupy the ruler's position. Therefore, since the rulers have ethical responsibilities that they are supposed

---

[33] Interestingly enough, part of this picture ill accords with Handlin's understanding of Lü. She writes that "In his search for an objective framework through which one could overcome conflicting claims to knowledge, Lü . . . let concern for 'principle' [that is, *li*] – which had dominated so many philosophical discussions – recede into the background" [Handlin 1983, p. 141]. It may well be that Liu was reading his own concerns into Lü, but that is a question for further study.

to carry out, they [must also] have *quanli* that they are supposed to enjoy. [1936a, III, p. 21b]

Rulers merit the *quanli* they receive because of the responsibilities they assume. Conversely – and perhaps more importantly – they are motivated by this *quanli* to take on and perform the responsibilities that come with ruling. It is important to realize, though, that Liu does not see *quanli* as simply a reward or incentive for rulers' performing their roles well. His point is rather that while the role of ruler is a difficult one, it is at the same time very fulfilling. *Quanli* is analytically distinct from its matching *yiwu* (responsibilities), but in reality they come together, a package deal. In another section of the *Essentials*, Liu quotes a famous saying of Wang Fuzhi (1619–92), a Qing-dynasty Confucian, which Liu feels expresses the relationship between responsibility and reward: "heavenly pattern (*tianli*) is in the midst of people's desires" [1936a, III, p. 20b]. Liu approves of this sentiment for reasons similar to those for which he cited Lü Kun. Wang is resisting the tendency of many Confucians to be suspicious of people's desires (*yu*), and instead recognizes the intimate relationship between the fulfillment of such desires and the exercising of moral responsibilities.

Unfortunately, a long parade of unscrupulous rulers in China's history took advantage of the power that they were granted as rulers to attempt to enjoy much more benefit than their usually meager performances of their responsibilities warranted. Liu calls this "the strong transforming their power into *quanli*" [1936a, III, p. 20b]. Liu says that he has the Chinese "Three Bonds" doctrine in mind as a specific instance of this evil, since the Three Bonds change what had been reciprocal relations into one-way relations [ibid., p. 21a].[34] Instead of balancing the loyalty subjects owed their ruler with the responsibilities the ruler owed his or her subjects, for instance, the Three Bonds speak only of the subjects' loyalty. The Three Bonds attempt to make legitimate, by recharacterizing as *quanli*, the unearned and unmerited benefits demanded by irresponsible rulers.

Liu's criticism of the Three Bonds echoes similar charges leveled a few years earlier by his contemporary Tan Sitong (1864–98). Liu is also echoing the views of Dai Zhen, discussed earlier as a central representative of the strand of neo-Confucianism that stresses the legitimacy of personal desires. Just prior to his comments about the Three Bonds, Liu

---

[34] The "Three Bonds (*san gang*)" are "the subordination of subject to monarch, child to parents, and wife to husband" [Liu 1990, p. 1].

cites several passages from Dai's writings in which Dai advocates recognizing that everyone has similar wants and desires, and that each allows his own to be manifested only to the degree that is compatible with similar manifestation on the part of others. Dai complains that modern rulers look down on real manifestations of pattern (*li*) – by which he means following and fulfilling the desires of the people – while using talk of "pattern" to justify all manner of repression [Liu 1936a, III, p. 20b].

I have already noted that Liu approves of Wang Fuzhi's view of the relation between human desires and the heavenly pattern. Liu adds, though, that Wang is too sanguine about the likelihood of rulers being able to resist the temptation to legitimize undeserved benefits. Wang simply stresses that rulers should follow the feelings of the people – and in so doing, follow the proper responsibilities for rulers as encoded in heavenly pattern. He ignores the legitimate personal spheres of the people, which include the fundamental "ability to act freely (*ziyou quan*)" [1936a, III, p. 12a].

Wang's problem, in short, is that he does not take the masses (*min*) seriously enough as people (*ren*). Liu believes that rulers' entitlement to appropriate benefits as part of their *quanli* is only a special case of the situation into which all people are born: We all have abilities that, when developed, provide satisfaction – that is, *quanli* – and simultaneously contribute to the general good. It is by developing and exercising these capacities that we use our ability to act freely. Citing Rousseau as his source, Liu asserts that "those who give up their ability to act freely give up that which makes them people" [1936a, III, p. 12a]. For a ruler to impose roles on people, or to deny them their *quanli*, is to fail to treat them as people.

As I have just indicated, though, the ability to act freely that we all have brings with it important responsibilities. Rulers, therefore, are not the only people responsible for the plight of society that Liu sees in his day: Most individuals have failed to exercise their abilities, so that they, too, may not merit whatever *quanli* they have managed to obtain. Liu explains:

People all have the ability (*quan*) to choose their own work (*zhiye*).[35] Let each person see where his or her nature [has made

---

[35] "*Zhiye*" is the standard term in modern Chinese for "profession," but in this context Liu's intention is much broader than our notion of profession, so I translate it as "work" instead.

him or her] complete. Choose [an area] in which his or her talents are strong as that on which to rely to order his or her life (*zhi sheng*). [When] all people can order their lives, then no one will again need to depend on what others give them; all will be "self-standing people (*zili zhi min*)." . . . Thus people's property cannot be invaded by the government. Thus self-choice of work is a responsibility that all individuals should carry out, and at the same time is the foundation of the *quanli* that all individuals enjoy. [1936b, I, p. 39a]

The idea is once again that built into our abilities, feelings, desires, motivational systems – in a word, our natures – is a path for us to follow, a proper way for us to fit into the larger societal pattern.

6.3 CONCLUSION

The perspective that allows us to make sense of all that Liu says about *quanli* is this: By adding "*quanli*" to his vocabulary, Liu was able to stress the importance of affirming both individual interests and abilities, and the satisfactions gained by exercising responsibilities, more easily than he could have without the concept of *quanli*. The idea that individuals have legitimate interests is not at all new to Confucianism; indeed, it is a prominent theme in a strand of Confucian writings with which Liu quite consciously identified. Be this as it may, the unsavory connotations of "personal" and of "desire" made affirming people's legitimate interests a difficult topic for Confucians, and one fraught with the possibility of misinterpretation. "*Quanli*" gives Liu new resources for dealing with this problem.

My contention, in sum, is that Liu's *quanli* does not represent a radical break with the Confucian tradition. Liu shares with other Confucian writers, with Liang Qichao, and with Rousseau the assumption that when properly understood, individual and group interests coincide.[36] Confucians have always believed that correctly understanding the kinds of creatures that we are and the kind of cosmos that we inhabit leads us to see that there is a single pattern of interactions between things in the cosmos that results in harmonious flourishing for all. There is room in this picture for differences between the pattern of my behavior and the pattern of your behavior, so long as they fit together to complement the

---

[36] Nathan has noticed this assumption in the writings of Liang and other twentieth-century constitutionalists; see [Nathan 1986, pp. 138f.] and [Nathan 1985, pp. 120–1].

overall pattern of human interactions. Thus my nature might have made me fit to teach college students, while someone else's might have prepared him or her to be an entrepreneur or a public servant. I will explore the plausibility of such visions of harmony in Chapter 8.

Liu's assertion that people may have to follow different paths in order to realize their natures has some Confucian precedent. Mencius had long ago argued that a division between those who labor with their minds and those who labor with their strength was both acceptable and even necessary [*Mencius* 3A:5]. His focus on the responsibility of individuals (*jishen*) to stand up for themselves, though, may sound un-Confucian. Mencius puts very little ethical responsibility on the shoulders of the masses (*min*): He says that if rulers fail to provide for the masses and then punish them when they act wrongly, the rulers have "trapped" the masses [*Mencius* 1A:7]. Theodore de Bary's *The Trouble with Confucianism* stresses this point, arguing that one of Confucianism's great weaknesses was its confining of ethical responsibility to a moral elite.[37] Without insisting that every Confucian agreed that ethical responsibility was solely a noble man's burden, we can conclude that Liu diverged here from the Confucian mainstream.

In the years immediately after writing the *Essentials* and the *Textbook*, Liu turned toward increasingly radical egalitarian views, becoming one of the leading spokespeople for anarchist ideology among the Chinese intellectuals in Tokyo. At the time he wrote the texts with which I have been concerned here, Liu had not yet completely rejected hierarchy, as can be seen in part by his continued assumption that the sovereign of the state would be an individual ruler. His views were evolving; he was, after all, only twenty-one years old when he completed the *Textbook*. It is at least fair to say that he identified with a strand of Confucianism that itself had mounted significant critiques of an overly rigid hierarchy, and that in his early writings on *quanli*, we can see some hints of a move beyond Confucian elitism altogether.

Liu's personal trajectory need not detain us further. Differences from Liang Qichao notwithstanding, I think it is clear that the two men's concepts of *quanli* shared a great deal. One's *quanli* were one's legitimate interests and abilities – legitimate, that is, so long as one worked to fulfill one's responsibilities to oneself and to others. I have argued in this chapter that we must see Liang's and Liu's concepts of *quanli* as emerg-

---

[37] [de Bary 1991, pp. 21–2, and ch. 6]. See also [Metzger 1977] on the weight of responsibility that Confucian intellectuals consequently bore.

ing out of their engagement with their contemporary realities and with particular aspects of their traditions. They draw on, interpret, and react to a range of Western writings, but this does not mean that they simply import one or another Western conceptualization of rights. The concepts they develop are significantly different from the Western ideas on which they draw. Neither laws, nor the potential for conflict between individuals and states, are as central to Liang and Liu as they are to their Western contemporaries, though both themes are still present. Part of the explanation for this is that both thinkers see *quanli* as a partial solution to China's need for greater national strength, as Marina Svensson has emphasized [Svensson 1996, ch. 5]. As I hope I have made clear, Liang and Liu also care about the *quanli* of individuals because of the ways that exercising *quanli* contributes to the legitimate good of the individuals themselves. It is now time to see how the story of Chinese rights discourse develops, and concepts of *quanli* change, as China moves toward the middle of the century.

7

Change, Continuity, and Convergence prior to 1949

THE TWO DECADES from the mid-1910s to the mid-1930s saw some progress and much frustration toward the realization of a stable, empowered state and society in China. During the decade and a half after 1935, China would be wracked by invasion and civil war, but 1915 through 1935 were years of enormous intellectual vitality in which theories that could help people to understand and improve their world were subjected to passionate debate and rigorous analysis. They were also years in which Western philosophies were interpreted and adopted with increasing sophistication. Numerous young people studied in and then returned from Western countries, and important American and European thinkers visited and lectured in China.

In such a context, *quanli* discourse underwent important changes. It lost most of its explicit connections to the Confucian tradition, which itself came under sharp, though often simplistic, attack. The flip side of this increased distance from Confucian vocabulary and sources of authority was the increasingly direct and complete engagement of Chinese writers with themes from contemporary Western rights discourse. If the Confucian source of *quanli* discourse and the Western stimulus to that discourse were of approximately equal importance during the earlier period we have discussed, that dynamic changes in the 1910s. Western writings are no mere stimuli, but become full-fledged participants in the debates over *quanli*.

Confucian voices and themes are not completely absent from the debate, however. During the anti-foreign demonstrations that break out in May 1919, it is Liang Shuming – soon to become famous as a champion of Confucian values – who defends the civil rights of the Chinese officials accused by demonstrators of being traitors [Alitto 1979, p. 72]. Liang's writings, in fact, offer an intriguing explanation for the partial

178

convergence of views about the content and scope of rights that emerges in this period: In his *Eastern and Western Cultures and Their Philosophies* of 1921, he argues that Western culture is becoming "sinicized" in reaction to individualistic excesses. While I do not believe that Liang's monolithic conceptions of Eastern and Western cultures can be sustained, it is true that many European and American authors did, in this period, advance theories of rights that were distinctly less individualistic and political than those of their predecessors. It is difficult to discern Chinese influence on these thinkers, but it is not at all hard to see why Chinese philosophers, even those who explicitly condemned Confucianism, might find such Western writings attractive. I will explore these convergences later in this chapter by juxtaposing Chinese ideas with those of John Dewey, an influential Western thinker who came to be well known in China.

In the previous chapter we saw certain commitments emerging as central to a shared conception of *quanli*, among them: (1) an ethical, rather than legal, grounding for *quanli*; (2) a positive content to *quanli*, in addition to negative restrictions; (3) a vision of personal and group *quanli* as harmonious with one another; and (4) a reciprocal relation between *quanli* and responsibilities. I will argue in this chapter that these commitments are retained by most participants in *quanli* discourse prior to 1949. My chief representatives of the period's writings will be Chen Duxiu and Gao Yihan, both prolific authors who began treating the subject of *quanli* in the mid-1910s. To summarize what will follow, Chen and Gao believe that *quanli* are the powers and benefits that an individual or group must enjoy in order to reach its ultimate goal – a goal which they tend to describe as the fulfillment of its personality (*renge*).

From among the many authors who make constructive contributions to Chinese rights discourse in this period, I have chosen Chen and Gao because of their centrality, representativeness, and sophistication. There are other writers from within the mainstream they represent whom I could have chosen; Luo Longji (1896–1965), a leader of the 1929 "Human Rights" movement that I mention briefly later, is a good example. Nor are Chen and Gao representative of all facets of their period's rights discourse; in particular, it will be important to contrast their views with those that conceive of rights as belonging only to adherents of certain ideologies, members of particular social classes, or followers of a given political party. I will treat these ideas, albeit somewhat briefly, near the end of this chapter.

Chen and Gao quite clearly do not sense any important conceptual difference between their ideas of *quanli* and the conceptions of rights employed by the Western writers with whom they are familiar. This might seem odd to someone versed in only one of the conceptions of rights popular at the end of the twentieth century: Several features of Chen's and Gao's conceptions differ substantially from what we might call the "Political Individualist" conception of rights, according to which rights are intrinsic features of all people but not of groups, and encompass only political, negative liberties. Chen and Gao, in contrast, see *quanli* primarily as means to further ends, and argue that they are as relevant to groups as they are to individuals. In addition, the scope of their *quanli* is significantly wider than that of Political Individualist rights, including economic and other benefits along with political powers such as the freedom to speak and participate in decision-making. I will nonetheless generally be content to translate their "*quanli*" as "rights" because, as we will see as this chapter develops, their usage corresponds quite closely to the ideas of rights held by many European and American writers in their day – and indeed, in our own, as I will discuss in Chapter 8. There are certainly multiple concepts that share the word "rights," and given the usage of someone like Dewey, not to mention Hobhouse and Laski, it seems pedantic to deny Chen and Gao the word.

Though Chen and Gao began as close colleagues with quite similar views, the two men's careers followed very different paths. Gao was a social liberal and an academic who remained as independent as he could from the day's politics; Chen felt compelled to engage in politics, becoming one of the cofounders of the Chinese Communist Party (CCP) in 1921. The rise of Marxism in China, signaled in part by the founding of the CCP, is a final issue with which this chapter will be concerned. Two themes can be detected in the writings of the era's Marxists about *quanli*: a critique of *quanli* as class-based and a conception of *quanli* as appropriately belonging only to progressive revolutionary forces. This latter idea actually comes out even more strongly in the works of those committed to the Nationalist Party (*Guomindang* or GMD), which shared with the CCP roots in the Leninist vision of a vanguard, revolutionary party. The last section of this chapter will look at each of these ideas and at the contexts in which they arise, including a brief look at the ambiguous attitudes toward rights expressed by Karl Marx himself.

7.1 CHEN DUXIU

After a thorough classical education, Chen Duxiu (1879–1942) went on to be a pioneering reform writer and activist, leader of the New Culture movement, dean of arts and sciences at Beijing University, and cofounder of the Chinese Communist Party. His subsequent life was less glorious – beginning with his dismissal as CCP Chairman in 1927 – but it is primarily with Chen in his ascendancy that I will be concerned. Chen's writings from this period present different challenges than the works of other thinkers I examine in this book; his many essays have been aptly characterized as "more than slogans but less than full-scale philosophy" [Zarrow 1996]. He is usually brief and polemical, rarely pausing to expound on the meanings of his central theoretical terms. Be this as it may, I find him to be an astute and coherent author, not easily pigeonholed as "nationalist," "individualist," "cosmopolitan," or any of the numerous other categories under which scholars have filed him.

One of the categories into which Chen is most often placed is radical anti-traditionalism [Lin 1979]. It is certainly true that Chen spent more of his time attacking various aspects of Confucianism[1] than did many of his contemporaries, such as Gao Yihan, who virtually ignored it. Be this as it may, Chen's immense knowledge of the tradition stayed with him throughout his life. He was a friend of Liu Shipei, and though he followed a very different path from Liu (who, it will be recalled, became increasingly conservative), it is plausible to think that Chen's interest in rights may have grown from roots similar to Liu's.[2]

Like many of his day, Chen began his public career immensely concerned over the fate of his nation. In an early article called "The Loss of the Nation," published between 1904 and 1905, Chen divided the nation's plight into three categories: loss of territory, loss of economic control (*liquan*[3]), and loss of sovereignty. The three are all interrelated, each of the first two having roots in the loss of sovereignty, which Chen defines as "the power of individual self-mastery" [Chen 1984b (1904), p. 51]. This phrase, which also appears in the slightly earlier essay "On the Nation" [Chen 1984a (1904), p. 40], is significant for its explicit use of "power

---

[1] My use of "Confucianism" here is purposefully vague. Chen aimed to refute those who saw the Confucian teaching (or perhaps religion; *ru jiao*) as needed in China; he also was critical of specific aspects of the historical tradition. Chen's most famous essay attacking Confucianism is translated in [Angle & Svensson 2001].
[2] See [Feigon 1983, pp. 11–15] and [Bernal 1976, p. 111].
[3] See the earlier discussion of this term in Chapter 4.

(*quanbing*)" where other authors so often leave it ambiguous whether "*quan*" means power or something more, such as authority or rights. Despite the fact that Li Hongzhang had already used *liquan* in a normative sense, as we saw earlier, in these early essays Chen's uses of *quan* seem not to express such normative commitments. Still, Chen is deeply concerned with the loss of self-control that the success of foreign incursions into China has meant. Significantly, he blames neither the foreigners nor the Chinese emperors, but instead the Chinese people for their fatalism and their stress on the family at the expense of the nation [Chen 1984b, pp. 53–5].

The charge that Chinese people neglect their nation both echoes the diagnoses of many of Chen's contemporaries (most famously, Liang's *On the New People*, discussed earlier) and foreshadows the complex analysis of individual and nation that Chen will develop in coming years. Even at this early stage, we can already see the two considerations that he will be at pains to harmonize. On the one hand, individuals need to be devoted to their nations. He believes this only natural, since true nations are made up of a people sharing a race, history, and culture: Citizens of a single nation are in a real sense all related to one another [Chen 1984a, p. 40]. In the constitution to the Anhui Patriotic Society, which Chen helped to establish in 1903, it was declared that individual freedom that "interfered with national welfare" was not to be permitted [Chen 1993 (1903), pp. 17–19]. On the other hand, in a 1904 article Chen praises the educational methods of the Ming-dynasty Confucian Wang Yangming for enabling the "free development of one's faculties," which alone leads to "an individual's true development" [Chen 1984c (1904), p. 62]. This development, in turn, leads "naturally to useful citizens" [ibid., p. 61]. The assumption that free development leads naturally to good citizens is the keystone of Chen's intellectual artifice at this point, and it is one that he rightly thinks he shares with the Confucian Wang. Although Wang never thought in terms of "citizens," he did believe that free development, under the stimulus of rites and music (both of which Chen discusses approvingly in his article), will lead "naturally" to moral adults.[4]

In the decade following these early articles, Chen was involved with other students of the "national essence" like Liu Shipei and Zhang Binglin, spent two years in Japan, spent two brief stints in the revolu-

---

[4] For Wang's views, see the full passage from which Chen quotes, translated in [Wang 1963, pp. 182–6].

tionary government of Anhui province, and helped to found Anhui University [Feigon 1983, pp. 74–95]. He entered the next stage of his career with essays he contributed first to the *Tiger Magazine* and then, starting in 1915, to the magazine he founded and edited, *New Youth*. Chen's famous essays in *New Youth* set the tone and much of the agenda for the New Culture movement.

In the opening article of *New Youth*'s first issue, "A Call to Youth," Chen writes that society is like a body: If allowed to grow old, it will wither; it needs the freshness of youth. Specifically, Chen enjoins the day's youth to take up the following charges: (1) Be self-masters rather than slaves. (2) Be progressive rather than conservative. (3) Be aggressive rather than withdrawing. (4) Be cosmopolitan rather than isolationist. (5) Be pragmatic rather than empty and abstract. (6) Be scientific rather than naively idealistic. The crucial section for my purposes is the first. It opens: "All people have the power to be self-masters (*zizhu zhi quan*), completely lack the right (*quanli*) to make others their slaves, and also completely lack the responsibility (*yiwu*) to become slaves themselves." In various ways this involves liberating ourselves: politically, religiously, and economically, as well as from patriarchy [Chen 1984d (1915), pp. 73–4]. Chen characterizes liberation positively as "completing one's free, self-mastered personality." Complementing these themes of self-mastery and freedom, he subsequently characterizes one's goal as "an individual, independent, and equal personality."

Although uniting with one's fellows and promoting the cause of one's nation receive little attention in this essay, we will see in a moment that they are never far from Chen's concerns, even if his thinking on this score has matured. It also is important to note that amidst all this talk of being liberated from various restrictions – all subsumed under the symbol of the slave – are hints of a positive ideal toward which Chen believes we should be moving. The passages just quoted contain three suggestions of a positive flavor. First, the word "completing (*wan*)" – in "completing one's . . . personality" – implies that there is an outline, an ideal, which we should be striving to complete. This meshes nicely with the second clue, namely the word "personality (*renge*)," which has a long history in European and particularly Hegelian thought of association with positive ideals. Of course Confucianism, too, emphasizes a positive personality ideal, though not by means of the word "*renge*," which is a Japanese neologism imported into China. We have already seen that *renge* played a role in Liang Qichao's understanding of *quanli*; from the beginning of the twentieth century, in fact, the term is quite widely associated with *quanli* [Svensson 1996, ch. 5]. The third point worth recognizing in this regard is that self-mastery has often, in both European and Confucian contexts, been used to explain how certain (higher) aspects of the self rule over other less significant parts. Self-mastery, that is, can be a key to either license or cultivation and control, depending on how it is interpreted.[5]

Let us now look at one way in which Chen fleshed out the personality ideal, albeit in a somewhat one-sided fashion. In "The Differences in the Fundamental Thought of Eastern and Western Peoples," Chen writes that there are two main races in the world, in two basic geographical groupings: the white in the West and the yellow in the East. The main differences are that (1) the West is warlike, the East craves peace; (2) the West is based on the individual, the East on family; (3) the West is based on law and pragmatism, the East on emotion and politeness [Chen 1984f (1915), pp. 97–8]. The article glorifies "individualism (*geren zhuyi*)," asserting that the goals of Western state and society are to preserve individual liberty, rights, and happiness – and no more. Freedom of thought and expression is for the development of individuality (*gexing*). Chen adds that Western theories of "national interest" and "social interest," while superficially in conflict with individualism, in fact are fundamentally aimed at consolidating the interest of the individual [ibid., p. 98]. The most striking section of the article is the last, in which Chen paints a remarkable picture of Westerners as living starkly law-based lives. He writes that "In the West, love and marriage are two different matters. Love is something common to the nature of all men and women, but when it comes to the relationship of husband and wife, this is a legal relationship, a rights-based relationship, and not purely an emotional relationship" [ibid., p. 99]. He pushes quite far the idea that relationships between all people in the West, even close family members, are based on impersonal legal standards, ultimately concluding that

> Putting primary emphasis on the rule of law and pragmatic considerations cannot but lead to mutual dislike born of harshness and scant empathy. However, the result will be that every individual in the society will rely on no one but him or herself, be ready to wage war, make independent calculations of benefit, achieve an independent personality (*renge*), each preserving his or her own, none interfering with another. [1984f, p. 100]

[5] The classic account of this theme is [Berlin 1970].

184

Chen sums this up as "starting with petty people, but ending with gentlemen," the exact opposite from what comes of the Eastern penchant for superficial politeness.[6]

While this essay paints a more extreme picture of individualism than Chen's other writings of the time, he is committed to the idea that self-interest is an important and appropriate concern for individuals. In an article from a few months later, he writes: "All human action treats the self as central; if one loses this [by adhering to Confucian slave-morality], what can be said for one?" [Chen 1984g (1916), p. 103]. Chen goes on to make explicit that such a loss renders it impossible for one to develop an "independent, self-mastering personality." After all, he adds, "From birth humans are self-regarding."[7] It is worth pausing to remind ourselves that this theme of humans being self-regarding is neither new nor at odds with all strands of the Confucian tradition. In Chapter 6 we looked at the explicitly Confucian-influenced discussions of this topic by Chen's friend and fellow student of the "national essence," Liu Shipei. Liu would probably have been appalled at the starkly legalistic picture of human relations that Chen described, but many other elements of Chen's picture would have been more congenial. This is not to imply that Chen himself saw these ideas as derived from, or even compatible with, Confucianism; in a 1916 essay, for instance, he asserts that Confucianism is incompatible with the complete moral and economic independence of individuals [Chen 1984h (1916), p. 153]. In a remark that will become important in a moment, as we look to the relation between *quanli* and Chen's turn to Marxism, Chen also adds that Western theories of individual independence take the economic independence of individuals – here meaning the ownership of property – to be fundamental [ibid.].

In any event, a balanced interpretation of Chen's ideas must take his somewhat extreme statements of individualism into account, but also cannot ignore the numerous more socially oriented assertions with which

[6] Chen's picture of Western rights-obsessed society meshes nicely with that of Liang Shuming, mentioned in the introduction to this chapter as a Confucian who discussed rights. While Chen apparently is endorsing the extreme individualism he describes, Liang sees it as a problem that results from seeking rights – which in 1921 he otherwise commends, though later in life he criticizes – in the way that Western cultures do. See the selection of Liang's writings translated in [Angle & Svensson 2001].
[7] See also "The Direction of Contemporary Education," in which he argues that we should develop both our animal and our human natures, since without the former we would be too yielding [Chen 1984e (1915), pp. 88–90].

they are often juxtaposed. The claim that "from birth, humans are self-regarding," for instance, is made in the context of arguing that people must nonetheless move beyond the relatively narrow confines of political parties, and devote themselves to "citizens' movements" [Chen 1984g (1916), p. 103]. Political parties in the mid-1910s were for the most part corrupt and powerless factions in a parliamentary system that was largely a sham. The New Culture movement in which Chen played a leading role was broadly anti-political. Chen argues that only inclusive citizens' movements are capable of large-scale social transformations, as evidence of which he cites the French and American revolutions and the Japanese Meiji Restoration. This idea that the people must unite in order to move the nation forward is given more explicit discussion in "The Direction of Contemporary Education." One of the directions in which Chen argues Chinese education must direct people is toward "populism (*weimin zhuyi*)." He explains that in feudal times, China (like other countries) lacked "group thought," since each person was individually under the command of the ruler. Gradually group thought developed, first in families, then in localities, then ultimately in nations – a stage which Chen says China has not yet reached. "Nationalism (*guojia zhuyi*)," though, can lead to an overconcentration of power in the hands of the rulers, and so to the invasion of the *quanli* of the people. Hence populism is born, wherein the people have sovereignty, whether or not there is a monarch [Chen 1984e (1915), p. 87].

Chen goes on to emphasize that he does not worship nationalism; in advanced countries, its defects have already been discovered. Still, he sees no route forward without first establishing a true nation. A true nation is devoted to the well-being of the whole collective, and "sacrifices a part of the *quanli* of individuals, in order to protect the *quanli* of the whole citizenry" [ibid., p. 87]. I believe that the framework here articulated helps us to understand how Chen's various remarks about individuals and the nation fit together, and should lay to rest some of the unprofitable debate about whether Chen is "nationalist" or "cosmopolitan."

We can sum up as follows. Chen sees that collectives like nations are formed of individuals, and the strength of the collective rests primarily on the strength and determination of the individuals. As he puts it in one place, "When people have come together to form a nation, if the personality of the individuals is elevated, then the personality of the nation will be likewise. If the power of the individuals is consolidated, then the power of the nation will be likewise" [Chen 1984g (1916), p. 103]. It thus makes sense for Chen to put so much stress on the need for independent individuals with lofty personalities, even while he also recognizes that nation-building will, at times, demand sacrifices of these same individuals. It remains in the individual's best interest to devote himself or herself to collective action because only when a nation has been established – with all the characteristics Chen has assigned to nations for years, including territorial integrity and economic control – will there be a stable enough entity to articulate and defend a constitution and legal system, both of which are necessary for the success of "populism."

I said "articulate and defend" because it is clear that Chen does not believe we have any rights outside of or prior to their social articulation, this despite his (somewhat idiosyncratic, by the standards of his day) frequent use of "*renquan*," which is often translated as "human rights." That is, Chen does not believe that we have "natural rights"; rights are things we gain in society. This does not mean that rights are simply granted by the state, though, nor that rights simply derive from law – the view often called "positivism" which we looked at in connection with Jhering in Chapter 6. Chen writes that "Law is for preserving current civilization, while the freedom of speech is for creating future civilization. Current civilization and law were produced by the criticism of earlier laws and civilization by the freedom of speech. Freedom of speech is the parent; laws and civilization, the child" [Chen 1984i (1919), p. 440]. Clearly current laws cannot justify our right to free speech; it is precisely against such laws that the right must be exercised. What, then, grounds our speaking out? I pointed out earlier that in one essay he says explicitly that the point of freedom of speech is to "develop individuality," and later in the same article he stresses the need to establish one's personality [Chen 1984f (1915), pp. 98, 100]. I conclude that *quanli* are not, for Chen, ours simply because they are natural, intrinsic goods, but rather because they are essential means to further ends that we value. We will see this understanding of *quanli* elaborated later in the writings of Gao Yihan.

Before I turn to Gao, I need to deal with one final aspect of Chen's thinking on *quanli*, namely its relation to his conversion to Marxism. Chen came increasingly to believe that social and especially economic constraints lay behind the failure of most Chinese to reach his ideal of an independent personality. In a 1919 article discussing John Dewey's conception of democracy (on which see more later), Chen notes that the aspect of Dewey's theory which directly seeks the equality of human personalities is "social democracy," which aims to do away with unequal class distinctions. Economic democracy, another element of Dewey's theory, similarly aims to equalize the rich and poor. Chen emphasizes that social democracy is his true goal, writing that while the other aspects of Dewey's vision – economic, political, and civil democracies – are important, they are ultimately "no more than tools for achieving our goal" [Chen 1984j (1919), pp. 429–30].

The following year he made the centrality of economic and social matters even more clear in a manner which recalls his statement from 1916 that economic independence is more fundamental than moral independence. He wrote that the enlightenment of the world's workers will come in two stages. First comes demanding better treatment, like shorter working hours; second comes demanding the rights to manage politics, production, and military affairs. The first stage "is still no more than begging for food. Only when individuals have their own food – and oil and salt and wood and rice and . . . so on – in their own hands, will the workers' rights finally be secure" [Chen 1984k (1920), p. 520]. Coupled with the evidence we have seen earlier, this statement helps to confirm the opinion of some contemporary scholars who have argued that a large part of Chen's interest in Marxism was his belief that independent personalities could be better developed and protected under Marxism.[8]

Once Chen openly committed himself to Marxism in 1921, he gave up talk of workers' rights: What was needed, he now believed, was a workers' revolution, after which rights would no longer be necessary, since all interests would be harmonized together in the workers' state that followed [Chen 1984l (1921)]. In making this assertion, Chen was following the lead of Marx himself, who believed that rights would be superfluous in a communist state, as I will discuss further in the final section of this chapter.

7.2 GAO YIHAN

The themes we have seen emerging in Chen's discussion of rights were by no means unique to him. This is important, since the language of others in one's community helps to institute the norms governing one's concepts. I now turn to Gao Yihan (1884–1968), a close contemporary of Chen whose views on *quanli* will help to flesh out what we can call the consensus position during the years currently under study.

---

[8] See [Ip 1994, pp. 48–9] and [Svensson 1998].

Gao was among the Chinese thinkers most familiar with Western political thought. He graduated from Meiji University in Japan in 1916, returned to China and was appointed a professor of political science at Beijing University in 1918, where he remained until 1926.[9] He subsequently taught at the Law School of the China National Institute of Shanghai, served as a member of the Control Yuan, and after 1949 was dean of the Law School of Nanjing University. He wrote widely on political theory, evaluating and synthesizing various trends in Western political thought. Rights figure extensively in Gao's writings; in addition to being one of the most subtle analysts of the general notion of rights writing in China, Gao was among the earliest and most influential advocates of economic rights. The writings on which I will draw range from his earliest essays discussing rights, in 1915, to his book *An Outline of Political Science* of 1930. In certain respects, as I will detail later, Gao's views evolved over this fifteen-year period, but the essential understanding of the role and importance of rights remained unchanged.

Rights, according to Gao, are a means rather than an end. In 1915, in the course of criticizing theories that take the absolute protection of people's rights to be the goal of the state, Gao writes: "Neither are rights the goal of human life; they are rather a road along which people desiring to attain their life's goal must travel" [Gao 1915c, p. 5]. Similarly, in a 1918 article Gao pointed out the flaws in nineteenth-century European justifications of populism, which were all couched in terms of rights and individual interest. Gao is certainly in favor of popular participation in government, but he insists that "rights and personal interest (*siyi*) are things on which human life relies, but not the goal of human life itself" [Gao 1918, p. 7]. Populist government needs to serve our ultimate goals if it is to be fully justified. I will turn in a moment to the question of our ultimate ends, but for now recognize that enjoying rights is, for Gao, a process whose value lies in the goals it enables us to achieve, rather than in any intrinsic feature of rights.

Despite the fact that Gao assigns rights only an extrinsic role, he still finds them to be fundamentally important to the good life that we all seek. This can best be seen via his discussion of self-sovereignty (*zizhu quan*), or more literally the power of being one's own master. This power is the essence of rights. It is the "*quan*" of "*quanli*." Gao realized that for one to be able to put this power into practice, one had also to have the

---

[9] This biographical sketch is based on [Hoh 1982 (1933), p. 122] and [*Asia Historical Dictionary*, vol. 3, p. 188].

material wherewithal to do so. In his earliest writings he treats this condition rather abstractly, speaking of the "ability to establish oneself (*zili zhi neng*)" [Gao 1916, p. 32]. By 1921, he was able to flesh this idea out more concretely, and we then find him writing of the importance – over and above political rights – of economic rights, if people are to be able to practice self-sovereignty [Gao 1921, p. 5]. In that essay he stresses that an abstract "right to freedom (*ziyou quan*)" is meaningless without the material ability to support oneself, attain an education, and the like. Gao points out the futility of telling the poor souls who cannot even find work pulling rickshaws – itself, he adds, an inhumane occupation – that they should freely choose an occupation. Before they can begin to put self-sovereignty into practice, they need a modicum of material well-being, on the basis of which they can seek training or other forms of education. Gao terms this requirement the "right to subsistence (*shengcun quan*)" [Gao 1921, p. 6].[10]

Self-sovereignty, then, means being able to act on one's will; it is that which sets us apart from animals and slaves [Gao 1915b, p. 6]. It is crucial to see, though, that for Gao self-sovereignty is not an end in itself. Gao is no Kantian. The goal we seek, for which self-sovereignty is a necessary condition, is a fully developed "personality (*renge*)." Gao emphasizes attaining and preserving one's personality throughout his career. In an early (1915) article he puts the importance of personality as follows:

> The state can ask of its people that they sacrifice their lives [in its defense], but it cannot ask that they sacrifice their personalities. . . . Personality is the master of rights. Without personality, rights would have nothing on which to rely; without rights, one is [no better than] an animal . . . and cannot be a citizen. [Gao 1915c, p. 4; see also Gao 1915b, p. 6]

What does it mean to say that "personality is the master of rights"? Simply that one's rights are in the service of one's personality, the fulfillment of which brings happiness [Gao 1916, pp. 4–5]. It is through exercising one's rights that one expresses one's will, which itself is a

---

[10] The demand for "the right to subsistence" became increasingly widespread in the 1920s. See [Lin 1922], which discusses the issues in terms very similar to Gao's. See also the discussion in [Svensson 1998, pp. 32–40]. My one difference with Svensson is over her insistence that concern for economic rights "had been virtually absent from Chinese human rights discourse" until the 1920s. I believe I have shown that while the phrase "right to subsistence" is new, the broad concern with material preconditions for the satisfaction of human desires had long been part of Chinese rights discourse.

manifestation of one's personality. In other words, without rights we cannot express our wills or our personalities. Without rights, our personalities would be suppressed. This is particularly important because our personalities are not given to us fully developed: We have potentials that we must strive to fulfill if we are to live full lives and attain happiness. Without rights, we cannot develop ourselves and thus lead stunted lives.

Individuals are not the only ones with personalities. The state and, especially in later writings, many other sorts of groups have their own "personalities" which they strive to fulfill; just like people, these groups also have rights on which their ability to develop their personalities depends. Conversely, individuals are also social creatures whose well-beings and personalities are inextricably linked to the groups to which they belong. Gao clearly takes it for granted that groups like the state have rights and responsibilities. In a 1918 article, for instance, he writes that the backers of "laissez-faire-ism" believe that "state rights (*guojia quanli*) and people's rights hinder one another; when state rights (*guoquan*) increase, the people's rights (*minquan*) cannot but retreat" [Gao 1918, p. 2]. Gao disagrees that these rights must be in conflict, but he accepts the idea that states have rights. In another article, we find him saying that "the state has rights against the people and people have rights against the state. The people have responsibilities toward the state, and the state has responsibilities toward the people" [Gao 1915c, p. 4]. In his 1930 book on political science, finally, Gao makes it explicit that groups like states also each have their own personalities, which we have already seen are the basis for having rights [Gao 1930, p. 72].

The reciprocal rights and responsibilities between states and people derive from the fact that each partly constitutes the other. States are simply groups created by people to serve the people's ends. States are not "natural" entities whose ends can be discovered scientifically; they are voluntary collections of people, and thus we have to look to the goals of human life if we are to discover the goals of a state [Gao 1915c, pp. 1–2]. Gao rejects views that call for individual rights to be sacrificed to the cause of state aggrandizement. If, as Gao believes, states and other groups nonetheless have their own wills and personalities, then the ends that they serve must be collective ends. Still, since individuals owe an important part of their personalities to the state (and, in Gao's later formulations, to other groups as well), they cannot but have responsibilities to it. Individuals are fundamentally connected with one another via the groups in which they mutually participate. I am an American. Part of what it is for my life to go well, for my personality to be fulfilled, is for America to do well, to achieve its (that is, our) collective goals. And since America is simply the collection of Americans, many of its goals will be unattainable unless Americans like myself make it our business to achieve them.[11]

In an early essay, Gao puts this relationship between individual and group in terms of working to develop one's "free will" so that it expresses the "general will" [Gao 1915a, p. 1]. This formulation points to some of the potential difficulties of the view, since I am surely not merely an American: My will and the personality it expresses differ on many points from those of other Americans. From early on, Gao is thus at pains to avoid the implication that individuals should sacrifice all for the state, as we will see in a moment. Gao does not believe that all of us ought to think and will alike. In early essays, he does argue that the result of unfettered, albeit socially informed, self-sovereignty will be a harmonious society expressing the general will. The surest way to social conflict, he writes, is for a government to try to repress the views or actions of some of its members [Gao 1915b, p. 6]. In 1916, he argues that individuals must make their own decisions about what is best for them, and contribute to communal decision-making through participation in governance [Gao 1916, pp. 4–5]. The business of the state is then to harmonize the various people, groups, and emotions in the interests of all, a goal Gao labels "justice."

As time went on, Gao became gradually less starry-eyed about the idea that the state can on its own harmonize all the people's disparate interests. In a 1926 article on Rousseau, for instance, Gao tempers his earlier enthusiasm for Rousseau's ideas about sovereignty and the general will.[12] Gao's central complaint about Rousseau is that his theory tries too hard to harmonize the freedoms of all people, with the result that in practice, it tends to assign all sovereignty to the state [Gao 1926, p. 69]. No matter what form of government a state adopts, it will thus (if Rousseau's theories are taken seriously) lapse into authoritarianism. This defect notwithstanding, Gao still argues that Rousseau's theories served an important historical role in helping states to unify their

---

[11] There are at least two situations which might pose exceptions: Certain goals might be achieved by the actions of those outside the group, even if group members do nothing; and some goals might result as the collective by-product of various different individual goals – the way the "invisible hand" is supposed to generate collective wealth, for instance.

[12] See, e.g., [Gao 1918] for a very positive portrayal of Rousseau.

populations. In the modern world, though, Gao sees such a side effect as no longer necessary, and thus wants to move beyond monistic theories of sovereignty.

The opposition to monistic sovereignty is a major theme of Gao's 1930 book *Outline of Political Science*. Gao presents the book as little more than a summary of recent trends in European political theory [Gao 1930, preface], but he is being modest. Throughout the book he weighs, compares, and assesses competing European schools of thought, arriving at a synthesis that is his own responsibility. He comes down in favor of pluralistic theories of sovereignty; that is, theories which ascribe the ultimate sources of authority not just to the state, but to other groups, such as labor unions, as well.[13] Gao explains that "humanity has various social purposes," only some of which are amenable to political, and therefore state, oversight. "Therefore there must be various groups, [each with its realm of sovereignty], if all [social purposes] are to be achieved" [Gao 1930, p. 76]. Gao adds that the state still has a role to play as mediator and harmonizer:

> On the one hand we acknowledge that the state's sovereignty cannot be absolute, and on the other hand acknowledge that the state's sovereignty is not entirely without use. It cannot be denied that each person feels loyalty to a particular set of groups, such that the state cannot expect to receive the complete loyalty of any individual. However, neither can it be denied that the loyalties of any given individual cannot avoid mutual conflict with those of any other individual, since the interests of the groups to which one gives one's loyalty cannot avoid mutual conflict with the interests of those groups to which another finds himself loyal. These facts are the reasons for which states exist. [Gao 1930, p. 87]

In a subsequent chapter he says that the mission of the state is to harmonize competing interests [ibid., p. 111]. Gao believes that thinking of the state as a mediator between distinct (if often overlapping) sources of sovereignty is fundamentally different from assigning all sovereignty to states. In addition to the point mentioned earlier about pluralistic sovereignty doing a better job achieving our varied "social purposes," Gao says that monist theories push people toward individual separation and ultimately conflict, while pluralistic theories tend toward cooperation and mutual aid [ibid., p. 79]. His idea seems to be that while people will

---

[13] For a European theorist's version of such a theory, see, e.g., [Cole 1995 (1915)].

not tend to have precisely the same interests and loyalties, when they owe their loyalties to a variety of overlapping sources, it will be evident that by working together they can better achieve their purposes. In contrast, refusing to help another will be, in at least some instances, like cutting off one's nose to spite one's face.

Gao, like Chen, recognizes that the harmonious development of people's personalities is not as simple as had once been thought – for instance by Dai Zhen or by Liu Shipei, though Gao of course does not mention any Confucians. We saw Chen struggle a little to say that both individual freedom and a flourishing, independent national group were vital. Gao's view evolves over time, ultimately reaching the theory of pluralistic sovereignty we just examined. For both thinkers, the most basic justification of rights is their role in the mutual fulfillment of individual and group personalities: Rights are the powers we must have and the benefits we must enjoy if we are to achieve our potentials. Political powers, like the ability to speak freely, and economic benefits, like the food and clothing we need, count more or less equally. Our unavoidably social existences, finally, explain the mutual importance of person to group and group to person, as well as the tight relationship between enjoying rights and shouldering responsibilities.

7.3 CONVERGENCE: JOHN DEWEY

It is now time to look at the writings of Chen, Gao, and their contemporaries from a comparative perspective. I suggested earlier that a certain amount of convergence can be discerned between Chinese writers on *quanli* in these years and their contemporaries in the West. Before considering what we should make of this convergence, let us first look at a prominent instance.

Most Western thinkers who have exerted influence in China have done so primarily via translations of their writings – often translations of which they were unaware. John Dewey (1859–1952) was an exception, and I choose to look at him for this reason: The explanation for the many resonances between his ideas and those of Chen and Gao cannot simply be that they read, and were convinced by, his writings. Prior to Dewey's arrival in China in May 1919, he had received little attention in Chinese scholarly circles, and none of his books or articles had been translated.[14]

---

[14] See [Keenan 1977, p. 11]. Hu Shi (1891–1962) had studied with Dewey before returning to China in 1917, and was instrumental in Dewey's invitation to visit China, but did little to promote Dewey's views prior to 1919; see [Grieder 1970, chs. 3–4].

During his two-year stay in China he gave numerous lectures (always assisted by a translator); transcriptions of many were published in newspapers and magazines. For reasons that will be clear as we proceed, Dewey's ideas resonated with some of the directions in which Chinese social and political discourse had been heading already, and his formulations were consequently embraced by many – even if, as we now know, China was simultaneously moving toward an increasingly polarized political world that would soon find Dewey's experimentalism irrelevant.

The most well known of Dewey's lectures were those on social and political philosophy, delivered in Beijing in November of 1919 and recorded by Gao Yihan, among others. As we look at Dewey's views, it will become apparent why Gao might have found them congenial, but in this regard it is important to recall that the majority of Gao's writings examined earlier were published before Dewey arrived in China: Gao was not influenced by Dewey; rather, he found in Dewey a kindred spirit. I should note that similarities between Dewey's ideas and Chinese thought have been remarked upon recently by David Hall and Roger Ames, who write that "Deweyan social theory . . . resonates in a striking manner with much classical and contemporary understanding of Chinese society insofar as Confucianism informs it" [Hall & Ames 1999, p. 117]. They base this conclusion on a comparison of Dewey's published writings with their interpretation of classical Confucianism; as such, its relevance to twentieth- and twenty-first-century Chinese society depends on the somewhat speculative premise that "Confucianism informs" such a society. I say this not to reject their hypothesis, but to suggest that my analysis here may complement their reasoning by showing how thinkers like Gao are reasoning within a discourse or tradition that has at least some of its roots in Confucianism.

Modern readers of Dewey's lectures are apt to find them frustratingly elusive when it comes to the sources or justifications of the goals he sets out. He says, for instance, that his social philosophy is superior to earlier ones since it "makes possible rational and dispassionate discussion of contending ends, and their evaluation in terms of probable advantage to the whole social fabric."[15] This is a criterion, if a vague one, but he says little about why we should choose it, other than because it is a method

---

[15] See [Dewey 1973, p. 83]. Chinese translations of Dewey's lectures, prepared with the help of his original English lecture notes, were published serially in *New Youth* magazine; those Chinese versions have since been translated back into English. I will

which will, he alleges, produce some concrete resolutions to concrete problems. Even if he is correct, though, why should we think of the resolutions toward which his theory directs us as correct? Similarly, in the next lecture, he begins by stating that the "ultimate criterion" for habits, customs, and social institutions generally was "the degree to which the matter being judged could contribute to the development and qualitative enhancement of associated living" [Dewey 1973, p. 90]. Again, this is a reasonably clear criterion, but why should we accept it? A few paragraphs later, Dewey says: "In these, as in all other aspects, the society which we desire is one in which there is maximum opportunity for free exchange and communication" [ibid., p. 92]. Who is "we"?

I do not mean to suggest that Dewey's text contains no hints of the answers to these questions. Before filling out his answers, I want to consider one possible answer which is instructive, though incorrect. Perhaps Dewey saw things like the "enhancement of associated living" as vital because they help us to realize basic human rights. He mentions human rights prominently in his discussion of the stages through which social reform proceeds. A society begins from tacit acceptance of the status quo, which is then challenged as society changes, and ultimately the reform achieves "fruition" [ibid., pp. 76–8]. Dewey discusses both the women's movement and the labor movement specifically, and says that a central component of the challenge these groups mounted had to do with "propounding the doctrine of natural rights," for the former, and "a conviction that they were entitled to certain human rights," for the latter. One can readily gain the impression from such passages that human rights are the standard against which societies are judged.

Such an impression is misleading. "Human rights" are crucial to the rhetoric of the challenge phase because they purport to be a standard independent of the values a society happens to have: That is why they are useful in justifying reform or revolution. This same feature, though, makes them incompatible with Dewey's pragmatist framework. He denies that there is any transcendent, culturally neutral set of rights that is ours by nature. If we examine the third stage of social reform, we will see this in practice. Dewey writes of the labor movement that, "In the third phase people became aware of the fact that the labor problem is not just one of individuals, but a social problem; that meeting the demands of the movement not only enhances the welfare of the indi-

generally cite the translated English versions, referring to the Chinese originals when necessary.

196

viduals involved, but promotes the welfare of the whole society" [ibid., pp. 78–9]. In general, he says, "it is only as the subordinate group gains numbers, strength, and public recognition that it becomes apparent that the things they demand can be defined as genuine social needs" [ibid.]. It is revealing that Dewey does not say that this final stage represents recognition of people's actual human rights; instead, he speaks of "social needs." This really returns us to our original question: What are these social needs, and by what standard are they assessed?

As I have said, Dewey does provide a few hints in his Beijing lectures as to what standard he is ultimately following. In the lecture on associated living, for instance, he writes that

> When people exist under arrangements which call for some to rule and others to be ruled, some to command and others to obey, integration of the society cannot proceed, nor can the society hope to remain stable, because this disparity of status and function breeds conflict and induces disorder. At the same time, this pattern of dominance-subservience makes the development of personality extremely difficult, if not impossible – and strangely enough, this is as true of the dominant group as it is of those in the subservient group. [1973, p. 92]

This passage criticizes certain social arrangements on two fronts: They make an integrated and stable society impossible, and they similarly render the "development of personality" impractical for all members of the society. A few pages later, Dewey echoes this latter concern, when he introduces his more specific arguments against authoritarian society by saying, "Let us look now at the effects upon human personality which may be observed in a society that fails to prize and seek the values of associated living" [ibid., p. 96]. "Personality" in the first passage, and "human personality" in the second, are both translations of "*renge*" [Dewey 1919, pp. 179, 181].

It appears as if the development of a flourishing personality – understood by Dewey's audience as "*renge*" – is at least a partial standard against which societal practices can be measured. Examination of Dewey's English texts reveals that this is in fact the case, and also that social integration, too, is related to satisfactory personality development. Dewey believed that moral questions only arise when one is faced with two or more incompatible values competing for one's choice. A decision in which one simply decides which of two actions would be more

197

pleasurable, for instance, is not moral but "technical." When one must decide between alternatives that cannot be measured on a single scale, one is faced with a genuinely moral situation. Dewey writes that in such situations, "the question finally at stake [is]: what shall the agent *be*?" He continues: "When ends are genuinely incompatible, no common denominator can be found except by deciding what sort of character is most highly prized and shall be given supremacy."[16] In fact Dewey tells us more than that the object of our moral choices should be improving our characters; he tells us what general standards to use in making such a determination. As Jennifer Welchman explains in detail, Dewey instructs us to choose ends which contribute to the formation of harmonious, flexible, and stable characters, since these are the characteristics which make for "true or moral satisfaction."[17] I might add that Dewey bases this conclusion on the idea that "the good life" is not some static goal, but the overcoming of an ongoing series of challenges, and argues that people with the kind of character or personality that he recommends will fare best in our ever-changing social world [ibid., pp. 162–6, 191]. "Personality" and "character" are basically equivalent for Dewey, both referring to the traits that centrally determine how we interact with our world.[18]

What, then, of rights? In his *Ethics*, they do not play an important theoretical role. He does offer a clue to his conception of rights, though, when he asserts that the highest virtue of social institutions is "effective freedom," by which he means "both freedom from interference by others as well as freedom to command resources essential for the realization of one's desires and aims" [Welchman 1995, p. 194]. Effective freedom, in other words, combines what we have come to think of as both positive and negative aspects. Given this understanding of freedom, we should expect that Dewey's view of rights will similarly encompass both negative limiting and positive enabling.

When we return to Dewey's Beijing lectures on social and political thought, we find that this expectation is fulfilled. Dewey writes that

[16] [Dewey 1978 (1908), pp. 194–5; quoted in Welchman 1995, p. 154].
[17] [Dewey 1978 (1908), p. 259; Welchman 1995, p. 163].
[18] See, for example, [Welchman 1995, p. 80], where the two words are used interchangeably. In the present context, it is also relevant that while "*renge*" was initially introduced as a translation of "personality," today it is typically translated as "character," with words like "*gexing*" or "*xingge*" used for "personality." I suspect this has to do with "personality" coming to be seen as fairly superficial and unrelated to morality, while "character" continues to be understood as a serious matter with moral overtones.

A right means the power which the individual has been granted to do something according to the law. He can do what he does because he has been granted the power by the law – by law which is supported and maintained by the power of the whole society. In other words, society buttresses the law and thus supports the power which the law grants to the individual person. . . . [Thus] the individual's freedom in law and in politics is the sum total of his various rights. [Dewey 1973, p. 148]

Implicit in this conception of rights as "powers" are the twin positive and negative aspects alluded to earlier: The right-as-power tells us that we are both permitted and enabled to do something.

A final important feature of Dewey's treatment of rights is the relationship between rights and responsibilities. In the Beijing lectures we read: "Every right enjoyed by an individual has as its obverse an obligation. For example, a person has a right to own property, but his right imposes upon him the obligation to respect the same right for each of his fellow men" [ibid.]. Dewey elaborates on this example, pointing out that respecting the right to property can entail things like using a contract when buying or selling, paying a tax on transactions, having deeds recorded, and so on. We see here the implications of Dewey's view that the enjoyment of a right is a power which therefore demands the support of a society's legal machinery. To have such rights, we must be members of a society which supports them, which means to actively participate in their fulfillment: These are the "obligations" that correspond to each right.[19]

The similarities between Dewey's ideas about rights and those of Chen Duxiu and Gao Yihan are marked and pervasive. When I noted at the outset of this chapter that neither of the Chinese thinkers had read Dewey – nor, for that matter, had Dewey read either Chinese author – I did not mean to imply that there were no common influences that might explain their similarities. It is at least the case that Chen and Gao read or read about many of the same Western thinkers that Dewey read: Hobbes, Locke, Rousseau, and others. Then, too, there is the idea that

---

[19] See also [Welchman 1995, p. 166], who summarizes a similar theme from Dewey's *Ethics*: "In choosing to be a moral agent, one must at the same time choose that the social institutions necessary to one's being a moral agent exist to sustain and enrich one's personhood. Now these social institutions cannot and will not exist unless individuals cooperate in their formation and continuation. Thus the exercise of social dispositions is necessary to one's attaining and sustaining personality."

Western thought was becoming increasingly, if implicitly, "sinified," as noted in the introduction to this chapter. To some uncertain extent, the convergence arose by coincidence: two strands within two traditions tending, for a time and for their own reasons, to be both locally prominent and globally similar. Out of such coincidences are larger communities made; in the writings and in the careers of all three men we can see the idea that we live in a shared world, with shared concerns, concretely exemplified. Finding ways to sustain such a feeling of community can be central to preserving a consensus on values, rather than allowing such a convergence to disintegrate. I will return to these themes in the book's final chapters. For now, let me turn to the aspect of global civilization toward which Chen himself turned, namely Marxism.

7.4 MARXISM AND LENINISM

Marxism has obviously been of enormous significance to twentieth-century China. It is during the period currently under discussion that Marxism takes root and flourishes in China; among other things, as noted earlier, the CCP is founded in 1921 by Chen Duxiu and others. My goal in this section is to explore to what extent Marxism and its derivatives influence rights discourse in China prior to 1949, and in particular to ask whether these ideologies change the ways that *quanli* was conceptualized. One answer, offered in a recent book by Robert Weatherley, is that Marxism serves primarily to confirm an already existing way of talking about rights which itself derives primarily from the Confucian tradition [Weatherley 1999]. While I do not deny that there are ways in which Marxism will come to reinforce certain preexisting themes in Chinese rights discourse, I think that saying this misses most of what is interesting about the relation between Marxism and rights discourse prior to 1949. First of all, a number of prominent Marxists launched critiques of those who advocated rights and human rights during the 1920s and 1930s. Second, the version of Marxism which had led to a successful revolution in the neighboring Soviet Union – namely, Leninism – was quite influential in China, not only on the CCP but also on the Nationalist Party (GMD). We will look at the idea that rights belong only to those with proper revolutionary pedigrees, which emerges in both of these groups, and look briefly at the debate that ensues between proponents of this idea and others committed to a broader conception of rights. Both the Marxist critiques and the Leninist innovations will have important consequences for the future of rights discourse in China.

Before turning to these specific issues, it will be helpful to review Marx's somewhat complicated attitudes toward rights.[20] To begin with, he was at best ambivalent about rights in pre-communist societies. His most famous discussion, in "On the Jewish Question," criticizes most types of rights for contributing to the atomization of self-centered bourgeois society; this was contrary to Marx's fundamental belief that humans are "species beings," flourishing only in society through their relationships with others [Marx 1978a (1843), p. 46]. He saw rights, that is, as reinforcing barriers between individuals: barriers that both protected us from, but also isolated us from, our fellow humans. I think that it is easy to see that Marx is correct, whether or not we share his belief in the fundamental relatedness of all people. Most obviously in contemporary American society, perhaps, the prevalence of rights language both protects individuals and individual behaviors, and reduces the desire or possibility for people to engage in more substantial ways.[21]

In other writings Marx did recognize the need for certain types of rights in pre-communist societies, such as the right of each to receive according to his or her labor, but even there he notes that, since individuals' abilities to labor differ from one another, this right is fundamentally unequal [Marx 1978c (1875), p. 530]. In the "highest phase of communist society," however,

> after the enslaving subordination of the individual life to the division of labor, and therewith also the antithesis between mental and physical labor, has vanished; after labor has become not only a means of life but life's prime want; after productive forces have also increased with the all-round development of the individual, and the springs of cooperative wealth flow more abundantly – only then can the narrow horizon of bourgeois right be crossed in its entirety and society inscribe on its banner: From each according to his ability, to each according to his need. [1978c, p. 531]

Goods will be plentiful, the needs of each can be satisfied, and none will need to fall back on claims of individual rights. Rights may have useful, if ambivalent, roles in societies that have not yet attained true

---

[20] Weatherley's summary of Marx's attitudes toward rights is quite helpful; see [Weatherley 1999, pp. 84–9]. For further discussion, see also [Waldron 1987] and [Lukes 1985].

[21] One analysis of this tendency is [Glendon 1991].

communism, but Marx suggests that in the long run, any need for rights is a signal of social problems that still need to be overcome.[22]

We have already seen how, as he moved toward Marxism, Chen Duxiu put increasing stress on the need for workers to enjoy the social and economic preconditions necessary for fulfilling their personalities. By the time he helped to found the CCP in 1921, he had stopped talking of rights altogether. This conclusion is certainly not necessitated by Marx's teachings, since China was still a long way from a true communist society. A consistent Marxist, that is, could well have demanded economic (and other) rights for all people. We also saw earlier that Gao Yihan, never a member of the CCP but certainly sympathetic to socialism, did in fact press the importance of fundamental economic rights. Tan Mingqian, like Chen an original member of the CCP, went beyond both Chen and Gao by explicitly criticizing the rights granted in the French Revolution – and implicitly criticizing many of the rights proposals made by liberals in his own day. The French Revolution was about the bourgeois wresting privileges from the aristocrats, but it did not institute genuine democracy because it did not realize true equality and freedom. Despite their sacrifices for the Revolution, proletarians gained no political rights; indeed, the rise of capitalism has meant that proletarians have lost any self-sovereignty (*zizhu*) that they ever had.[23] Tan argues that the real spirit of contemporary democracy lies in two things, equality and freedom. True equality requires giving people equal opportunities, and thus true freedom means allowing for both the satisfaction of one's own self-regarding desires and the similar satisfactions of others: All people must have equal opportunities, if freedom is to be meaningful [Tan 1920, pp. 588–9]. Like thinkers that we have seen before, in other words, Tan looks to a balanced solution between self and other, and self and group; he never suggests that for some reason the group's interests must take precedence over those of individuals.

A decade later, other members of the CCP raised their voices in criticism of a new round of liberal demands for human rights. Three prominent liberal thinkers wrote a series of articles in the *Crescent* magazine which criticized the GMD government's meager efforts to institutionalize protection for human rights. Since several other scholars have

---

[22] Elsewhere Marx implies that while antagonisms arising from social and economic relations will disappear in communist society, individual antagonisms (like lovers' quarrels) may remain, leading some scholars to speculate that rights might still have a limited role [Marx 1978b (1859), p. 5].

[23] See [Tan 1920, p. 586]. This article has been translated in [Angle & Svensson 2001].

recently written about this "Human Rights movement," I have chosen not to focus on it in this chapter; suffice it to say that in various ways, these writings continued to exemplify the trends and conceptualizations that I sketched in earlier sections of the chapter.[24] In any event, the criticism leveled against rights in 1931 is important because it makes explicit the idea, implicit in Chen Duxiu's silence about rights after 1921, that revolution, rather than constitutional revision, is the only route to full equality and freedom for the proletariat.[25]

A second feature of the 1931 communist criticism of liberal rights proposals is the idea that the CCP should be struggling for the rights of members of a certain class, rather than for the rights of all. Tan Mingqian's earlier article had explicitly condemned any hegemony of one class over another, but later critiques move away from this position. In fact, a wide range of articles published starting in the 1920s advocated what came to be called "revolutionary people's rights (*geming minquan*)," which were opposed to "human rights (*renquan*)." In light of the bitter struggles that eventually occurred between the GMD and the CCP, culminating in the civil war of 1945–1949, it may be surprising to learn of the considerable cooperation between the two parties in the early 1920s and of their initial ideological similarities. The eventual differences between them were enormous, certainly, but in the early 1920s both were explicitly revolutionary parties, and both were developed, with advice and financing from the Comintern, along Leninist lines [Spence 1990, pp. 334–41].

"Revolutionary people's rights" were granted only to those committed to the goals of the revolution. The declaration from the GMD's first nationwide conference stated that "All individuals and groups that truly fight against imperialism can enjoy all freedoms and rights; whereas all those who betray the nation, deceive the people, and are loyal to the imperialists and warlords, regardless of whether it is as a group or as an individual, may not enjoy these freedoms and rights."[26] As one theorist who had helped to found the CCP but then switched to the GMD explained, the GMD's "ideal is surely the realization of political equality, but in order to attain true equality, it is necessary to pass through a period of temporary inequality. . . . We know that to accomplish true

---

[24] See [Svensson 1996], [Narramore 1983], [Spar 1992], and [Fung 1998] for discussion. Two of the most important essays from the movement are translated in [Angle & Svensson 2001].

[25] See [Peng 1983 (1931), pp. 111–12]. This essay is translated in [Angle & Svensson 2001].

[26] Quoted in [Zhou 1928], which is translated in [Angle & Svensson 2001].

equality, we first have to clear away its obstacles and do away with those who damage equality" [Zhou 1928, p. 13]. This same idea, that rights need to be restricted to those with proper revolutionary ideals, can be found in some documents associated with the CCP. It is noteworthy, though, that leaders of the CCP came to be more inclusive during their subsequent struggles against the GMD – an inclusiveness that they explained in terms of the various stages through which the revolution had to pass. We thus find Mao Zedong writing in 1940 that "It should be laid down that all landlords and capitalists not opposed to the War of Resistance shall enjoy the same human rights, property rights, and right to vote, and the same freedoms of speech, assembly, association, thought, and belief, as the workers and peasants" [Mao 1991 (1940), p. 768].

There is nothing in particular about Chinese culture and Russian culture that would have led one to predict that their political discourses would converge in the mid-twentieth century. Yet converge they did, which for a time led to considerable engagement among thinkers, authors, artists, and others from the two nations. Like the convergence between Chen and Gao, on the one hand, and Dewey, on the other, this later convergence does not last: As political and other circumstances change in the two nations, they begin to evaluate things increasingly differently. In Chapter 8 I will be looking at some of the ways in which contemporary Western rights theorists might be able to engage with their Chinese counterparts, and I will suggest that we once again see some grounds for convergence. It is worth bearing in mind, therefore, the fragility of such convergences. A convergence is really just the beginning of the process of building and maintaining consensus on key normative matters.

8

Engagement despite Distinctiveness

RIGHTS DISCOURSE HAS CONTINUED to develop in China since the establishment of the People's Republic in 1949. As we might expect, given the ambivalent attitude that Marxism has toward rights, the developments have been neither simple nor continuous. In addition, while we have certainly seen some tensions between different ideas of rights in the pre-1949 period, contestation over who has rights, and what rights are, becomes even more prominent in the years since then. Be that as it may, most participants in Chinese rights discourse continue to conceive of rights in ways that will be familiar from earlier in the century.

This chapter has two goals. To begin with, I aim to assess the extent to which recent Chinese thinking about rights substantiates the first of Liu Huaqiu's claims, with which the book began: Do we in fact find in China today a distinctive conception of rights? Chapters leading up to this one have made clear that Chinese discussions of rights emerged and developed in a distinctive way, sharing some but not all features with developments outside China. Among other factors, concerns over the satisfaction of legitimate desires, the construction of a nation within which individuals could flourish, and the protection of individuals' abilities to develop their personalities all played important roles in the Chinese discourse. Here I will argue that this distinctiveness continues down to the present day. I will look at three aspects of Chinese rights discourse, each familiar from previous chapters, and show the extent to which each continues to be an important, if not uncontested, part of the way in which rights are conceptualized. The three aspects are (1) the ways in which rights are related to interests, (2) the degree to which different people's rights are can be harmonized, and (3) the interrelation between economic and political rights.[1]

We will find variation and argument within each aspect. Recall that such differences can reflect two quite different processes. On the one hand, the way that our many commitments are interwoven tells us that we should always expect differences in meaning, though these differences need not, as we saw in Chapter 2, stand in the way of communication. On the other hand, this successful communication depends in large part on cooperating within the communal structure of norms. When communities fracture and central dimensions of people's commitments become contested, a second kind of difference in meaning arises, this latter kind with the potential to jeopardize successful communication, particularly if some parties to the disagreement resist recognizing the formation of different linguistic communities. Although we will see some hints of this latter process, it will nonetheless appear against the background of considerable consensus.

Not only is there considerable consensus within Chinese rights discourse, but there is also more cross-cultural similarity than is often recognized. Calling Chinese rights discourse "distinctive" is very different from calling it "unique." We have seen in previous chapters that Chinese rights thinkers have regularly drawn on and interpreted various Western writings and concepts; I argued in Chapter 7, for instance, that there was a significant convergence in 1920s rights discourses, East and West. A strong version of Liu Huaqiu's first claim, according to which Chinese rights discourse is fundamentally different from Western treatments of rights, cannot be sustained. On the other hand, Chinese rights discourse is not merely an imperfect attempt to mirror Western ideas. If we reinterpret Liu to be saying simply that Chinese ideas about rights have developed in accord with Chinese concerns and practices, and that Chinese concepts of rights over the years have differed in important ways from many Western conceptions of rights, and finally that there are important continuities within Chinese rights discourse, even down to the present day – if we understand Liu thus, then we should affirm the first of his claims.

---

[1] I select these three from among a larger set of features distinctive of, though not unique to, Chinese rights discourse. Others of these features – such as a stress on both group and individual rights, a reciprocal relation between rights and duties, or a priority on substance instead of process – will come up in the following discussion, but I will not focus on them.

In addition to cautiously affirming the first of Liu Huaqiu's two claims, this chapter continues the process of dealing with his second claim – namely, that foreign conceptions of rights should not be imposed on China. As I have just suggested, Chinese rights discourse is not now, nor has it ever been, as sealed off from other cultures' rights discourses as Liu Huaqiu might believe. Chinese rights discourse has a coherent history and is made up of Chinese concepts and concerns, but this does not have to mean that Chinese and Western rights discourses are "isolated" from each other, in the sense introduced in Chapter 3. In fact there are significant grounds for cross-cultural dialogue, and perhaps for mutual learning, within each aspect of rights discourse on which I focus. This chapter demonstrates that genuine engagement is both possible and desirable.

Before turning to my three specific aspects of recent Chinese concepts of rights, it may be helpful to rehearse rapidly the historical settings in which these discussions have occurred. As I have been throughout the book, I continue to be very selective about which individuals and texts I have chosen to discuss; my goal is to illustrate important themes – often in some depth – rather than to write a complete history. Explicit discussions of rights over the last twenty-five years have taken place in several contexts. Best known are the two political movements which were subsequently suppressed by the government: the Democracy Wall movement in the winter of 1978–79 and the Tiananmen democracy movement in the spring of 1989. The United Nations serves as the focus of a second set of contexts. China has played roles there which include criticized aggressor (e.g., for its role in Tibet in 1959), leader of non-aligned and Third World nations in their efforts to move beyond colonial legacies and develop as independent nations, and participant in efforts of Asian nations to shape international human rights discourse through their notion of "Asian values." It was primarily in this last role, in fact, that Liu Huaqiu made the statement with which this book began. A third context is academic discourse, principally since 1990. These writings cover a spectrum, ranging from those which have informed or closely followed the government's position, as articulated in its white paper of 1991, to a variety of less orthodox positions, some rather critical of the official stance. I will draw on several essays that fit into this category in the analysis to follow.[2]

---

[2] For references to some literature on this period, see Section 1.1 of my Introduction.

8.1 RIGHTS AND INTERESTS

In a groundbreaking article, the American philosopher and legal scholar Randall Peerenboom has argued that contemporary Chinese human rights theorists understand rights as a kind of interest. He contrasts this with the view of many American philosophers that the nature of rights is deontological (based on moral duties), rather than utilitarian (based on interests); that is, "rights precede interests, both in the sense that rights trump interests and that rights are not based on utility or social consequences but on moral principles whose justification is derived independently of the good" [Peerenboom 1995, p. 361]. Peerenboom also identifies and criticizes a tendency among contemporary Chinese theorists to assume that individual and collective interests, and thus individual and collective rights, will not conflict. He explicitly connects this latter idea with the continuing appeal of ideas from the Confucian tradition, arguing that the central role of rites (*li*) in the tradition helps to explain the "enduring appeal of the utopian myth of harmony," which has "blind[ed] rulers and reformers alike to the realities of disharmony, [and thus] retard[ed] the development of a strong theory of rights" [Peerenboom 1998, p. 251].

In this section I will explore the relation between rights and interests, putting off the question of harmony until the next section. As Peerenboom would no doubt acknowledge, rights and interests may have more complex interrelations than his simple framework of utilitarian versus deontological rights theories suggests. Spelling out these different possible relations will help us to understand what Chinese rights theorists may be saying when they link rights and interests. I show that Chinese theories can be understood along lines similar to a prominent Western theory which, I argue, is in certain ways superior to the Western theories on which Peerenboom focuses. I also argue that this alternative Western theory is vulnerable to an objection to which Chinese theorists might help it respond.

8.1.1 Western Theory on Rights as Protected Interests

Many contemporary Western rights theorists take interests to be central to the idea of rights. Some who do this are indeed utilitarians, which I will define precisely in a moment, but it is crucial for my purposes to note that many philosophers who tightly link rights and interests are not utilitarians. In order to better understand, and ultimately engage with,

Chinese thinkers who talk about rights as a type of interest, we need to review the range of perspectives that Western thinkers take on this question.

Utilitarians believe that (1) the right actions to take are those that best promote people's interests, and (2) all interests can be measured on a single scale, typically that of utility or pleasure. For it to be right to respect someone's rights, therefore, utilitarians hold that the rights in question must maximize interests.[3] We ought to respect property rights, on this view, because the institution of property leads to more utility (or pleasure) than any alternative institution. It is a bit misleading to say that utilitarians believe that rights are interests. It is indeed in our interest to have rights, since – according to the utilitarian rights theorist – when rights are respected, our interests are maximized. That is, rights are a particular way of promoting or protecting our interests. Of course, "our" here refers to the entire group whose members enjoy the rights in question; it might maximize my own interests to have a unique right to anyone else's property, but such a right is unlikely to maximize all of our interests, summed together, so utilitarians would reject it.

Contemporary Western philosophers have raised a variety of objections to the utilitarian approach to rights. Among other things, they question whether there really is a single scale on which all our diverse interests can be ranked, as well as whether rights that are justified only by their promotion of interests can adequately protect us from competing interests. These are complicated matters, and while it is clear that some forms of utilitarianism fail to meet such challenges, other forms may fare better.[4] Rather than delving into such matters, my purposes will be better served by introducing an account of how rights can protect interests that does not depend on specifically utilitarian reasoning.

As a starting point, consider the following statement by Ronald Dworkin, which Peerenboom quotes as an example of Western (anti-utilitarian) rights discourse: "A right is a claim that it would be wrong for the government to deny an individual even though it would be in the general interest to do so" [Dworkin 1977, p. 269]. Dworkin often puts this in terms of rights "trumping" interests. Another author whom

---

[3] This sentence makes clear the difference, sometimes forgotten, between that which is right (to do), on the one hand, and rights, on the other.

[4] Traditional *act utilitarianism* seems particularly vulnerable to the second challenge; see [Lyons 1994]. *Rule utilitarianism*, if plausible on other grounds, may fare better. See [Gibbard 1984] and [Pettit 1988] for related arguments.

Peerenboom sees as representative of American rights discourse puts the point this way: "Rights are one thing; interests are another; and when they collide, rights are trumps" [Pennock 1981, p. 5].

The simple theory suggested by these two quotes might be thought to explain satisfactorily the sense in which someone's right can protect her interests. Consider Mary, the owner of a single-family home with a drive-way leading up to her garage.[5] She has a right to use her driveway – it is her private property – which cannot, at least in ordinary circum-stances, be violated by her neighbors, even if parking in her driveway would be convenient for them. In Dworkin's language, her right "trumps" other people's interests, so she does not need to worry about a daily weighing of her interest against those of her neighbors. Even if their interests in parking in the driveway seem stronger than hers on a given day, her right still trumps their mere interests.

In fact, however, this simple theory is far too strong. It is also a cari-cature of Dworkin's actual view, though perhaps not of some of the other theories that Peerenboom cites.[6] Certain kinds of interests ought to be able to override at least certain kinds of rights. The drivers of emergency vehicles, for instance, are typically justified in parking in the driveway. The general interest served by allowing such breaches of rights is too strong – and perhaps the interests being protected in such cases too weak – for the right to "trump" in such cases. A close examination of Dworkin's views shows that he, too, recognizes that rights are not *always* trumps. He writes:

> Someone who claims that citizens have a right against the Govern-ment need not go as far as to say that the State is *never* justified in overriding that right. He might say, for example, that although citizens have a right to free speech, the Government may override that right when necessary to protect the rights of others, or to prevent a catastrophe, or even to obtain a clear and major public

---

[5] This example is inspired by [Lyons 1994].

[6] In addition to Pennock, cited earlier, Robert Nozick has put forward a well-known view which is, in my view, much too strong for the reasons stated here. See especially [Nozick 1974, pp. 29–30]. Philip Pettit is incorrect when he argues that Dworkin's trumps are equivalent to Nozick's "side constraints" in [Pettit 1987]. Pettit notes in passing that Dworkin's trumps can be "partial" while Nozick's constraints are equivalent only to "total trumps" [p. 10]. He proceeds to ignore this difference, however, which if fully rec-ognized vitiates his conclusion that rights on either account are "untradeable against certain other goods" [p. 11]. This seems true of Nozick but not of Dworkin, except perhaps for what Dworkin calls "fundamental rights."

benefit (though if he acknowledged this last as a possible justification he would be treating the right in question as not among the most important or fundamental). What he cannot do is say that the Government is justified in overriding a right on the minimal grounds that would be sufficient if no right existed. [Dworkin 1977, pp. 191–2][7]

Now it is one thing to say that one right can override another; bridge players are familiar with the fact that a higher trump defeats a lower trump. Allowing that certain strong interests can defeat at least some rights, though, suggests that "trump" may not be the best metaphor for Dworkin's understanding of rights: In bridge at least, even the ace of a non-trump suit will lose to the deuce of trumps.

I will say more about this in a moment, but for now let us note that Dworkin recognizes the requirement that rights be protective, since there must be some grounds, like the neighbor's convenience on a given day, insufficient to override a right. At the same time, Dworkin wants to allow that at least some rights (albeit not fundamental ones) can themselves be overridden by general interests. Finally, notice that the citation from Dworkin with which we began, "A right is a claim that it would be wrong for the government to deny an individual even though it would be in the general interest to do so," is, taken out of context, ambiguous. It might mean that *no* general interest can outweigh a right, which seems to be Peerenboom's reading, or it might mean that rights cannot be outweighed by merely *minimal* increases in the general interest. We have now seen that this latter interpretation is surely what Dworkin intends.

The substance of Dworkin's view, in short, seems to provide the notion of (limited) protection of interests that we are after, but the metaphor of rights as trumps is misleading. It may be apt for "fundamental" rights, but we are after a way of understanding the way that rights can protect interests in general, not in some narrower range of cases. In search of a more widely applicable view, let us turn now to the views of Joseph Raz. Raz's work is relevant for several reasons. First, though he is a leading proponent of the view that rights are grounded on interests, he is no utilitarian. He is a value pluralist: He believes that there is an irreducible

---

[7] See also [Dworkin 1977, p. 366]: "No alleged right is a right (on my account) unless it overrides at least a marginal case of general collective justification; but one right is more important than another if some especially dramatic or urgent collective justification, above that threshold, will defeat the latter but not the former."

plurality of goods (e.g., pleasure, autonomy, virtues, etc.) and that no calculation of consequences can measure individual well-being [Raz 1986,
chs. 11–13]. Second, he has introduced the notion of a "protected reason"
that may provide a satisfactory account of the kind of protection which
rights afford to interests. Third, he has views on the harmony between
individual and collective interests that will be important to my discussion of those topics in subsequent sections of the chapter.

Raz defines a right as follows: "'X has a right' if and only if . . . an
aspect of X's well-being (his interest) is a sufficient reason for holding
some other person(s) to be under a duty" [1984, p. 195].[8] In other words,
one has a right whenever one has an interest that is sufficiently important to ground a correlative duty.[9] Rights are not the same as interests,
but the two bear intimate relations to one another. We can say that while
rights are not themselves protected interests, they are that which protects interests. Specifically, they do this by grounding duties, which Raz
explains via the idea of a "protected reason." Protected reasons are, as
their name implies, more than mere reasons. Mary's interest in being able
to park in her driveway whenever she wants is a reason for her neighbor not to park there, but it is not a protected reason. Protection comes
from the addition of what Raz terms an "exclusionary reason," which is
a reason to refrain from acting for certain other kinds of reasons [1990,
p. 39]. Raz says that authoritative directives are examples of "protected
reasons," since receiving an order from a superior gives one *both* a reason
to act *and* a reason not to act on other sorts of reasons (like fatigue or
disagreement with one's superior). Raz writes:

> In deciding whether one ought to obey the authority's directive, one
> ought to exclude all the reasons, both for and against [the act], which
> were within the jurisdiction of the authority. One ought to weigh the
> directive in the balance with whatever reasons, for or against the act
> it requires, [that] are outside the authority's jurisdiction, adding to
> them whatever reasons arise out of the duty to support just institu-
> tions in the situation at hand. [1990, p. 192]

---

[8] See also [Raz 1986, p. 166]; chapter 7 of [1986] is identical with [1984].

[9] See [Raz 1984, pp. 199–200] on ways of understanding the "correlativity" between rights
and duties with which Raz disagrees. Also note that while Raz's phrasing here might
imply that only X's interests count toward grounding the right, he makes clear elsewhere
that the interests of others are often harmoniously interwoven with individual interests,
and that the combined weight of these interests typically grounds rights. See [Raz
1992].

While the idea of jurisdiction may need some further spelling out, it is clear that we have an idea here well-suited to the kind of limited protection of interests that we have already seen rights play.

Thinking back to Mary's situation, her interest in parking in her driveway, as well as the common interest in private property (as explained later), grounds her right to so park. By recognizing her right, we understand her neighbors, among others, to be under duties not to park in Mary's driveway. We can now flesh out the neighbors' duties with the idea of a protected reason as follows: The neighbors' duties are both reasons for them not to park in Mary's driveway, and reasons for them not to consider a range of reasons for (or against) parking there. The neighbors' convenience when unloading groceries, for instance, is a relevant reason that could be taken into account if this were a mere balancing of interests. Since Mary's interest is protected by a right, this convenience cannot be considered.

Other considerations, outside the "jurisdiction" of Mary's right, can be considered. We might imagine that the jurisdiction in question covers everyday interactions in normal situations. Ambulances, fire trucks, and perhaps even moving vans represent abnormal intrusions into the neighborhood, and we can readily see how the interests they represent might be appropriately weighed against Mary's interest in a free parking space. If we see these abnormal situations as falling outside the jurisdiction of Mary's right, that is, her right may – in such special cases only – play no role in the balancing of reasons beyond providing a simple reason to let her park. In these cases, in other words, Mary's interest is no longer protected.

Raz's account of the ways in which rights protect interests has many virtues. Unlike Dworkin's notion of "trumps," it provides a consistent account of how and why interests are protected across a range of rights. It is easy to see, for example, that those rights we take to be "fundamental" have wide jurisdictions, some protecting the relevant interest against even the greatest social benefits. Still, my goal here is neither a complete defense of Raz's theory nor a thorough critique of Dworkin's. I am instead interested in understanding the general texture of the relations between rights and interests posited by leading Western rights theorists. As we turn now to Chinese rights theories, we will see that rights are taken by most theorists to protect interests in a manner quite consistent with Raz's ideas.

8.1.2 *Chinese Interests*

Based on what we have seen in previous chapters and what I will discuss in the balance of this one, it is clear that the dominant view of rights, both now and throughout the history of Chinese rights discourse, has been that rights are closely tied to interests. Indeed, we saw that "*quanli*" was originally adopted as an equivalent for "rights" in large part because it readily expressed the ideas of both legitimate powers and legitimate benefits or interests – ideas with which one strand of the Confucian tradition had been concerned for centuries.

To grant this tie between rights and interests is not the same as agreeing with Peerenboom that Chinese theorists today understand rights *as* interests, nor does it concede that their theories are utilitarian. As we saw earlier, there are several ways to understand how rights might relate to interests. I argue here that contemporary Chinese thinkers see rights as protecting interests in a manner compatible with Raz's theory. Chinese theories are not as vulnerable as Peerenboom believes them to be, nor need they be weak.

I will start by looking at what an important representative of the activist strand of Chinese rights discourse has said about the relation between rights and interests. The most significant outpouring of theoretical writings by activists critical of the government occurred during the 1978–9 Democracy Wall movement. The writings ranged from big-character posters to sophisticated essays in underground magazines; the range of perspectives one finds in these different sources is almost as varied.[10] The most famous of the radical activists from Democracy Wall was Wei Jingsheng, editor of the magazine *Explorations*. Wei believes that the rights people have are "inherent," rather than "bestowed" on them by the state [Wei 1980b, p. 142]. He writes that "From the moment one is born, one has the right to live and the right to fight for a better life." This does not mean that rights are natural and eternal, as those terms are often understood in Western rights discourse; Wei adds that

> At the same time human rights only exist in relation to other things, for people do not live in a vacuum but are surrounded by other things and relate, directly or indirectly, to their environment. Thus,

---

[10] See [Seymour 1980] for translations of many important documents, and [Guang 1996] for helpful analysis.

human rights are limited and relative rather than unlimited and absolute. This limitation constantly grows and changes with the development of the history of mankind and with man's quest to tame and control his surroundings. [1980b, p. 142]

Wei believes that rights are closely related to the idea of equality. This is one of the ways in which rights are relative to our social environments; Wei believes that human rights are those assurances or protections that can be given to all people equally. He says that "Rights are opportunities to be recognized by the external world" [ibid., p. 143], which in another essay he suggests means the "conditions [necessary] to lead a normal life" [Wei 1980a, p. 65]. He is adamant that rights are not guarantees of anything, but simply equal opportunities to satisfy one's desires and live well. In a remark that I will examine more closely later when I turn to the issue of harmony, Wei concludes that "On the basis of freedom," democracy and human rights "encourage voluntary cooperation and achieve unity of relatively unanimous interests" [Wei 1980b, p. 145].

Nowhere in his work from the Democracy Wall era does Wei address more clearly the status or origin of rights. Right are protections of the fundamental capacities or interests which all humans have and need in order to pursue their aims, though these capacities and aims can change over time, and rights will change with them. Wei's final remark about seeking a unity of interests shows that justifying rights in terms of interests is not far from his mind, though he does not make that connection explicit. Wei was in jail throughout the 1989 Tiananmen movement, but wrote a letter from jail on June 15, 1991, about human rights that has been published in the United States. In the letter he stresses that, contrary to government claims that rights are bestowed on people solely by state laws, "human rights . . . have objective standards that cannot be modified by legislation and cannot be changed by the will of the government." He goes on to characterize them as "natural" and "instinctive," though he still recognizes their basis in "primary-level social relations" – namely, the social relations which "emerge from man's basic nature" rather than those which are "stipulated or manufactured by man" [Wei 1997, pp. 167, 175].

Wei seems to have moved some distance from his position of a decade earlier, since this talk of instinct and natural rights is less amenable than his earlier formulations to justifying rights by their contribution to, or protection of, interests. While his is an important voice in the overseas activist community (since 1999 he has been living in exile abroad), it is now time to look at what less radical academics publishing in China have said about interests. I will begin with Li Buyun, a legal scholar who is the associate director of the Chinese Academy of Social Sciences' Human Rights Research Center. In a well-known article published in 1992, Li writes that "The foundation of rights are interests. In essence, the relationship of rights and duties between people is a kind of inter-est-relationship" [Li 1992, p. 11].[11] He qualifies this by noting that interests should never be considered in isolation from social and productive relations, and that these relations change as social forms evolve. The existence of social relationships, in fact, leads directly to the need for rights:

> Social relations between people are the source of people's "due rights (*yingyou quanli*)" and the grounds for the production and development of human rights. . . . The existence of social relations is a premise on which the existence of human rights rests. If an individual existed in complete isolation, he would not need anything in the form of rights and duties to mediate (*tiaozheng*) the various kinds of contradictions and conflicts of interests that arise between people. [Li 1992, p. 11]

Rights, in this formulation, "mediate" between different interests. Li does not say more about how this mediation is to take place. The basic idea is rather clear, however: Some interests win out over others on account of their connection to rights. In the idiom I was using earlier, we would say that rights protect certain interests and not others.

As we saw earlier, there is an important difference between saying that rights protect interests, and that rights are merely one kind of interest that can be weighed against others. Protected interests – whether we follow Raz or some other account – typically cannot be compared with other kinds of interests. Li sees that "due rights" must defend certain interests from incursion in order for healthy social relations to exist. Where, though, do due rights come from? Li writes that

> People's due rights, and the duties that exist in tandem with them, come about in part through the concrete reflection of the principles of laws and other social regulations, and in part through the manifestation in actual social relations and social intercourse of

---

[11] This entire essay is translated in [Angle & Svensson 2001].

216

acceptance of and support for the people's moral, social, and political concepts, as well as their traditions, habits, and customs. [Li 1992, p. 9]

That is, due rights emerge from social practices, rather than from any one transcendent source (like natural rights) or foundational ethical principle (like utilitarianism's "greatest good for the greatest number"). To determine what norms should guide us, we look to the norms implicit in our actual practices.[12]

Li is not the only one to explicitly connect rights and interests. Zhang Wenxian, a law professor at Jilin University, says that "rights are a means by which the state, through passing legal regulations . . . allows people to choose and acquire interests that are within the scope of a state's interests" [Zhang 1992, p. 38]. He adds that

When the state establishes or utilizes law to proclaim various kinds of rights, it has already weighed individual, collective, and social interests in accord with the people's general will and publicly acknowledged standards of value. Individual and collective rights, like social rights, thus internally manifest the unification of individual, collective, national, and even human fundamental interests, [and thus] all are affirmations of legitimate interests. [1992, p. 40]

There is clearly much here of relevance to the topic of harmony, which I will take up later. For now, let us concentrate on what is being said here about interests. Zhang goes on to point out that there are proper and improper interests, but no improper rights. When we have a right to something, therefore, we can certainly conclude that the thing is in our interest, and we can further conclude that it is *properly* in our interest: It accords with the general will and public standards of value. As such, we might expect that interests which have been "affirmed" by rights cannot be straightforwardly weighed against interests which have not been so affirmed. As was the case with Li Buyun, rights for Zhang are not a special type of interest, but rather a protective device which applies to certain kinds of interests and not to others. By saying that we have rights to these interests, we mark them off as not tradeable against other types of interests. Whether interests protected by rights can be

---

[12] Pragmatic justifications of normative ideas have been studied fairly intensively by recent Western philosophers, and while Li clearly leaves a great deal to his readers' imaginations, I (for one) am quite sympathetic to such an approach. For some discussion, see [Lovibond 1983] and [Brandom 1994].

overridden by other interests also protected by rights – that is, by other legitimate interests – is a topic I will take up later.

The role Zhang gives to the state in stipulating rights, and the explicit mention of the law, deserves some comment. Later in the article Zhang agrees with other theorists that "due rights (*yingyou quanli*)" are more fundamental than legal rights.[13] When we compare this notion of due rights with Zhang's earlier statements, we see that the earlier quotations deal with idealized legal rights. Zhang explains that "the concept and advocation of due rights guides legislators; so long as conditions allow it, [they] ought to promptly establish the citizens' due rights as legal rights. If the actual situation allows for people to enjoy one hundred percent of their rights, then they shouldn't be given only ninety percent" [p. 42]. There are no countries, he says, with perfect systems of legal rights; all are constrained by the need for further economic and political development and cultural progress. This is not yet the place to assess claims like this. Suffice it to say here that even when we take on board Zhang's distinction between legal and due rights, it still makes sense to say that rights (in general) are grounded on interests, but are not simply interests themselves.

As we did with Li Buyun, we can ask how one knows what a person's due rights are. Zhang says that due rights are "the rights-needs (*quanli xuyao*) and rights-claims (*quanli yaoqiu*) of the people of a specific society that are produced based on their particular conditions of social and material life and on their cultural tradition. They are the rights people ought to have in order to be people" [Zhang 1992, p. 41]. This parallels the view of Li Buyun, with the striking addition of that last sentence, which resonates strongly with rights discourse from earlier in the century. As we saw once again in Chapter 7, Chinese theorists have regularly seen rights as defining the interests needed to be a whole person. Zhang in fact elaborates on this theme, writing that the rights of "person and personality (*renshen renge*)" are the logical point of departure for human rights, since they define what is necessary for both natural and social existence [ibid., p. 46].

A third essay that expands on the themes we have just seen is "On the Individual-based Properties of Human Rights" by Luo Mingda and He

---

[13] While there is considerable agreement on this subject among contemporary Chinese scholars, even a decade ago this would have been controversial. Prior to the 1990s, most Chinese publications dismissed the idea of moral (or normative) rights, holding that rights were merely legal grants by the state. See discussion in [Li 1992].

Hangzhou. The explicit target of Luo and He is the tendency among their contemporaries to place too much weight on the collective or "*gong* (general)" dimension of rights, and too little on the individual or "*si* (self-regarding)" dimension [Luo & He 1993, p. 56]. Luo and He begin by arguing that the category of "*quanli*" is, logically speaking, a summary of two social phenomena: *quan* or power and *li* or interests [ibid., p. 56]. This is a nice example of the ways in which Chinese theorists clearly understand themselves as working within a Chinese discourse, rather than as outsiders commenting on a foreign discourse (about "rights"). In any event, Luo and He say that *quan* and *li* are intimately linked because whether one receives one's due interests can often depend on one's powers. They write that "seeking rights is in fact seeking the interests that correlate with a [certain] share of power" [ibid., p. 56]. Rights are a means to secure certain interests; rights give us the power, in other words, to protect these interests.

I said a moment ago that Luo and He see themselves as resisting a tendency to place too little weight on the "self-regarding" dimension of human experience. They are not egoists, however. Interests must be understood in social contexts. They distinguish between "self-interest (*zili*)" and "selfishness (*zisi*)," for instance, as follows: "selfishness is when one tries to take for oneself interests that are legally (or rationally) enjoyed by all or by others" [ibid., p. 56]. I would say, therefore, that they are striving to strike the same balance that theorists have been aiming for from the very earliest moments of explicit discourse about *quanli* in China: recognizing legitimate interests while not giving in to selfish egoism. What makes something a "self-interest," which seems to be by definition legitimate, is that it exists in harmony with the goods appropriately enjoyed by others and by the entire collectivity.

Unlike Zhang Wenxian, Luo and He do not restrict the applicability of rights to legitimate interests. Rights simply protect interests; if there are "selfish interests," rather than "self-interests," then the rights are illegitimate. Luo and He argue that "human rights (*renquan*)" are the same for all people in a given historical era, and are simply those rights which all can simultaneously enjoy. If one's rights exceed what all can enjoy in a given historical era, then these rights are called "privileges (*tequan*)" rather than human rights, and one is liable to have one's privileges forcibly taken from one by the collective will [ibid., p. 59]. They explicitly connect the enjoyment of privileges with selfishness (*si*) [ibid.].

For something to be a human right, then, it must pass two tests. First, it must be something that can, at a given level of development, be enjoyed by all. Hidden in this formulation is the idea that it be in each individual's interest: something relevant not just to a few people, but so basic as to be relevant to anyone. This leads Luo and He frequently to characterize human rights as based on those interests necessary for "people to be people (*ren zhi wei ren*)" [e.g., p. 56], nearly the same formulation we saw Zhang use a moment ago. Second, for something to be a human right, it must also be protected so that people actually enjoy the interest in question; otherwise, it would simply be a human interest, not a human right.

One of the central themes of Luo and He's essay is that we should understand "human right" in this way because doing so gives us the best understanding of the historical development of, and current challenges facing, human rights. They assert that subjective self-interest has, appropriately, been the engine driving the development of human rights through the ages, from slaves versus masters to feudalism to capitalism [ibid., p. 59]. The levels of interests enjoyed were rising from age to age, but disparities drove the historical process on. They stress that even in socialist states, self-interest-driven human rights movements are necessary and appropriate to fight bureaucratism, corruption, and so on.

To any who would argue that a gradual awareness of our true natural rights has driven these historical developments, they respond that while "natural rights" has been a useful slogan, it has no more basis in "nature" than a mouse would have if he claimed a right to life when pursued by a cat [ibid., p. 57]. Like both their predecessors and their contemporaries, Luo and He are concerned to ground normative discourse on concrete, tangible interests rather than on questionable metaphysics. They add that self-interest (as they have defined it) does not work behind the scenes to realize itself, independent of human will. Abstract rights based on interests of which people are not conscious are really no rights at all, since the "power" component is missing. Sounding a theme that is strikingly reminiscent of Liang Qichao ninety years earlier, they argue that we must be conscious of our self-interests, and thus of our rights. We must claim and exercise these rights, for only then will the rights be real and the aims they seek come within our grasp.[14] Luo and He conclude that the lack of rights consciousness among Chinese citizens is a greater obstacle to modernization in China than any institutional failings. Development depends on awakening the people to their self-interests [p. 61].

[14] Some rights, like those of children, might have to be claimed by others on their behalf.

While in many ways they agree with their Confucian and communist forebears on the evils of selfishness, they believe that the goods of self-interest must be emphasized so that the people will embrace their just rewards and society can struggle forward.

8.1.3 Engagement

We have not found unanimity in Chinese rights discourse on the subject of the relation between interests and rights, nor on the larger issue of the origin of rights. I have used Wei Jingsheng to represent some of the changes that have occurred in the last quarter-century, including a movement toward the idea that we have rights simply because they are innate features of our humanity. As I noted earlier, although Wei is now in exile abroad, the writings that I have drawn on were written in China and based, according to Wei, solely on Chinese sources (Marxist and otherwise). We might expect to find even larger differences between a thinker like Li Buyun, on the one hand, and Western rights theorists, on the other.

Indeed, this is what Peerenboom finds when he contrasts Chinese utilitarian thought with Western deontological thought. On close inspection, though, we have found something both different and more complicated. First of all, Chinese thinkers are not best understood as utilitarians. Many participants in contemporary Chinese rights discourse clearly believe that we have rights because they are necessary to protect certain interests, and thus that rights have an extrinsic value, in that they are means to achieving valuable ends – such as realizing our legitimate, non-selfish interests. Nowhere do these theorists suggest, though, that rights are justified solely by their contribution to overall utility. Instead, they tend to tie the idea of legitimate interests together with the notion of "being a person" or achieving "personality." They explain how we know what it is to "be a person" in much the same way that they say we know what rights we ought to have: through reflection on the ways we inhabit our physical, social, and cultural environments. Implicit in these practices are ideals for which we strive and norms to which we seek to hold ourselves. These ideals and norms, and thus rights and notions of personality, are the dynamic products of the ways we live in our environments. Where there are economic, social, or cultural differences among different groups, these authors maintain, we should expect to find at least some differences in norms, and thus some differences in conceptions of rights.

It is striking that while there are such cross-cultural differences – on which more in a moment – there are nonetheless also strong cross-cultural resemblances. Peerenboom's deontologists are far from holding the day in Western rights theories; as we saw earlier, the writings of Joseph Raz provide but one example of a Western theory which is neither deontological nor utilitarian, and which bases rights centrally on interests. We can also see that Raz's views engage rather well with those of his Chinese contemporaries, raising questions that further development of the latter's ideas might answer.

Think, then, of the dimensions of difference and similarity that we have uncovered in this chapter so far: some striking similarities between earlier and contemporary Chinese theorizing; some equally striking cross-cultural similarities, which, however, exist side by side with important differences of the kinds to which Peerenboom points. Nor is difference confined to cross-temporal or cross-cultural dimensions. Wei shows us that the meaning of rights is contested even within contemporary Chinese discourse, and to a lesser extent there are differences among Li, Zhang, and others.

A great strength of Brandom's view of conceptual meaning, and the principal reason I have chosen it for the abstract, linguistic basis of my account, is its ability to help us understand these various dynamic differences. It emphasizes the ways in which what we say can mean different things while still allowing us to communicate, and this because of the ways in which communication is a shared, cooperative practice. Our many differences will never go away, but they can change and be reduced when we cooperatively engage with one another. Community means holding one another to shared norms, even if the norms apply differently thanks to differences in material commitments. Engagement means seeking to learn from one another, without abandoning our own community and our own norms – even if we allow them to change as seems appropriate (from our own perspective). I will pursue these themes further in the book's Conclusion. For now, I will end this section with an example of how engagement might lead to mutual learning. We will see that just as Li and his contemporaries may have something to learn from a Western theorist like Raz, so Raz may benefit from considering the Chinese theorists' views.

Recall that Raz defined a right as "'X has a right' if and only if . . . an aspect of X's well-being (his interest) is a sufficient reason for holding some other person(s) to be under a duty." We then explored Raz's suggestion that the distinctive protective function of rights can be understood on analogy to the idea of a "protected reason," which both gives us a reason to do something and excludes other reasons from consideration. Mary's right to park in her driveway means that her (and our – see later) interest in private property is a sufficient reason for holding others to be under a duty to allow her to park, which can be interpreted as these others having protected reasons to let her park, which means that they both (1) have a reason to let her park and (2) cannot consider other sorts of reasons not to let her, like their momentary convenience.

That's certainly a mouthful . . . and perhaps it is the right way to understand the nature of our duties to Mary. Certainly it seems to capture the sense in which rights seem to protect interests, as we discussed earlier. Notice, though, how quickly "rights" dropped out of that analysis. Based on what I have said so far, at least, rights seem to do no more than signal when duties, and thus protected reasons, are warranted. But do we really need the idea of rights for that? Why not just say that in certain sorts of cases, people's interests create duties for others to protect them? Isn't it redundant to speak of rights?

Raz believes that rights are not simply the passive flip side of duties, in part because he says that rights can dynamically create new duties in new situations. The right to education can ground certain sorts of duties in, say, a rich American suburb, but very different duties in a poor American inner city [Raz 1984, pp. 199–200]. One can see his point, but it is not clear why we cannot just say that individuals' interests in education can generate different duties in different circumstances. Raz's account seems to have no central motivation for all our talk of rights, and given his explicit goal of capturing our everyday use of the term [Raz 1992, p. 141], this seems to be a serious shortcoming. What is the point of saying that interests can ground *rights*, which then lead to duties?

In a famous article, Joel Feinberg asked what would be missing in an otherwise morally exemplary world which was devoid of the notion of rights. His answer is that the world would lack the activity of "claiming" for oneself, on which, he argues, self-respect is based. Feinberg believes that

> Having rights enables us to "stand up like men," to look others in the eye, and to feel in some fundamental way the equal of anyone. To think of oneself as the holder of rights is not to be unduly but properly proud, to have that minimal self-respect that is necessary to be worthy of the love and esteem of others. Indeed, respect for persons . . . may simply be respect for their rights, so that there

cannot be one without the other; and what is called "human dignity" may simply be the recognizable capacity to assert claims. [Feinberg 1970, p. 252]

A world without rights – and more importantly, a world in which we could not claim or assert our rights – would be a world with neither self-respect nor respect for others.

Craig Ihara has recently argued that Feinberg overstates his case; Ihara grants that rights-claiming may be one route to self-respect, but insists that Confucianism, while making no mention of rights, does have "a significant and interesting conception of human equality and human worth, [and] respect for persons and proper pride might plausibly be thought to arise out of these human capacities and their exercise" [Ihara in press]. Ihara suggests that whenever one can "assume a basic cooperativeness and honesty, or . . . reliable impartial authority or mechanism," then individual rights may be less important or even unnecessary for human self-respect [ibid.]. Only when communities break down, common goals are forgotten, and "the desire for individual advancement or other forms of competition dominate, [will] each person want and need individual safeguards or rights" [ibid.]. Ihara concludes that moral systems devoid of rights might not be "practical" in the modern world, but that this is a different failing from the kind of moral unacceptability for which Feinberg had argued.

I believe we should agree with Ihara that claiming rights need not be the only route to self-respect and human dignity, unless those notions are defined so narrowly as to beg the question against a non-rights morality like Confucianism. Ihara's conclusion, however, is based on too sanguine a view of moral reality, and we can see this by looking back at Chinese rights discourse. At least as early as the beginning of the twentieth century, Chinese thinkers argued that the Chinese people needed to develop "rights consciousness." As we saw earlier, Liang Qichao and others believed that their contemporaries needed to put more stress on individual achievement and individual interests. This idea is repeated, in almost the same words, by Luo and He in the article we examined a short while ago. Luo and He argued that rights take on reality through being claimed; people must awaken to their self-interests for them and their entire nation to progress morally, socially, and economically.

The idea that we have rights only if we claim them, which may have originated with Jhering, makes particularly good sense in light of the pragmatic theories about the origin of rights which, as we have seen, most contemporary participants in Chinese rights discourse hold. If the norms to which we hold ourselves are implicit in our practice, then what we do – whether or not we recognize our interests and claim our rights – matters. This is not to say that what we do wholly determines what rights we have; it is possible that we can have important interests which merit protection without always being aware of it. Our commitment to the importance of such interests may, for a time, be implicit in others of our commitments, rather than fully explicit. Still, as Luo and He argue, it is more convincing to see the ever-broadening scope of rights as a process of new rights being created when new groups articulate and claim their legitimate self-interests, rather than as a process of the gradual discovery of the natural rights that we have all always had.

The upshot of all of this is that Raz can borrow an answer to my query from the Chinese tradition. Rather than say, with Feinberg, that we care about rights because they provide the only route to self-respect, he should say, with Liang and the rest, that we care about rights because only this kind of caring assures that rights and their correlative duties will exist at all, and thus that our important self-interests will be protected. Now I do not mean to imply that such an answer settles this matter conclusively; my proviso a moment ago about the possibility of being unaware of important interests, for instance, may suggest that more needs to be said to clarify how this affects the underlying argument. Be this as it may, my main point here is to illustrate the ways in which Chinese and Western theories can apparently engage productively with one another.

8.2 RIGHTS AND HARMONY

I have already noted that Peerenboom believes the stress on interests in Chinese rights discourse to be related to a belief in the ultimate harmony of all interests. It will be worthwhile, therefore, to take a brief look at contemporary Western views of harmony and conflict as they relate to rights. I will then turn to recent Chinese views, focusing on the difference that emerges between thinking that interests – and the rights which protect them – can be unified, and thinking that they can be harmonized. At the end of this section I argue that harmony is a reasonable goal to seek within a community that shares at least certain common goals or traditions.

8.2.1 Conflict versus Harmony in Western Theorizing

I begin with Dworkin, who announces: "The concept of rights, and particularly the concept of rights against the Government, has its most
natural use when a political society is divided, and appeals to cooperation or a common goal are pointless" [Dworkin 1977, p. 184]. Dworkin
thus strongly implies that rights have their central applications in cases
of conflict between an individual's interest and the interests of others. At
some level this must be true: We have seen that rights protect interests,
and the notion of "protection" makes little sense unless the interests are
being protected from someone who has a conflicting interest. Dworkin's
discussion of rights as "trumps" over common interests, however, implies
more than just a local conflict between two people; it suggests that rights
regularly protect people against claims based on common goals or the
common interest. We have also already noted that Peerenboom believes
that Chinese rights discourse downplays the real conflicts at the root of
our rights.

Raz disagrees, at least in part. He sees rights as most commonly and
naturally grounded in a harmony of interests between individual right-
holders and others in their societies. His target is the view, implied in
Dworkin's statement, that the "special function" of rights in moral or
political thought is to "represent the individual's perspective or interest
against the general or public good, or against the claims, demands, or
requirements of others generally" [Raz 1992, p. 127]. Raz begins by
asking why rights are given more weight than the interests of the right-
holders involved would seem to justify. We saw earlier that it is essential
to the idea of rights that one's right to something count for more than
just the degree to which one's interests are served by that something:
Mary's right to park in her driveway is stronger than her mere interest
(at a given moment) in parking. Why? Dworkin's answer – and the
answer that would be given by any of the theorists on Peerenboom's list
of Western, deontological rights theorists – is that such protection serves
to ensure the dignity of the individual.[15]

Raz argues instead that rights tend to serve common interests or goals
at the same time that they serve individual interests. He writes that "the
weight of the right does not match the weight of the right-holder's interest which it serves, because . . . the right is justified by the fact that by

---

[15] See [Dworkin 1977, p. 198]. Dworkin believes that the point of rights is a combination
of protecting human dignity and promoting political equality.

serving the interest of the right-holder it serves the interest of some others, and their interest contributes to determining the weight due to the right" [Raz 1992, p. 133]. Other people's interests contribute to the justification of the right, in other words, when they are "harmoniously interwoven with those of the right-holder" [ibid., p. 134], which Raz takes to be the normal case.

Let us consider one of Raz's examples:

> The right of free expression is among the foundation stones of all political democracies. [It] serves to protect the interest of those who have it and who may wish to use it to express their views. It also serves the interest of all those who have an interest in acquiring information from others. But here again the right serves the interests of those who are neither speakers nor listeners. Everyone who lives in a democracy is affected by the fact that this is a society enjoying a free exchange of information. One may go one step further. If I were to choose between living in a society which enjoys freedom of expression, but not having the right myself, or enjoying the right in a society which does not have it, I would have no hesitation in judging that my own personal interest is better served by opting for the first option. [1992, p. 137]

He adds that for certain people – politicians, writers, and the like – this right means a great deal to their daily lives. For most others, though, it has little direct impact, and "it rightly means less to them than their success in their chosen occupation, the fortunes of their marriages, or the state of repair of their homes" [ibid.].

To the extent Raz is successful in explaining the weight we place on rights by highlighting the ways in which individual rights serve common interests, he relies on the existence of a "wide-ranging consensus" on what the common good is, which consensus he takes to derive in part from "the background of a common tradition" [ibid., p. 141]. In an effort to make the continued existence of such traditions plausible, Raz stresses that heated rhetoric and public controversy are not equivalent to fundamental conflict. He concedes that occasionally there is conflict between individual and common interests, but insists that the primary relation between them is "supportive" [ibid.].

I believe there is much truth in Raz's analysis: Individual and common interests do tend to reinforce one another in harmonious ways, and this helps us to understand the weight we place on individual rights. For this to be plausible, it is crucial that we distinguish between "common interests" and "state interests," where "state" is understood to apply to the government and bureaucracy. The interests of a nation's rulers will usually diverge from the common interests of the whole collectivity: Most obviously, it may well be in the rulers' interests, but perhaps not in the collective's, for those particular rulers to remain in power. As we will see later, there is a decent argument to be made for the importance, to Chinese individuals as well as to the Chinese people collectively, of a stable and independent nation-state. This is different from saying that an unchanging government is good for those in the government. If we are to understand Raz and like-minded Chinese theorists charitably, we must keep this difference in mind.

I am troubled by one aspect of Raz's argument. He draws a stronger conclusion than he needs to, and this stronger conclusion is vulnerable to criticism on several grounds. In order to be clear on just what I think we should take from Raz, let me quickly explore these problems. Raz summarizes his argument as having two stages: (1) "the protection of individual . . . rights serves the common good," and (2) "the common good served by those rights is, in the majority of cases, more important to individuals than the enjoyment of their own . . . rights." This leads him to the conclusion that (3) "therefore . . . the status the rights enjoy in the liberal democracies is due to their contribution to the common good" [ibid., p. 136]. This conclusion, however, simply does not follow from the two premises. It certainly follows from (1) and (2) that *part* of the justi-fication for the status that rights enjoy comes from their contribution to the common good, but nothing Raz has said requires the stronger conclusion.

More importantly, (3) as it stands seems to deny that an individual's interest in dignity or autonomy plays an important role in grounding rights. But Raz himself, in other writings, assigns a high priority to "autonomy-based duties" [Raz 1986, p. 408]: Autonomy is a central con-stituent of our well-being, and our interest in autonomy thus grounds both duties and rights. In addition, Raz's (3) seems to leave no room for rights in cases where individual and common interests *do* conflict – even though his discussion of our interest in autonomy could readily ground such rights.

Neither of these criticisms is telling against Raz's main point, which is simply that the individual and common interests that ground rights are typically "harmoniously interwoven." He simply needs to more carefully qualify the ways in which he states this conclusion. I thus substantially agree with the following characterization of his argument:

Little has been said [here] to challenge directly theories such as Nozick's [1974], which start from first principles to derive propositions sustaining a view of rights in which their conflict with the interests and moral claims of others [is] central. But enough has been said to suggest that such views are radically revisionary. They gain no support from a balanced understanding of our concept of rights, nor from the role of rights in our moral and political culture. [Raz 1992, p. 141]

Once again, this is completely consistent with having shown only that common interests are a substantial, but not total, explanation of the weight we place on individual rights.

8.2.2 Chinese Harmony

Turning now to Chinese theorizing about the relation between rights and harmony, I begin with activist discourse from 1978 to the present. A contemporary scholar has written that while there were some important differences between the Democracy Wall movement and the Tiananmen movement, there was a particularly strong continuity between them in their "inadequate attention to the conflictive nature of interests" [Guang 1996, p. 426]. In each case, he says, democracy "became a symbol of harmony of interests instead of a means for reconciling differences" [ibid., p. 429]. To a certain extent I agree with this analysis, but as we work through what both activists and scholars have said along these lines, we will see that there is an important distinction between trying to remove all differences and create a unity of interests, on the one hand, and respecting at least some differences while creating a harmony of interests, on the other.

Consider, for instance, what Wei Jingsheng said about democracy in his "The Fifth Modernization":

Democracy regards harmony with individuality as its basic condition of existence; essentially, this is a form of cooperation. Nobody can find any form of totalitarianism without suppression of individuality and enslavement of people. Similarly, nobody can find any form of democracy without a foundation of harmony of the individuality of the majority of citizens. [Wei 1980a, p. 58]

Similarly, in another article from the same period, he writes that

229

> In actual life, different people have different ideas. If people are not free to live and do things as they wish, it is impossible to have large-scale cooperation on a voluntary basis or to establish a cooperative social structure. Hence, to begin with, democracy must be a social system that protects freedom. On the basis of freedom, it must encourage voluntary cooperation and achieve unity of relatively unanimous interests. [Wei 1980b, p. 145]

I take it that the "unity" to which Wei here refers is part of the larger harmony that he seeks: When people with different ideas and interests manage to establish a harmonious social structure, some subset of their interests will, presumably, turn out to overlap and thus be unified. As I will later discuss further, though, such a unity ought not be seen as essential to a harmony of interests.

The scholar cited a moment ago also notes that activists in 1989 "shunned 'special rights and interests' and claimed to be 'spokesmen for the entire nation and the vanguard of social justice'" [Guang 1996, p. 428]. He adds that the hunger strikers represented the extreme of self-sacrifice in the name of a collective goal. I agree that we see in these instances evidence of a belief in the unity of all interests. At the same time, as this scholar recognizes, some 1989 activists did explicitly talk of "pluralism." In a speech delivered by Ren Wanding, the founder of the China Human Rights League in 1978 and again active in the 1989 movement, pluralism was highlighted:

> I maintain that the long-term goal of China's democratic movement must naturally be the nonviolent reform of the present social-political structure of unified, centralized party leadership. This structure must be supplanted by a pluralistic social-political structure, a pluralistic democracy, a pluralistic culture, and a pluralistic nation. [Ren 1990 (1989), pp. 122–3]

Ren does not go into much more detail about what he means by "pluralism," other than to make clear he envisions some form of multi-party democracy – a view which, however, did not resonate with all members of his audience [Han 1990, p. 121]. Ren sees pluralism as opposed to unity, but does not explicitly raise the issue of harmony. Let us turn now to academic discourse in the 1990s and see how these themes are developed.

Zhang Wenxian, whose thoughts on the relation between rights and interests we have already discussed, is among those who touch on our current topic. Recall that Zhang wrote

When the state establishes or utilizes law to proclaim various kinds of rights, it has already weighed individual, collective, and social interests in accord with the people's general will and publicly acknowledged standards of value. Individual and collective rights, like social rights, thus internally manifest the unification of individual, collective, national, and even human fundamental interests, [and thus] all are affirmations of legitimate interests. [Zhang 1992, p. 40]

Zhang also implied that what the state was doing when it engaged in this weighing of interests and determination of the general will was discovering people's "due rights," which its policies would attempt to realize, as legal rights, to the extent possible.

What does it mean to say that rights "internally manifest" the unity of all interests? Raz's talk of the ways in which individual and collective interests can be "harmoniously interwoven" together suggests one gloss. Just as for Raz rights are justified by the support they receive from different types of interests, so for Zhang rights emerge when individual and collective interests can be jointly protected. There is an important difference between the two views, however: Where Raz speaks of "harmonization," Zhang says "unification." As I will later discuss further, harmony allows for – indeed, depends upon – difference in a way that unity does not. One way of reading the claim that rights are based on the unification of interests is that rights would protect individual interests only insofar as they did not differ from a collectively determined (or state-determined) standard. In addition, as we will explore in a moment, to the extent that interests are thought to be unifiable, rights can cease to seem worth pursuing at all.

The relationship between rights and harmony has been addressed most explicitly in contemporary China by Xia Yong, a professor at the Chinese Academy of Social Sciences. In the concluding chapter to his *The Origins and Foundations of Human Rights: A Chinese Interpretation*, Xia argues that human rights and harmony not only can, but also ought to, come hand in hand.[16] Xia takes as his stalking horse the assertion that Confucian concern with harmony explains the lack of rights talk in the Chinese tradition. He begins by citing several examples of harmony in nature, and then asserts that harmony is actually the basis of the

---

[16] This chapter is reprinted, as "*Renquan yu Zhonguo Chuantong* (Human Rights and the Chinese Tradition)" in [Xia 1996]. I follow the original pagination.

universe, including both humanity and society. He thus applauds the Confucian equation of harmony with "spontaneity (*ziran*)," which he contrasts with the Western idea of nature – as in "natural law" – as a transcendent source of meaning and order imposed from outside of concrete reality [Xia 1992, p. 187].

It is easy to see what Xia means by saying that spontaneous harmony is the basis of the universe, though we might sometimes be more tempted to speak of "equilibrium" than "harmony." Anything that persists in the world does so by maintaining a kind of harmony with its environment. Xia mentions the relations between plants and the seasons, for instance; I note that it is only a short step from here to the classic statement in *Xunzi* of the need for humans to similarly harmonize with the seasons (in planting and harvesting, to cite a basic example) if they are to thrive.[17] Any balanced account of these matters, of course, must also take change into account. Evolution gives us an example of gradual change; attempts by humans to transform our physical environments or to increase crop yields are examples of more rapid changes. Still, the former makes sense only within a framework of success coming from harmonizing with one's environment (albeit perhaps even better than a predecessor), and the latter can succeed only if the new arrangement establishes a new harmony. Both of these are consistent with Xia's idea of harmony that is spontaneous, thus emergent, thus neither pre-configured nor eternal.

Xia sees various sorts of struggle or competition (both theoretical and practical) as central to Western political and moral theory, and as central to the emergence of the idea of rights. An important premise of rights, he argues, is the separation and independence of its subjects: In order to hold rights, people must be distinct from one another, and perhaps even have distinct interests [ibid., p. 182]. Xia looks at traditional Chinese economic, political, and cultural realities, and in each case finds evidence for inadequate separation between people to ground full-fledged rights. On this basis he tentatively concludes that an overemphasis on harmony was an obstacle to the development of rights thinking in traditional China, but Xia clarifies his finding in the essay's final section. Harmony and human rights, he concludes, are not incompatible; after all, he has argued that harmony is central to all natural and social processes. Xia even stresses that the traditional system of *lifa* (rites and laws) was not itself

---

[17] See *Xunzi* 17.

the problem. Instead he lays blame at the feet of the concrete culture that produced both the *lifa* system of values and, partly through those values, exaggerated the role of harmony in society at the expense of recognizing the realities of conflict. Xia suggests that in principle, *lifa* and human rights can coexist, though the particular culture (and class society, etc.) that produced the ideas behind *lifa* was indeed inimical to human rights. Xia's fundamental idea seems to be this: Systems of social norms are not free-floating, but rather are produced in, and tend to reinforce, particular systems of social and economic organization. In a way, this is just an application of his claim about the ubiquity of harmony, for if a value system and its concrete social and material environments are not in some kind of equilibrium, one or both will change or be rejected. This insight has roots in Marxism, but one need not be a Marxist to accept its wisdom.

How should we think about human rights and the Chinese tradition, then? Xia's answer is that, first, the traditional social-economic-political structure did pose barriers to the development of human rights discourse. Xia wants to stress, though, that the obstacles were less the values themselves than the concrete institutions. He insists that something very like those values (*lifa*) is compatible with human rights, and thus all that would be required to support such a combination, we can conclude, is a social structure congenial to them.

This may sound very speculative, but Xia actually has two such social structures in mind: contemporary China and the contemporary West. Xia notices that harmony comes from a proper balance between separation and connection. Too much separation leads to atomism or individualism (in a pejorative sense); too much connection leads to unity (*"heyi"* and *"yitong"* in Chinese) [ibid., pp. 188–90]. He believes that in the West, competition and conflict are overdeveloped. Moving toward embracing harmony would mean moderating these tendencies, but would not require rejecting human rights. China, according to Xia, traditionally had little sense of opposition or separation, and this has been even more true under many of the last fifty years of communist rule. Now that Xia has introduced the contrast between unity and (mere) harmony, we can more precisely diagnose China's difficulty: Rather than too much harmony, we should instead say that its values and its social structures have pressed for unity. Xia's solution to this is to embrace difference to the degree necessary for harmony and human rights to flourish, without going all the way to the selfish individualism he sees rampant in the West.

8.2.3 Engaging Harmony

As we reflect on the Chinese views just outlined, I think that the central question which we have to answer is what to make of the differences between rights views that aim at unity, aim at harmony, or accept conflict. The first, as I have already hinted, I believe we should find problematic; the last, which I will associate with Dworkin for present purposes, is clearly at odds with much Chinese theorizing about rights. If Chinese theorists are to be able to articulate and sustain a distinctive conception of rights, then I believe a great deal will rest on the notion of harmony.

Xia Yong, at least, insists that there is a crucial difference between unity and harmony. Unity leads to stability through making everyone the same; harmony seeks the same end through accommodating differences. In an essay called "Confucian Harmony and Freedom of Thought," Peerenboom has looked at the question of harmony which, as I noted earlier, he believes to lie at the core of China's trouble with rights. Much of what Peerenboom says about harmony is very astute, and I will draw on his analysis in a moment. Peerenboom is convinced, though, that harmony ultimately collapses into unity. He argues that Chinese thinkers have held that harmony must be sought through "persuading, cajoling, and manipulating others" to come to share a single vision of the good, and this "single vision" seems to him to require a "Confucian utopia where the interests of the individual and the community coincide" [Peerenboom 1998, pp. 240, 250–1]. Only Western-style deontological rights, he concludes, support "pluralism" by serving as "anti-majoritarian" trumps to keep collective interests from overpowering the conflicting, divergent interests of individuals.

I do not want to deny that some Chinese thinkers and many Chinese leaders have, throughout Chinese history, attempted to impose a uniformity of thinking and valuing. Peerenboom begins his article with a quote from Deng Xiaoping: "We have stressed the need for the strengthening of Party leadership, democratic centralism, and centralization and unification. The most important aspect of centralization and unification is the unification of thought. This is essential if we are to have unity in our actions."[18] My question is whether the kind of unification sought by Deng

---

[18] [Deng 1992, vol. 1, p. 286]; quoted in [Peerenboom 1998, p. 234]. Donald Munro has emphasized the tendency of Confucian thought to seek single-minded unity; see both [Munro 1988] and [Munro 1996].

is aimed at harmony, or whether harmony and unity really are two distinct goals, as Xia Yong has argued.

I think that the seeds of an answer to this question that supports Xia Yong's view are contained in Peerenboom's own definition of "harmony." He writes that "harmony is a contextual concept at odds with the idea of a single, objective, universal normative order. The goal is to combine the diverse elements of the many members of a particular society at a particular time into a single, cohesive whole" [Peerenboom 1998, p. 240]. Harmony is like pluralism, in other words, because both reject the idea of a single, objective, universal normative order. Many versions of the unity idea, in contrast, assume precisely such an order as a way to justify their goal. Still, Peerenboom is bothered by the fact that while harmony posits no single normative order that stands for all time, it does seem to require that at any given point in time, a way of reconciling all interests into a "single, cohesive whole" must exist. Thanks to this second kind of singularity, Peerenboom apparently sees unity and harmony as equally problematic.

They are not. Unity demands sameness of thoughts and interests; harmony does not. The "diverse elements" to which Peerenboom refers can think differently from one another, and their interests can diverge. To choose a simple example, members of a family all have different interests, in addition to there being interests which the family as a collective may have, but which individuals may or may not recognize as their own. Jane and her husband Tim want to succeed in their different careers; her success in hers contributes little to his success in his, and may even lead to greater conflicts: Her increased need to travel or longer hours at the office might increase the time he needs to spend away from his office with their children. If they were only two professionals who had been thrown together by chance, there might be little hope for harmony to emerge. Luckily, families' members do not (in general) conceive of themselves so narrowly. In addition to being an accountant (let us suppose), Tim is a husband, father, brother, son, and so on, and he recognizes interests and commitments that go along with each of these relationships. He cares about his wife's professional success for all kinds of reasons, and cares about his children's well-being for many more. Jane is bound up in a similar net of relationships, with the result that the two of them can probably balance, compromise, tweak, and (perhaps) cajole their way to a harmonious "cohesive whole." For now, at least. There will be more work to do when she gets a promotion, or he gets a job offer, or whatever.

The contrast between this example of harmony and a case of unity is stark, because unity would require that everyone's interests be the same. One way of imagining this would be to suppose that everyone in the family had to be committed to Tim's professional success. Perhaps other values and interests would be allowed, but only insofar as they did not conflict with this overriding goal. Is it good for Tim's career for him to take a job in Beijing? Then off the family goes, with nary a thought – if their interests and commitments really are unified – to friends, family, or jobs left behind. While moves like this are all-too-familiar parts of recent American life, the psychological picture that unity requires is unsettling, to say the least.

Before reflecting on these contrasting examples, we should pause to consider how relevant family-based examples really are. In the end, issues of rights come up more often in contexts like our diverse, hetero-geneous state, rather than our more homogeneous families. While Chinese Confucians have long relied on an analogy between family and state, contemporary critics have argued that there are important differ-ences between them – one of which might be that the state is more likely to be a site of irreconcilably conflicting interests.[19] States may in fact be better than families at sustaining themselves in the face of deep conflict and despite an absence of shared values; for one thing, states can rely on coercion to a degree usually not found in families. To say this is not to admit, though, that states are immune to the kind of harmony here dis-cussed. The many ways in which our interests overlap with those of others in a state provide much the same fertile ground for balancing, compromising, and cajoling as that found in a family, in ways that I will touch on later. It bears remembering, finally, that Raz's original claims were made with respect to the citizens of states.

To what degree can people's values differ from one another without impairing their ability to achieve harmony? This is the core issue for Peerenboom; he writes that achieving harmony "requires a common value structure. The role of government and particularly the ruler is to establish the basis for such a common value structure by providing ideological guidance and moral leadership" [1998, p. 241]. "Common value structure" is importantly ambiguous. Recall that Raz, too, speaks of a "wide-ranging consensus" on what the common good is, which

---

[19] For two perspectives on the problems with extending Confucian norms from family to state, see [Yu 1994, p. 27] and [Ci 1999, pp. 334–5].

consensus he takes to derive in part from "the background of a common tradition." Does this, too, end up collapsing into a unity of interests? I think not. Harmony is a solution to potentially conflicting differences that emerges out of particular configurations of values, traditions, and social and economic conditions. In Xia Yong's biological analogies, there is no reason to think that common interests predate the emergence of a harmonious equilibrium in an ecosystem; similarly, if a harmonious reconciliation of diverse individual interests and various collective interests is possible in a given situation, that need not be based on any prior agreement. Indeed, as Peerenboom says, leadership in traditional China, at least, was "predicated on a heightened capacity to perceive patterns in the diversity, to discern possibilities for order where others see only endless chaos" [ibid.].

This may sound extraordinarily idealistic, perhaps depending on sage rulers to make it work. According to neo-Confucian theory, that may have been true. But I think that contemporary Chinese rights theorists have something rather different in mind when they talk of harmony. Or at least, I believe that the tradition of Chinese rights discourse has made available other, more plausible options, whether or not they are what Xia Yong intends. The first thing to consider is the fairly consistent characterization by twentieth-century rights theorists of the sorts of interests that we ought to prioritize when seeking to arrive at a harmonious solution. Again and again we have seen reference to fulfilling one's "personality (*renge*)" and to protecting that which enables us to be persons (*zuoren*). This is not the place to explore in detail these criteria, but it is important to note that their open-ended guidance should be helpful in achieving harmony. This is one level – the existence of a common vocabulary in terms of which to describe our interests – on which "the background of a common tradition" is important.

Second, recall the ideas of Gao Yihan about harmony, discussed two chapters ago. An obvious route to harmony, suggested by my husband-and-wife example, is negotiation: Where we have diverse but overlapping interests, free and cooperative negotiation is perhaps more likely than any other means to reach a harmonious solution. This idea is implicit in some of Gao's early writings, as indeed it is in Wei Jingsheng's "Fifth Modernization." Gao recognized, though, that differences in power can make negotiation problematic. His solution, building on the ideas of his contemporaries in England and elsewhere, was pluralistic sovereignty: Give different bodies in society legitimate powers, rather than reserve all sovereignty for the state. I believe that this once again demonstrates the difference between harmony and unity as goals; those who advocate the latter want to arrogate all power to the state, since only a complete monopoly on legitimate power can lead to unity, as the earlier quotation from Deng Xiaoping recognizes.

It might be objected that notions like "personality" are too diffuse to ground an effective regime of rights; haven't the experiences of the last seventy-five years amply demonstrated the vulnerability of such rights conceptions to state manipulation? Doesn't harmony in the end collapse into unity, in practice if not in principle? It seems to me that the answers to these questions depend in large part on whether a rights regime that is based on the idea of harmonizing interests like "personality" can be successfully institutionalized: whether they can, in the terms current in China, be transformed from due rights into legal rights. The difficulties with institutionalizing rights regimes in twentieth-century China have had many causes, not least the fact that many power-holders have explicitly sought unity, rather than harmony, which has precisely the drawbacks that Peerenboom identifies. To look at only a single example, consider that Sun Yatsen (1866–1925), the founder of the Nationalist Party and widely acclaimed as the father of modern China, favored "revolutionary rights," which meant rights only for those who were committed to a particular revolutionary program.[20]

Such difficulties with institutionalizing a rights regime in China apply just as much to conflict-based models as they do to harmony-based ideas, so perhaps the latter are no worse off than the former. My central contention here is that the agreement on vocabulary ("personality" and so on) that we have seen may suggest that there is a conception of the common good rich enough to underwrite a wide range of rights in something like the manner that Raz suggested earlier in this chapter. Questions about how much of a "common tradition" is required for harmony to be achievable and about how much common tradition contemporary Chinese can be said to share need careful study. It seems clear, at the very least, that those who believe China can develop an effective rights regime based on the distinctive concept of rights I have been examining here must face squarely the issue of whether the Chinese have, or can re-manufacture, such a common tradition.

---

[20] See Chapter 7 for its discussion of "revolutionary rights" in the thought of both nationalists and communists. See also the essays by Sun and Zhou Fohai in [Angle & Svensson 2001].

Finally, does a stress on the role of harmonized interests in justifying rights imply that there are never conflicts of interest between individuals and larger groups? Before I answer these questions, recognize that while there may be considerable disagreement about how best to realize goals like the fulfillment of personality, Raz cautions that we should not "equate controversy with conflict of interests" [1992, p. 141]. Vigorous argument can often be about how best to realize ideals, rather than representing fundamental differences over the ideals themselves. This is not to say that all appearances of conflict are mirages. Raz makes it quite clear that such conflicts persist. While "the range and nature of common goods" constrain the "channels which define the well-being of individuals," this nonetheless "leaves ample room for occasional conflicts between individual well-being and the common good" [ibid.]. Interests which conflict with the common good can also be protected by rights, so long as there are adequately strong reasons for doing so. Raz's main point, which I believe he shares with his Chinese contemporaries, is that most rights – including those which most obviously protect individuals against the state – are not grounded on conflicts with the common good, but rather on an essential harmony.

8.3 POLITICAL VERSUS ECONOMIC RIGHTS

As a final perspective on the idea that Chinese and Western conceptions of rights differ from one another, let us now look at whether Chinese ideas of rights, and especially of human rights, put greater stress on economic rights than do their counterparts in the West. First I will explore the degree to which there is a real difference along this dimension between Chinese and Western rights views. We will see that while there is some truth to the idea, things are considerably more complex and contested, in both China and the West, than this simple dichotomy suggests. Second, I will look at the arguments some Chinese have used to justify putting economic development, as well as national independence and sovereignty, ahead of full-fledged political freedoms. These arguments are rarely taken seriously by Western analysts, who see them as merely excuses for political repression by China's leaders. Without wanting to deny the possibility of such motives, I will strive to consider the Chinese arguments more carefully, looking to see whether viewing the arguments in the context of China's tradition of rights discourse helps to illuminate their appeal.

8.3.1 Complex Reality

The claim that Chinese rights concepts put more weight on economics than do Western ones is typically put in a very strong form: Chinese views emphasize economic rights at the expense of political freedoms, while Western views focus solely on political rights and ignore economic ones. Each side, according to this understanding of the difference between China and the West, privileges one form of rights over the other. There is indeed a certain amount of truth in this characterization: Numerous representatives of the United States government have downplayed or even rejected the idea of economic rights over the last twenty-five years, and Chinese government documents and spokespeople have argued that "subsistence rights (*shengcun quan*)" – a primarily economic notion – are more fundamental than political freedoms. As we look into these ideas, though, we will see both that other participants in Western rights discourse hold views at odds with that of the United States government, and that Chinese views on this topic are complex and internally contested.

One of the touchstones for United States governmental policy on economic rights is the International Covenant on Economic, Social, and Cultural Rights, passed by the United Nations General Assembly in 1966. The Carter administration made a concerted effort to have the covenant ratified by the U. S. Senate in 1978, with no success. Even though the Carter administration favored ratification, their understanding of the substance of the covenant suggests that they did not view its provisions as rights-claims on a par with political rights. In a variety of forums, the administration argued that the covenant was no more than a "statement of goals to be achieved progressively," imposing no obligation other than "work[ing] toward the eventual achievement of . . . minimum standards."[21]

If the Carter administration implicitly undermined the status of economic rights, the Reagan administration made it explicit. A 1981 State Department memorandum "endorsed the unqualified rejection of economic, social, and cultural rights as 'rights,'" and asserted that "human rights were to be explicitly defined for the purposes of future U.S. foreign policy as 'meaning political rights and civil liberties'" [Alston 1990,

---

[21] Quoted in [Alston 1990, p. 377].

p. 372]. Since 1981, this policy has been repeated and elaborated but has not been significantly changed.

That, then, is the truth in the notion that Western concepts of rights do not include economic aspects. If "West" meant "United States government," and if we looked only at current views – ignoring, for instance, the "economic Bill of Rights" advocated by the Roosevelt administration in 1944 [Alston 1990, p. 387] – then perhaps the notion could be sustained. Many Americans outside of the government and many leaders and scholars in other Western nations, however, reject the U. S. government's conception of rights. To begin with, virtually all Western governments except the United States have ratified the covenant.[22] Economic rights have been championed by many of these states for years, both in international arenas like the United Nations and in domestic legislation. The Universal Declaration of Human Rights, in addition, makes explicit a variety of economic and other non-political rights, showing no awareness of the idea that economic rights are somehow less than equal partners with their political brethren. A number of Western and (in particular) American scholars, finally, have argued that economic rights are just as important as political rights.[23]

Only a quite narrow range of "Western" contributors to rights discourse, in short, endorse the idea that political rights are more important than economic ones.[24] Given the ways in which the U.S. government puts its resistance to economic rights in terms of denying that such "rights" create any obligations, it seems likely that an important motive for the policy is not wanting to foot the bill for realizing the economic rights of the rest of the world. Whatever we make of this reasoning, and whether or not we think it a likely result of recognizing an equal partnership between economic and political rights, I want to turn now to looking at the complexities underlying the Chinese position(s) on this issue.

Most Chinese commentators on rights over the last ten years, both in and outside of government, have said that political, economic, and other rights are interdependent and equal. In his remarks to the 1993 Vienna

[22] For the most recent data on which countries have signed which treaties, see ⟨http://www.unhchr.ch/data.htm⟩.

[23] The best-known such account can be found in [Shue 1996 (1980)].

[24] Be this as it may, Chinese commentators regularly assert that the "West" looks solely at political rights; see, for example, [Liu 1996a, p. 122]. Given the power of the U.S. government to influence international initiatives, this view of the West is perhaps understandable.

World Conference on Human Rights, for instance, Ambassador Liu Huaqiu asserted that "The concept of human rights is an integral one, including both individual and collective rights. Individual rights cover not only civil and political rights but also economic, social, and cultural rights. The various aspects of human rights are interdependent, equally important, and indispensable" [Liu Huaqiu 1995, p. 214]. Similar statements can be found in Chinese academic discourse, as when a professor at the Chinese Academy of Social Sciences writes that "Developing countries hold that [civil and political rights, on the one hand, and economic, social, and cultural rights, on the other] are interrelated and interdependent and both necessary for safeguarding personalities" [Liu 1996a, p. 122; see also translation in Liu 1996b, p. 110].

Despite the fact that Chinese analysts, by and large, claim equal importance for the various kinds of rights, government spokespeople and most academics go on to argue that in China's particular situation, some rights must be pursued before others. Liu Huaqiu adds, immediately after the passage quoted in the previous paragraph, that "For the vast number of developing countries to respect and protect human rights is first and foremost to ensure the full realization of the rights to subsistence and development" [Liu Huaqiu 1995, p. 214]. The government's white paper on human rights of 1991 similarly says that "To solve their human rights problems, the first thing for the Chinese people to do is, for historical reasons, to secure the right to subsistence" [Information Council 1991].

Before pausing to consider what exactly the "right to subsistence" is, it is important to see that the official argument does not stop here. The white paper maintains that "Without national independence, there would be no guarantee for the people's lives" [ibid.], while Liu Huaqiu says that "As a people that used to suffer tremendously from aggression by big powers but now enjoys independence, the Chinese have come to realize fully that state sovereignty is the basis of the realization of citizens' human rights" [Liu Huaqiu 1995, p. 215].[25] The argument is: Without the right to subsistence, no other human rights; without national independence, no right to subsistence; without state sovereignty, no national independence – and the white paper throws in "national strength" and "national stability" as further necessary conditions [Information Council 1991]. What should we make of this?

---

[25] For excellent discussion of the background to these and other official statements of Chinese human rights views, see [Kent 1999, pp. 155–60].

8.3.2 Analysis and Engagement

In light of the foregoing, the following questions present themselves. First, can a good case be made for the U.S. government view that economic rights are not genuine rights? Next, what exactly is the "right to subsistence"? Third, can a good case be made for its being, at least in the particular circumstances of China and other developing countries, the "first thing" to which Chinese people should attend – especially in light of the commitment, acknowledged by all who make that claim, to equal and interdependent political and economic rights? Finally, if the importance of the right to subsistence is sustained, can a similarly strong case be made for linking it to national independence and state sovereignty?

Arguments against granting economic rights the status of rights fall into three categories: first, those based on the political effects of such a recognition; second, historical arguments; third, conceptual arguments. In the first category belong considerations like charges that a recognition of economic rights will confuse international human rights discourse, take attention away from the real priorities of political rights, and allow rogue regimes to excuse political rights violations in the name of promoting economic rights.[26] In general, these seem simply to beg the question against economic rights. If there are such rights, shouldn't they receive our attention?

Historical arguments to the effect that rights emerged out of the Anglo-American ethical and political tradition, which did not countenance economic rights, are problematic for two reasons. First, economic rights can be found in that earlier tradition, and certainly in more recent documents like the Universal Declaration. Second, as I have demonstrated throughout this book, even though historical research can be invaluable in clarifying how concepts should be understood, it is nonetheless true that concepts within normative traditions can and often should change over time.

Conceptual arguments, finally, tend to be based on the distinction between "negative" and "positive" rights. The former are supposed merely to involve leaving people alone, as when we refrain from torturing them; the latter require positive action on our part, as when we provide someone with an education. Positive rights have been criticized

---

[26] So argued U.S. Assistant Secretary of State Elliott Abrams, for instance. See [Alston 1990, p. 373].

both for requiring government infringement on people's private domains and choices, and for identifying rights without clearly specifying the people or bodies who hold the duties to fulfill those rights.[27] This distinction between positive and negative rights has been effectively criticized by Henry Shue, who demonstrates the ways in which virtually all rights have both positive and negative aspects [Shue 1996 (1980), ch. 2]. Joseph Raz's understanding of rights, discussed earlier at some length, emphasizes the ways in which rights can generate different sorts of duties in different contexts, which undermines the objection that there is no single, clear duty-holder in cases of positive rights [Raz 1984, p. 212]. I conclude that there is little to be said for the view, currently affirmed by the U.S. government, that economic rights are not genuine rights.

The next question is what the Chinese mean by a "right to subsistence."The Chinese term is the right to "*shengcun*," which in various contexts can be translated as "subsist," "exist," or "live." "Live" and "exist" do not fit the contexts in which the right to *shengcun* is discussed. The right to *shengcun* is not about merely existing or merely being alive. It is about living in a fuller sense: having food, shelter, clothing, access to health care, and even, in some formulations, some considerable political and cultural opportunities. It is glossed in publications like the 1991 white paper as including both "the basic guarantee of life and security" and a guarantee of the "basic means of livelihood" [Information Council 1991].[28]

The importance of such a right, with particular focus on its economic aspects, has long been recognized in China. I discussed one of the earliest formulations of "*shengcun quan*" earlier, in the context of Gao Yihan's view of rights. I believe we have seen ample evidence that even before the term "*shengcun quan*" was coined, participants in Chinese rights discourse tended to view material well-being as an important part of people's rights. Before explicit rights discourse began, the Confucians on whom I focused in Chapter 4 were very cognizant of people's need to fulfill their legitimate desires. Economic matters were at the heart of most nineteenth-century discussions of *quanli*. At the beginning of the

---

[27] Citations to and critical discussions of these claims can be found in [Alston 1990, p. 373] and [Shue 1996 (1980), ch. 2].

[28] [Kent 1993, p. 223] and [Kent 1999, p. 157] both argue that the phrase "*shengcun quan*" ought to be translated "right to existence," because the Chinese notion encompasses both physical security and minimal material well-being. Since, however, "subsistence" includes existence (physical security), while "existence" does not include subsistence (minimal material well-being), I find her argument puzzling and unconvincing.

twentieth century, Liang Qichao stressed that we ought to struggle for our ethically legitimate interests, among which subsistence concerns must surely rank highly. Liu Shipei argued for the importance of a right (and responsibility) to work in order for people to be "self-standing people." Chen Duxiu, finally, put increasing stress on the need for individuals to have economic, in addition to political, independence. Unlike some contemporary analysts, therefore, I believe that concern with something very like *"shengcun quan"* has a rich and strong connection to the prior tradition of rights discourse in China.[29]

My third question is whether a good case can be made for the priority which writings like the white paper put on the right to subsistence. Given my answer to the question about whether we ought to recognize economic rights as rights, the issue here is not whether there is a right to subsistence, nor even whether such a right is of extreme importance. I shall presume that it is. Instead, we need to ask whether the realization of other rights should be put on hold while the right to subsistence is pursued single-mindedly. The white paper asserts that "It is a simple truth that, for any country or nation, the right to subsistence is the most important of all human rights, without which the other rights are out of the question" [Information Council 1991]. The text then argues that thanks to a long period of semi-colonial exploitation, among other reasons, China today is not yet in a position to guarantee the "basic means of livelihood" to its people, and so it must focus its efforts on realizing this goal.

The argument's first premise, that without subsistence guarantees, the enjoyment of other rights is impossible, calls to mind the following argument of Gao Yihan's. Gao endorses the idea of a right to choose one's own work, but adds that without provision for training and the free time to seek a job, such a right is meaningless to many. He writes that "Pulling a rickshaw is in itself an inhumane job, but under the conditions of today's China, there are those who cannot even find work pulling rickshaws. Isn't telling such people to freely choose their work like telling

---

[29] [Kent 1999, p. 156] suggests that the Chinese got the idea of a right to subsistence primarily from Henry Shue's 1980 book *Basic Rights*, which had been quite influential in international discussions of human rights. [Svensson 1998] discusses the appearance of the "right to subsistence" in the 1920s, but argues that it was a new idea, derived primarily from Western socialist doctrines. I do not want to deny that these various sources have been important to the way the idea was articulated, in the 1920s or the 1990s, but do want to insist that we not view this as a novel addition, wholly without precedent, to Chinese rights discourse.

those so poor that they haven't enough to eat to go and choose the finest delicacies for their nourishment?" [Gao 1921, p. 5]. In Chapter 7 we also looked at the early Marxist Tan Mingqian's assertion that proletarians gained no political rights from the bourgeois political revolutions because there was not a genuine equality of opportunity. In the main I find these arguments compelling: Without the level of economic well-being sought via the right to subsistence, it is difficult or impossible to enjoy in practice political rights to which one might be entitled in principle.

This does not yet lead to the conclusion sought by the white paper, however. That argument turns on what arrangements are likely to lead to the actual enjoyment of rights, which opens up the question of whether a single-minded focus on satisfying subsistence needs is likely in practice to lead to the realization of the right to subsistence and subsequently to other rights. Here the claim made by members of the U.S. government that economic rights can serve as an excuse to avoid political rights takes on more relevance: It is not a good argument against economic rights being rights at all, but it can also be interpreted as a plea that we look with suspicion on any reasons advanced for failing to satisfy political rights. Even so, it still does not amount to an argument against the white paper's conclusions.

To assess the claims in the white paper, we need instead to ask: Does the articulation and enforcement of political rights, to one degree or another, help or hinder the realization of basic economic rights? Answering this question is of course an enormous undertaking, requiring both careful theoretical work and extensive empirical research. Amartya Sen is famous for his argument that famines do not occur in democracies, since pressure from the free press and opposition parties leads to steps being taken to alleviate possible famines – even in cases where food shortages are much more severe than in non-democratic countries that have experienced famines.[30] China's horrendous famine during the Great Leap Forward of 1959–62 is arguably a case in point: Under pressure from, or in the grip of, ideological goals, information about production did not flow freely, leading the government to take no action to mitigate food shortages until far too late. Sen notes that Mao Zedong himself said in 1962 that

---

[30] [Sen 1999] is one of his most recent and wide-ranging discussions of this thesis. See especially his chapter 7.

Without democracy, you have no understanding of what is happening down below; the situation will be unclear; you will be unable to collect sufficient opinions from all sides; there can be no communication between top and bottom; top-level organs of leadership will depend on one-sided and incorrect material to decide issues, thus you will find it difficult to avoid being subjectivist; it will be impossible to achieve unity of understanding and unity of action, and impossible to achieve true centralism. [Quoted in Sen 1999, p. 182; see Mao 1976, pp. 277–8]

Mao's understanding of democracy is obviously a far cry from multi-party, participatory democracy, nor does he suggest that any political rights are needed to carry out his vision of democracy. In light of discussions earlier in this chapter, it is interesting to see him endorsing "unity" as his ultimate goal. Sen, on the other hand, believes that more than information exchange is needed; rights to political participation lead to officials having incentives to act on the information they receive, or else risk the wrath of the electorate.

Even this brief discussion of the relevance of political rights to subsistence makes clear the complexity of the issues involved. Are political rights the only solution to famines, or would a solution like Mao's notion of democracy have been enough? Do other factors about the relevant societies matter? We can also turn these questions on their heads: Are there ways in which the pursuit of political rights impedes the realization of economic rights, as the white paper's argument implicitly assumes? How are these balanced against whatever economic gains might come from enforcing those same political rights? There should be ample room for engagement here between scholars both East and West on issues that to one degree or another matter to all of us.

Before we leave this issue, I must add that there is an essential difference between being provided with subsistence and having a right to subsistence. Slaves, to borrow a trope from earlier Chinese rights discourse, may be given the means to subsistence by their masters, but they have no rights. Free people, according to one common formulation, have moral claims to that which each of them needs "to be a person." The need to stand up and claim one's due, rather than passively waiting for things to be given one, has been a theme of Chinese rights discourse throughout the twentieth century. As we have seen throughout this book, Chinese rights theorists have almost always placed significant importance on political rights. Whatever we eventually discover about the relation between political rights and economic development, it may well be that to enjoy a *right to* subsistence requires the ability to claim things, and that political rights are necessary preconditions for such abilities.

My final question in this section is whether a case can be made for the linkage which many contemporary Chinese writings on rights seek to establish between the right to subsistence, on the one hand, and national independence and state sovereignty, on the other. Whether or not subsistence can be justified as the sole pursuit of China's human rights policy, pursuing the right to subsistence is surely of extreme importance; indeed, economic development is a central goal of almost all contemporary states. If its realization depends on national independence or state sovereignty, then we should concur with some, if not all, of the conclusions of the white paper. I have just noted the difference between merely enjoying subsistence and enjoying the right thereto; China's experience with imperialism and colonialism suggests that we need to consider this distinction not just with respect to individuals, but also for the Chinese people more generally. Chinese intellectuals have long felt that, like slaves, the legitimate interests of the Chinese people as a whole were paid little heed by their European "masters." National independence was and still is seen, therefore, as a route to securing not simply subsistence, but the right to subsistence.

A second and related theme has been the reciprocal relationship between an individual and his or her group. Unlike nineteenth-century rights discourse, Chinese rights thinkers in the twentieth century have consistently recognized the importance of individual rights. They tend nonetheless to stress the mutual entailment of individual and group rights. Individual rights are only operative in a well-functioning group, so each individual's rights depend, in part, on the fulfillment of his or her responsibilities to the group. In this regard it is especially important not to conflate the state with the nation, nor to ignore the various intermediary groups which are also important to individual and larger-group flourishing. State sovereignty may well contribute to national independence, but nothing in the current argument suggests that the power of the state should be seen as an end in itself. As Gao Yihan argued in 1915, the state is a means to people's ends, and must always be assessed in this light.

Taken together, the considerations in the previous two paragraphs make a case that in today's world, national independence and state sovereignty are required for people to enjoy the right to subsistence. If they are necessary conditions, though, they are not sufficient on their own. An all-powerful state in which the people have no voice may provide no guarantee of their right to subsistence. We can agree that political rights without subsistence rights are empty, but effective subsistence rights seem likely to depend on political rights. We may well agree with the white paper that groups' rights are essential to securing the equally essential right to subsistence, but I suspect most will dissent from its relegation of political rights to a secondary status.

In each of the main sections of this chapter, I have engaged with positions put forward by contemporary Western and Chinese rights theorists. At the same time, though, I have agreed, at least in part, with Liu Huaqiu's claim that Chinese conceptions of rights are distinctive – not simple imitations of one or another Western idea. If the concepts are at least somewhat different, on what grounds was I able to engage with both? From what perspective was I arguing? These are the questions that I will endeavor to answer in the book's final chapter.

9

Conclusions

THIS BOOK HAS REVOLVED around two questions: whether China can be said to have its own concept of rights, and whether countries with their own concepts of rights are immune from criticism phrased in terms of foreign rights concepts. Liu Huaqiu answers both of these questions in the affirmative. My own answers should now be clear. First, there have been both continuities and changes in the ways that rights have been conceptualized over the course of China's rich and distinctive rights discourse. These concepts are certainly China's "own": The contexts within which they have emerged and been contested are central episodes in China's cultural and political history, and they have always drawn importantly on preexisting concepts and concerns – even when they have criticized some of the commitments central to those existing values. Second, we have seen that the only way a community can unilaterally declare its values and practices immune to the scrutiny of others is through "parochialism," which also cuts off that community from making legitimate demands on others. As I will explain later, the activities of China's government, to say nothing of other Chinese actors, make it clear that they do not think of their values as parochial. This means that China cannot be immune from criticism, though it is no guarantee that any accommodation, much less constructive engagement, will be forthcoming between the Chinese and other communities. My goal in this Conclusion is to fill out my answers to these questions by making explicit the linked philosophical, historical, and normative conclusions for which I have argued in this book, and to review the evidence (and, where appropriate, the values) on which they are based.

The grounds for these conclusions and the scope of their appeal vary from one to another. For instance, consider the following two propositions: (1) We should conclude that China has a rich and distinctive rights discourse. (2) We should seek an accommodation of differences with one another in a spirit of toleration, and on that basis engage one another on as many levels as possible. These two claims are among the conclusions for which I argue in this final chapter, but let us reflect on the identities of the "we" that figure in each of the two propositions. I hope that all readers join me in this reflection, and similarly I hope that all readers join me in endorsing (1). My reasons for believing (1), which I have spelled out over the course of the book and will summarize momentarily, are reasons that I believe everyone should accept. Insofar as they depend on specific epistemic norms – for instance, that one should not simply assume that all peoples share a certain stock of inflexible concepts – I believe that all should endorse these norms, and I believe that all or virtually all of my readers do share my commitment to them. Proposition (1) may be controversial, but the kind of evidence I have given for it should not be.

I also hope that most or all of my readers join me in affirming proposition (2), but I do so on slightly different grounds. Unlike the first claim, which appeals to all people in the same way, this second claim appeals to members of two different communities, and might do so on different grounds for each. In fact more than two communities are embraced by this second "we": This is a proposition that I put forward for inspection and endorsement by all parties concerned with Chinese human rights theory and practice. Unlike the case with (1), endorsement of (2) may arise from a variety of perspectives, for a variety of reasons. As I made clear in the Introduction, I am not arguing that universal Reason demands that we seek consensus; if it makes sense to each of us to tolerate, accommodate, and engage with one another, it must make sense on the basis of our own values. These values, of course, are not immutable – the very processes of accommodation and engagement under discussion may lead us to change our values in small or large ways. Communities are also regularly divided about some of their values, so that some members may endorse (2) wholeheartedly while others accept it grudgingly, or not at all. Be all this as it may, accepting (2) means that one's own values – including perhaps one's norms for dealing with internal conflict – endorse its acceptance.

The perspective I offer here on who "we" are and whether "we" will endorse all my conclusions rests ultimately on my commitment to taking seriously the claims of people who are not obviously parts of my community. Taking their claims seriously does not mean acceding to them if they are wrong, but it does mean making room for their commitments in my understanding of how we can communicate, and perhaps even reason, with one another. The burden of Chapters 2 and 3 was to provide such an understanding, which can be summarized as three philosophical theses: concepts are inferentially articulated commitments; pluralism emerges from varying degrees of conceptual distance; and the consequence of pluralism is a menu of strategies one might find it sensible to adopt toward others, depending on one's values and one's situation.

It is crucial to see that I am not arguing for linguistic determinism, as that has been traditionally understood. Language use is a good window on the commitments our practices institute, but language itself is never determinative. My "pluralism" is about what is possible, and perhaps even likely, given our contingently different histories, but it is in no way necessary. Indeed, I have suggested that we may all have reasons to want to overcome pluralism, at least in many areas of our life. (In other areas, pluralism may enhance our lives without appreciable cost.) Let us also keep in mind that I have, for all practical purposes, rejected the utility of thinking of others' languages or values as "incommensurable" with our own.

Among the strategies with which I have suggested one might respond to pluralism, parochialism is a particularly important instance. Recall that one responds parochially to others when one refuses to grant them normative competence based not on the failure of the others to satisfy some generic criterion, but solely because they are "not us."[1] This is especially significant in light of Liu Huaqiu's claim that China is immune to foreign criticism, since one way to be immune is to refuse even to consider granting others normative competence on parochial grounds – as I suggested earlier that Americans may have done to Japanese-Americans during World War II. Parochialism is not consistent with making demands of the others, though: If they are *ex hypothesi* denied normative competence, then they cannot see the reasons to act as we say they should. Therefore, if Chinese have made arguments about what others should and should not do, they are not treating the others parochially, and thus are denied the option of defending their own values in parochial fashion. And there is ample evidence that Chinese, both within the government and without, have argued over the years about values. From statements at the United Nations and other international forums to individual popular or scholarly essays, Chinese have consistently engaged with others in non-parochial terms. That still leaves a whole range of

---

[1] See Section 3.1.

options, as spelled out in Chapter 3 and discussed subsequently, but parochialism is not an open route to Liu's desired immunity.

In the middle chapters of the book, I have established at least four large theses, each related in part to Liu's claim about Chinese distinctiveness. First, I have argued that one strand of the neo-Confucian tradition played a constructive role in the development of Chinese rights discourse. This argument spanned three chapters, as we looked first at the neo-Confucians themselves, then at ways in which their concerns played into the nineteenth-century origins of rights discourse – not least in Japan – and finally at the degree to which important thinkers at the beginning of the twentieth century picked up these same themes as they developed their ideas about rights. Subsequent rights discourse, of course, is almost completely devoid of positive references to Confucianism. The subsequent discourse can nonetheless be seen as developing many of the earlier themes, as we have seen as recently as Chapter 8, in the ways that contemporary Chinese rights theorizing maintains a strong tie between rights and people's interests.

The second and third theses that I have in mind are as much methodological as they are historical: Historical traditions like that under study here are contingent, dynamic, and often interrelated with other such traditions; and we should interpret these traditions from the inside, adopting what Cohen calls a "China-centered" approach. I suggested in the book's Introduction that a failure to adequately recognize the dynamism and interrelations of traditions was a problem with Alasdair MacIntyre's theoretical account of these matters; a strength of my account, I believe, is the way in which its understanding of traditions and its detailed historical studies of such a tradition mutually support one another. The aspect of "China-centered" history which I have emphasized is analyzing Chinese concepts in their home contexts, though without being blind to the ways in which they have been related to, or even derived from, interpretations of foreign texts and terms. This approach has of course been supported at numerous points by my more theoretical contentions about the natures of concepts and of moral pluralism.

My final historical argument concerns the distinctiveness of Chinese rights discourse. I believe that this study conclusively proves that China has been the site of a robust and distinctive discourse about rights. One of the best and most recent bits of evidence for this is the way in which recent Chinese rights theorists, as we saw in the previous chapter, have analyzed the word "*quanli*" into its constituent parts and discussed rights in those terms. I have nonetheless been careful to say "distinctive" rather than "unique": As we should expect from what I just said about the interrelations among traditions, Chinese rights discourse has never been hermetically sealed off from other developing traditions of rights discourse. Instead, it has been in continuous contact with such traditions, drawing on a wide variety of sources, as they were interpreted and deemed relevant in China. Once we give up the idea that there is but a single proper concept of rights, and realize that communication is possible even if we do not all share precisely one meaning, we come to see that not only is there a distinctive Chinese discourse about rights, but also there is a distinctive American discourse, a French discourse, and so on. All interact, all are dynamic, all are internally contested. Some are closer to one another than others, in part because some bear closer kinship relations, having been born of the same, or at least similar, parents – such as the Latin natural-rights tradition or Roman law. On the other hand, many are different enough to raise the issue of pluralism: How should those committed to different moralities interact with one another?

As I have already suggested, answers to this question must be understood slightly differently than the various theses that I have rehearsed up until this point. The difference is not that answers to this latest question depend on shared norms while the earlier claims do not: The philosophical and historical claims do depend on commitments to what counts as good evidence and good argument. The difference is that I am more confident that my readers share with me standards of argument and evidence than I am that (all) readers will share my moral commitments. For some readers, therefore, the normative conclusions to which I now turn will simply be articulations of that to which they are also committed, while others may see some of these conclusions as challenging assertions.

On several general points I believe there should be widespread agreement. Where grounds for engagement exist, as they surely seem to in this case, we should pursue engagement vigorously – and we should do so on as many simultaneous horizontal planes as possible. As I argued earlier, horizontal engagement between members of sub-groups will often offer the best opportunities for mutual granting of normative competence and for mutual learning. If one is a Chinese politician, then a fellow politician from Sweden, say, may be best suited for conveying the concepts, constraints, and commitments that characterize the larger (internally contested) moral arena in Sweden. This is because the Swedish politician will share more with his or her Chinese counterpart than would a

Swedish stockbroker, and because the Swedish politician must, at the same time, remain engaged with others in his or her home community – the dimension I have called vertical engagement.

Add to this my claim that the logic of engagement pushes toward consensus, and one can see the appeal of overlapping horizontal engagements. Engagement pushes toward – but does not guarantee – consensus, since full-fledged engagement depends on granting each other normative competence. We each expect the other to feel the pull of the sorts of reasons we find compelling. As I think through your reasons and you think through mine, each (ideally) with an open mind, I am likely to be swayed by your good reasons and you by mine: Remember that if we have granted each other normative competence, that means that we reason about values in the same way, and thus that we should find the same sorts of reasons "good." Since I have made no claims about there being a single moral truth to which all who reason in the same terms must converge – perhaps these things are underdetermined by the available reasons – I cannot claim that engagement will inevitably lead to consensus. Still, the pressures it exerts seem likely to push in that direction. Engagement helps us toward consensus in a second sense, as well: It nudges us toward ever richer or thicker consensus. I argued earlier that a thin consensus, based on thin values, can be unstable, and thus that we have reason to seek a more sustainable agreement.[2]

Another idea with which all may agree is that the distinction between thick and thin values may often be a useful tool, but it is not a panacea. There may be universal agreement that corruption is a bad thing, but international attempts to do something about it may still founder on the variety of distinctive interpretations to which "corruption" is open in different communities. The thin version of corruption on which all agree may still be enough to ground some practical measures, or at least – as discussed in the Introduction – to encourage local activists to pursue implementation of their own laws against corruption. Thin values also come very close to what I called in Chapter 3 "norms of accommodation," and their importance in this guise cannot be neglected. Norms of accommodation are values in accord with which groups agree to interact, even though both sides feel internally that the accommodative norms are inferior to their own values. Engagement is all very well, but it promises no immediate or even long-term results, so accommodations will continue to be very important.

---

[2] See Section 3.2.3.

A final general observation before turning to more specific normative claims: We cannot neglect the roles that power and politics play in shaping discussions of values. It is regrettable but inevitable that considerations of power influence what people say and do not say. The idea that such matters may shape our decisions is implicit in the framework I developed in Chapter 3: We base our judgments of what stance to adopt toward others, I said, in part on the costs entailed by the various alternatives. Sometimes these costs will keep us quiet: If I stand to be harmed for speaking out, I may keep quiet; in other cases, I may want to speak but have no means to communicate widely. In still other cases the costs push us to speak or act, despite scruples we may feel, such as if we make repressive or even parochial demands in an effort to keep a powerless sub-group from suffering still greater wrongs. This last case is complicated by the difference that may exist between the sub-group's norms and those of their oppressors: The former may welcome our intervention, while the latter find it repressive. This can help us to justify our actions to ourselves, but does not wholly dispense with their repressive nature. Pressuring the Chinese government on behalf of dissident intellectuals in China may sometimes fall into this category.

Most of the conclusions one can reach about how to react to the influence of power upon value discourse must be highly contextual and carefully balanced. There is at least one general thing we can say, though, which is that most of us will have good reasons to resist any attempts to monopolize a discussion, to cut off engagement, or to end efforts to establish dialogue. Given that moral traditions are dynamic and their differences merely contingent, we all have reasons to engage with others in the hope that they will come to think more like us, or that we will see reasons to become more like them – or both.

This is of course a very abstract consideration, unlikely to sway an unreflective dictator. In this context it would be well to note that the idea of dialogue over human rights has come under some criticism in recent years by non-governmental organizations like Human Rights in China (HRIC). They worry that dialogue will "displace other methods, including multilateral action at the UN and public censure" [HRIC 1997]. They point out that the government of the People's Republic of China (PRC) has recently welcomed "dialogue" while rejecting "confrontation," but the activities by members of the international community that have led to improvements in human rights conditions in China have almost exclusively been those which the Chinese government labels as confrontational. HRIC suggests a range of criteria for implementing successful dialogues, and concludes that "dialogue without pressure is nothing but appeasement and will merely serve to degrade the authority of international human rights standards" [ibid.].

I find myself largely in agreement with HRIC on how government-to-government dialogues should be conducted, and join them in rejecting the way that the PRC government has distinguished "dialogue" from "confrontation." Frank criticism is an appropriate part of dialogical engagement with one another, so long as both sides are open to such discussions. To their credit, HRIC recognizes that all governments "engaging in dialogue should be prepared to discuss their own human rights records"; in my terms, this is a necessary precondition for granting normative competence to one's dialogue partner, without which engagement cannot proceed. We must not resist discussion of our own shortcomings if we ask others to discuss theirs. This is a lesson the U.S. government would do well to heed carefully: Its refusal to take seriously Chinese criticisms of the U.S. human rights record does little to promote the kind of dialogue here envisioned.

It only remains to add that the dialogues described by HRIC are far from the only form of dialogue that should be encouraged. Horizontal engagement should be pursued wherever possible. Opportunities for engagement increase every day as global interconnections increase and communication technologies improve. In each context, we should value the respect that grounds toleration, and thus we should seek an accommodation of our differences in a spirit of toleration. I argued earlier that Gibbard is wrong to assert that the endorsement of mutual respect is something intrinsic to normative discussion or to our shared human natures. Be this as it may, I do value such respect, and believe that others should as well. We should all value it because it makes for better communication and engagement, and because valuing treating others in ways they find legitimate manifests a kind of empathy with others which is itself valuable. Too often those of us in a position to influence public views about other nations – including scholars, the media, and authorities in both the United States and China – demonize or harangue rather than working toward open, balanced understandings and criticisms. The power of the market to shape our media, no less than the power of political leaders, needs to be carefully watched if we are to work toward a real accommodation, and perhaps ultimately consensus.

Now consider the provisional outcomes of the detailed engagement which I undertook in the preceding chapter. Several features of that discussion bear highlighting. First, it is evident that I thought it appropriate to grant normative competence to contemporary Chinese rights theorists, academics and activists alike. It seemed to me that the kinds of reasoning in which they engage are perfectly accessible to us. I also proceeded as if they would grant competence to me and to the thinkers on whom I drew. This is up to them, of course, and in practice will have to wait on the publication of that chapter, or this whole book, preferably in Chinese.[3] My reasons for believing that they will take seriously my questions and my arguments are several: (1) I take pains to draw on aspects of Western rights discourse that mesh particularly well with Chinese concepts; (2) I endeavor to demonstrate the potential for mutually fruitful dialogue, and emphasize my (our) openness to genuine two-way engagement, by stressing an area in which Western theory may stand to learn something from its Chinese counterpart; (3) it seems to me that the kinds of reasons to which I appeal are similar to the kinds of reasons on which they rest their own positions.

As I made clear in the previous chapter, my primary goals were to illustrate the possibility and potential fruitfulness of an open dialogue about rights. I consider the specific theses at which I arrived to be beginnings, rather than conclusions, of arguments. Thoughtful engagement between Western and Chinese thinkers, comparatively common seventy years ago, is only just beginning to be revived. As I have emphasized, this engagement needs to take place alongside as many other levels of engagement as possible, and all of us who are engaging all of them also need to talk among ourselves and reflect on the various and tentative conclusions to which we come. I endorse Liu Huaqiu's pluralism, though perhaps not in a way he would wholly recognize, but I reject his isolationism. It is certainly true that there is no abstract vantage point from which one can "think of the human rights standard and model of certain countries as the only proper ones and demand all countries to comply with them." It does not follow, however, that I cannot ask of you to comply with my values – or else to convince me why you should not. Rather than giving us reason to end discussion, our differences with the Chinese should serve as a challenge to all of us to work toward a position of agreement superior – as judged from each of our perspectives – to where any of us stands now.

[3] I presented parts of Chapter 8, under the title "Toward a Cross-Cultural Dialogue on Rights and Interests," at an international conference on political philosophy in Beijing in April 2001. The terms in which the paper was discussed suggested a mutual granting of competence.

Bibliography

Alitto, Guy S. 1979. *The Last Confucian: Liang Shu-ming and the Chinese Dilemma of Modernity*. Berkeley: University of California Press.

Alston, Philip. 1990. U.S. Ratification of the Covenant on Economic, Social, and Cultural Rights: The Need for an Entirely New Strategy. *American Journal of International Law* 84:2. 365–393.

Ames, Roger T. 1997. Continuing the Conversation on Chinese Human Rights. *Ethics & International Affairs* 11. 177–205.

——. 1988. Rites as Rights: The Confucian Alternative. In: Rouner, Leroy S., ed. *Human Rights and the World's Religions*. Notre Dame: University of Notre Dame Press. 199–216.

Angle, Stephen C. 1994. Concepts in Context: A Study of Ethical Incommensurability. Ann Arbor: University Microfilms.

——. 1998. The Possibility of Sagehood: Reverence and Ethical Perfection in Zhu Xi's Thought. *Journal of Chinese Philosophy* 25:3. 281–303.

——. 2000. Review of *The Discourse of Human Rights in China* by Robert Weatherley. *Journal of Asian Studies* 59:3.

——. In press. Pluralism in Practice: Incommensurability and Constraints on Change in Ethical Discourses. In: Michael Barnhart, ed. *Varieties of Ethical Perspective*. Lanham, MD: Lexington Books.

Angle, Stephen C.; Svensson, Marina, trans. and ed. 1999. On Rights and Human Rights: A Contested and Evolving Chinese Discourse, 1900–1949. *Contemporary Chinese Thought* 31:1.

——. 2001. *The China Human Rights Reader*. Armonk, NY: M. E. Sharpe.

Anonymous. 1966 (1897). Zonglun (總論). Xiangxue Xinbao (湘學新報). Taipei: Hualian chubanshe.

Asia Historical Dictionary (ヤジヤ歴史事典). 1960. Tokyo.

Ayer, A. J. 1936. *Language, Truth, and Logic*. London: Victor Gollancz.

Baehr, Peter R.; van Hoof, Fried; Liu Nanlai; Tao Zhenghua, eds. 1996. *Human Rights: Chinese and Dutch Perspectives*. The Hague: Martinus Nijhoff.

Bauer, Joanne R.; Bell, Daniel A., eds. 1999. *The East Asian Challenge for Human Rights*. Cambridge: Cambridge University Press.

Benedict, Ruth. 1934. *Patterns of Culture*. Boston: Houghton Mifflin.

259

Berlin, Isaiah, Sir. 1970. *Four Essays on Liberty.* New York: Oxford University Press.

Bernal, Martin. 1976. Liu Shih-p'ei and National Essence. In: Furth, Charlotte, ed. *The Limits of Change.* Cambridge: Harvard University Press. 90–112.

Biagioli, Mario. 1990. The Anthropology of Incommensurability. *Studies in the History and Philosophy of Science* 21:2. 183–209.

Blaustein, Albert P.; Clark, Roger S.; Sigler, Jay A., eds. 1987. *Human Rights Sourcebook.* New York: Paragon House.

Bourdieu, Pierre. 1974. The Economics of Linguistic Exchanges. *Social Science Information* 16:6. 645–668.

Braisted, William Reynolds, trans. 1976. *Meiroku Zasshi: Journal of the Japanese Enlightenment.* Cambridge: Harvard University Press.

Brandom, Robert. 1994. *Making It Explicit: Reasoning, Representing, and Discursive Commitment.* Cambridge: Harvard University Press.

Brook, Timothy. 1998. *The Confusions of Pleasure: Commerce and Culture in Ming China.* Berkeley: University of California Press.

Brooks, E. Bruce; Brooks, A. Taeko. 1998. *The Original Analects: Sayings of Confucius and His Successors.* New York: Columbia University Press.

Brown, Chris. 1999. Universal Human Rights: A Critique. In: Dunne, Tim; Wheeler, Nicholas J., eds. *Human Rights in Global Politics.* Cambridge: Cambridge University Press. 103–127.

Chan, Joseph. 1995. The Asian Challenge to Universal Human Rights: A Philosophical Appraisal. In: Tang, James T. H., ed. *Human Rights and International Relations in the Asia-Pacific Region.* London: Pinter.

1997. An Alternative View. *Journal of Democracy* 8:2. 35–48.

1999. A Confucian Perspective on Human Rights for Contemporary China. In: Bauer, Joanne R.; Bell, Daniel A., eds. *The East Asian Challenge for Human Rights.* Cambridge: Cambridge University Press. 212–240.

2000. Thick and Thin Accounts of Human Rights. In: Jacobsen, Michael; Bruun, Ole, eds. *Human Rights and Asian Values: Contesting National Identities and Cultural Representations in Asia.* Richmond, UK: Curzon. 59–74.

Chan, Wing-tsit, trans. 1963. *A Sourcebook in Chinese Philosophy.* Princeton: Princeton University Press.

1989. The Principle of Heaven and Human Desires. In: *Chu Hsi: New Studies.* Honolulu: University of Hawaii Press.

Chang Chia-ning. 1991. Elements of International Law: Conditions of Formation and Problems of Translation (『萬國公法』成立事情と翻訳問題). *Translation Theory* (翻訳の思想). Tokyo: Iwanami shoten; vol. 15.

Chang Hao. 1971. *Liang Ch'i-ch'ao and Intellectual Transition in China.* Cambridge: Harvard University Press.

1987. *Chinese Intellectuals in Crisis.* Berkeley: University of California Press.

Chen Duxiu 陳獨秀. 1993 (1903). A Draft for the Anhui Patriotic Society (安徽愛國會擬章). In: *Selected Essays of Chen Duxiu* (陳獨秀著作選編). Shanghai: Renmin chubanshe; vol. 1.

1984a (1904). On the Nation (説國家). In: *Selected Essays of Chen Duxiu* (陳獨秀文章選編). Beijing: Sanlian shudian; vol. 1.

1984b (1904). The Loss of the Nation (亡國篇). In: *Selected Essays of Chen Duxiu* (陳獨秀文章選編). Beijing: Sanlian shudian; vol. 1.

1984c (1904). An Explanation of Wang Yangming's Fundamental Ideas on Elementary Education (王陽明先生訓蒙大意的解釋). In: *Selected Essays of Chen Duxiu* (陳獨秀文章選編). Beijing: Sanlian shudian; vol. 1.

1984d (1915). A Call to Youth (警告青年). In: *Selected Essays of Chen Duxiu* (陳獨秀文章選編). Beijing: Sanlian shudian; vol. 1.

1984e (1915). The Direction of Contemporary Education (今日之教育方針). In: *Selected Essays of Chen Duxiu* (陳獨秀文章選編). Beijing: Sanlian shudian; vol. 1.

1984f (1915). The Differences in the Fundamental Thought of Eastern and Western Peoples (東西民族根本思想之差異). In: *Selected Essays of Chen Duxiu* (陳獨秀文章選編). Beijing: Sanlian shudian; vol. 1.

1984g (1916). 1916 (一九一六年). In: *Selected Essays of Chen Duxiu* (陳獨秀文章選編). Beijing: Sanlian shudian; vol. 1.

1984h (1916). The Way of Confucius and Modern Life (孔子之道與現代生活). In: *Selected Essays of Chen Duxiu* (陳獨秀文章選編). Beijing: Sanlian shudian; vol. 1.

1984i (1919). Law and the Freedom of Thought (法律與言論自由). In: *Selected Essays of Chen Duxiu* (陳獨秀文章選編). Beijing: Sanlian shudian; vol. 1.

1984j (1919). The Foundation of Practicing Democracy (實行民治的基礎). In: *Selected Essays of Chen Duxiu* (陳獨秀文章選編). Beijing: Sanlian shudian; vol. 1.

1984k (1920). The Laborer's Enlightenment (勞動者底覺悟). In: *Selected Essays of Chen Duxiu* (陳獨秀文章選編). Beijing: Sanlian shudian; vol. 1.

1984l (1921). Discussing Anarchism (討論無政府主義). In: *Selected Essays of Chen Duxiu* (陳獨秀文章選編). Beijing: Sanlian shudian; vol. 2.

Chen Lai 陳來. 1999. The Ethics of Confucianists and the Value of Human Rights (儒學倫理與"人權"價值). *International Confucian Research* (國際儒學研究); vol. 6.

Chen Que 陳確. 1979a. Scholars Take the Ordering of Life as Fundamental (學者以治生為本論). In: *Collected Writings of Chen Que* (陳確集). Beijing: China Bookstore Press; vol. 1.

1979b. Discussion of Self-Regard (私説). In: *Collected Writings of Chen Que* (陳確集). Beijing: China Bookstore Press; vol. 2.

Cheng, Anne. 1997. Nationalism, Citizenship, and the Old Text/New Text Controversey in Late Nineteenth Century China. In: Fogel, Joshua A.; Zarrow, Peter G., eds. *Imagining the People: Chinese Intellectuals and the Concept of Citizenship, 1890–1920*. Armonk, NY: M.E. Sharpe.

Cheng I-fan 程一凡. 1984. Gu Yanwu's View of Personal Benefit (顧炎武的私利觀). In: Institute of Modern History, Academia Sinica, eds. *Proceedings of the Conference on Modern Chinese Statecraft Thought* (近世中國經世思想研討會論文集). Taipei: Academia Sinica.

Ch'ien, Ssu-ma. 1994. Neinhauser, William H., Jr., ed.; Tsai-fa Cheng et al., trans. *The Grand Scribe's Records*. Bloomington: Indiana University Press.

Chow, Kai-wing. 1994. *The Rise of Confucian Ritualism in Late Imperial China: Ethics, Classics, and Lineage Discourse*. Stanford: Stanford University Press.

Chu Ron-guey. 1998. Rites and Rights in Ming China. In: de Bary, Wm. Theodore; Tu Wei-ming, eds. *Confucianism and Human Rights*. New York: Columbia University Press. 169–178.

Ci Jiwei 慈繼偉. 1999. The Right, the Good, and the Place of Rights in Confucianism (從正當與善的區分看權利在現代西方和儒家思想中的差異). *International Confucian Research* (國際儒學研究); vol. 6.

Cohen, Paul A. 1984. *Discovering History in China: American Historical Writing on the Recent Chinese Past*. New York: Columbia University Press.

Cole, G. D. H. 1995 (1915). Conflicting Social Obligations. In: Stapleton, Julia, ed. *Group Rights: Perspectives Since 1900*. Bristol: Thoemmes Press.

Crawford, Andrew. 1997. A Revolution of Ideas: The Baba Tatsui Synthesis. Wesleyan University Senior Essay. Unpublished.

Dai Zhen. 1990a. Ewell, John Woodruff, Jr., trans. *Evidential Commentary on the Meanings of Terms in Mencius*. Ann Arbor: University Microfilms.

1990b. Chin, Ann-ping; Freeman, Mansfield, trans. *Tai Chen on Mencius: Explorations in Words and Meaning*. New Haven: Yale University Press.

戴震. 1995. Zhang Dainian, ed. *Complete Works of Dai Zhen* (戴震全書); vol. 6.

Dardess, John W. 1983. *Confucianism and Autocracy: Professional Elites in the Founding of the Ming Dynasty*. Berkeley: University of California Press.

Davidson, Donald. 1984a (1967). On the Very Idea of a Conceptual Scheme. In: *Inquiries into Truth and Interpretation*. Oxford: Clarendon Press. 183–198.

1984b (1975). Thought and Talk. In: *Inquiries into Truth and Interpretation*. Oxford: Clarendon Press. 155–170.

1986. A Nice Derangement of Epitaphs. In: LePore, Ernest, ed. *Truth and Interpretation: Perspectives on the Philosophy of Donald Davidson*. Oxford: Basil Blackwell. 433–446.

de Bary, Wm. Theodore. 1979. Sagehood as a Secular and Spiritual Ideal in Tokugawa Neo-Confucianism. In: de Bary, Wm. Theodore; Bloom, Irene, eds. *Principle and Practicality*. New York: Columbia University Press.

1988. Neo-Confucianism and Human Rights. In: Rouner, Leroy S., ed. *Human Rights and the World's Religions*. Notre Dame: University of Notre Dame Press. 183–198.

1991. *The Trouble with Confucianism*. Cambridge: Harvard University Press.

1998. *Asian Values and Human Rights: A Confucian Communitarian Perspective*. Cambridge: Harvard University Press.

Deng Xiaoping. 1992. *Selected Works of Deng Xiaoping*. Beijing: Foreign Languages Press.

Dewey, John. 1919. Transcript of Dr. Dewey's Lectures on Social and Political Philosophy, Part 6 (杜威博士講演錄：社會哲學與政治哲學〔六〕). *New Youth* (新青年) 7:2.

1973. Clopton, Robert W.; Ou, Tsuin-chen, trans. *Lectures in China, 1919–1920*. Honolulu: University of Hawaii Press.

1978 (1908). Boydston, Jo Ann, ed. *Ethics*. Carbondale: Southern Illinois University Press.

Donnelly, Jack. 1989. *Universal Human Rights in Theory and Practice*. Ithaca: Cornell University Press.

1997. Conversing with Straw Men while Ignoring Dictators: A Reply to Roger Ames. *Ethics & International Affairs* 11. 207–213.

Dowdle, Michael W. 2001. How a Liberal Jurist Defends the Bangkok Declaration. In: Bell, Lynda S.; Nathan, Andrew J.; Peleg, Ilan, eds. *Negotiating Culture and Human Rights*. New York: Columbia University Press.

Dworkin, Ronald. 1977. *Taking Rights Seriously*. Cambridge: Harvard University Press.

Elman, Benjamin A. 1984. *From Philosophy to Philology: Intellectual and Social Aspects of Change in Late Imperial China*. Cambridge: Council on East Asian Studies, Harvard University.

1990. *Classicism, Politics, and Kinship: The Ch'ang-Chou School of New Text Confucianism in Late Imperial China*. Berkeley: University of California Press.

2000. *A Cultural History of Civil Examinations in Late Imperial China*. Berkeley: University of California Press.

Fay, Brian. 1987. *Critical Social Science*. Ithaca: Cornell University Press.

1996. *Contemporary Philosophy of Social Science: A Multicultural Approach*. Oxford: Blackwell.

Feigon, Lee. 1983. *Chen Duxiu: Founder of the Chinese Communist Party*. Princeton: Princeton University Press.

Feinberg, Joel. 1970. The Nature and Value of Rights. *Journal of Value Inquiry* 4.

Fikentscher, Wolfgang. 1977. *Methoden des Rechts*. Tübingen: Mohr.

Fingarette, Herbert. 1972. *Confucius – The Secular as Sacred*. New York: Harper & Row.

Finnis, John. 1980. *Natural Law and Natural Rights*. Oxford: Clarendon Press.

Fodor, Jerry; Lepore, Ernest. 1992. *Holism: A Shopper's Guide*. Oxford: Basil Blackwell.

Fukuzawa Yukichi. 1969. Dilworth, David A.; Umeyo Hirano, trans. *An Encouragement of Learning*. Tokyo: Sophia University.

Fung, Edmund S. K. 1998. The Human Rights Issue in China, 1929–1931. *Modern Asian Studies* 32:2. 431–457.

Gao Yihan 高一涵. 1915a. On the Republic and Young People's Consciousness (公和國家與青年之自覺). *New Youth* (新青年) 1:1–3.

1915b. The Social Contract and the Basis of the Nation (民約與邦本). *New Youth* (新青年) 1:3.

1915c. On the Country Not Being the End of Life (國家非人生之歸宿論). *New Youth* (新青年) 1:4.

1916. Utilitarianism and Life (樂利主義與人生). *New Youth* (新青年) 2:1.

1918. On the Changes in the Three Great Political Ideologies in the Modern World (近世三大政治思想之變遷). *New Youth* (新青年) 4:1.

1921. The Problem of People's Rights in Provincial Constitutions (省憲法中的民權問題). *New Youth* (新青年) 9:5.

1926. Rousseau's Doctrines of People's Rights and State Rights (盧梭的民權論和國權論). *Dongfang Zazhi* (東方雜誌) 23:3.

1930. *An Outline of Political Science* (政治學綱要). Shanghai: Shenzhou Guoguang she.

Geertz, Clifford. 1973. *The Interpretation of Cultures.* New York: Basic Books.

Gibbard, Allan. 1984. Utilitarianism and Human Rights. *Social Philosophy and Policy* 1:2.

1990. *Wise Choices, Apt Feelings.* Cambridge: Harvard University Press.

Glendon, Mary Ann. 1991. *Rights Talk: The Impoverishment of Political Discourse.* New York: Free Press.

2001. *A World Made New: Eleanor Roosevelt and the Universal Declaration of Human Rights.* New York: Random House.

Goodrich, L. Carrington; Fang, Chaoying, eds. 1976. *Dictionary of Ming Biography.* New York: Columbia University Press.

Graham, A. C. 1958. *Two Chinese Philosophers.* London: Lund Humphries.

1989. *Disputers of the Tao: Philosophical Argument in Ancient China.* Chicago: Open Court.

Graham, A. C., trans. 1981. *Chuang Tzu: The Seven Inner Chapters and Other Writings.* London: George Allen & Unwin.

Greiff, Thomas E. 1985. The Principle of Human Rights in Nationalist China: John C. H. Wu and the Ideological Origins of the 1946 Constitution. *China Quarterly* 103. 441–461.

Grice, H. P. 1989. Meaning. In: *Studies in the Ways of Words.* Cambridge: Harvard University Press. 213–223.

Grieder, Jerome B. 1970. *Hu Shih and the Chinese Renaissance.* Cambridge: Harvard University Press.

Grotius, Hugo. 1990 (1625). On the Law of War and Peace. In: Schneewind, J. B., trans. and ed. *Moral Philosophy from Montaigne to Kant.* Cambridge: Cambridge University Press.

Gu Yanwu 顧炎武. 1959a. On the Prefecture-County System (郡縣論). In: *Collected Prose and Poetry of Gu Yanwu* (顧亭林詩文集). Beijing: China Bookstore Press; vol. 1.

1959b. On Licentiates (生員論). In: *Collected Prose and Poetry of Gu Yanwu* (顧亭林詩文集). Beijing: China Bookstore Press; vol. 2.

Guang, Lei. 1996. Elusive Democracy: Conceptual Change and the Chinese Democracy Movement, 1978–79 to 1989. *Modern China* 22:4.

Haakonssen, Knud. 1996. *Natural Law and Moral Philosophy: From Grotius to the Scottish Enlightenment.* Cambridge: Cambridge University Press.

Habermas, Jürgen. 1985. McCarthy, T., trans. *The Theory of Communicative Action.* Boston: Beacon Press.

Hall, David L.; Ames, Roger T. 1999. *The Democracy of the Dead: Dewey, Confucius, and the Hope for Democracy in China.* Chicago: Open Court.

Han Minzhu, ed. 1990. *Cries for Democracy: Writings and Speeches from the 1989 Chinese Democracy Movement.* Princeton: Princeton University Press.

Han Tan 韓菼. 1827. Five Plans (擬策五道). In: He Changling; Wei Yuan, eds. *Statecraft Writings of the Imperial Dynasty* (皇朝經世文編); vol. 12.

Handlin, Joanna F. 1983. *Action in Late Ming Thought: The Reorientation of Lü K'un and Other Scholar-Officials.* Berkeley: University of California Press.

Hansen, Chad. 1997. The Asian Values Debate and the Moral Synthesis Goals of Comparative Philosophy. Online at ⟨http://www.hku.hk/philodep/ch/aparights.html⟩, accessed 3/13/01.

He Qi (Ho Kai). 1992 (1887). To the Editor of the China Mail. In: Xu Zhengxiong, *The Development and Divergence of Late Qing People's Power Thought* (清末民權思想的發展與歧異). Taipei.

和啟; Hu Liyuan 胡禮垣. 1994 (1901). *True Interpretation of the New Policies* (新政真詮). Shenyang: Liaoning People's Press.

Hegel, G. W. F. 1991. Nisbet, H. B., trans. *Elements of the Philosophy of Right.* Cambridge: Cambridge University Press.

Hoh Chih-hsiang, ed. 1982 (1933). *Who's Who in China.* Hong Kong: China Materials Center.

HRIC. 1997. The Dialogue Debate: A Strategy for Advancing Human Rights or a Way of Evading Responsibility? *China Rights Forum.* Fall issue.

Hsu, Immanuel. 1960. *China's Entrance into The Family of Nations: The Diplomatic Phase, 1858–1880.* Cambridge: Harvard University Press.

1983. *The Rise of Modern China.* New York: Oxford University Press.

Huang, Philip C. 1972. *Liang Ch'i-ch'ao and Modern Chinese Liberalism.* Seattle: University of Washington Press.

Huang Zongxi 黃宗羲. 1985 (1663). Waiting for the Dawn (明夷待訪錄). In: *Complete Works of Huang Zongxi* (黃宗羲全集). Hangzhou: Zhejiang Ancient Text Press.

1993. de Bary, Wm. Theodore, trans. *Waiting for the Dawn.* New York: Columbia University Press.

Hummel, Arthur W., ed. 1970 (1943). *Eminent Chinese of the Ch'ing Period.* Taipei: Ch'eng Wen Publishing Co.

Hymes, Robert P. 1986. *Statesmen and Gentlemen: The Elite of Fu-Chou, Chiang-Hsi, in the Northern and Southern Sung.* Cambridge: Cambridge University Press.

Ihara, Craig K. In press. Are Claim Rights Necessary? A Confucian Perspective. In: Shun, Kwong-loi; Wong, David B., eds. *Confucian Ethics: A Comparative Study of Self, Autonomy, and Community.* Cambridge: Cambridge University Press.

Index to Xunzi (荀子引得). 1986. Shanghai: Shanghai Ancient Text Press.

Information Council of the State Council. 1991. *Human Rights in China.* Beijing.

Ip, Hung-Yok. 1994. The Origins of Chinese Communism. *Modern China* 20:1.

Jensen, Lionel M. 1997. *Manufacturing Confucianism: Chinese Traditions and Universal Civilization.* Durham: Duke University Press.

Jhering, Rudolf von. 1872. *Der Kampf ums Recht.* Vienna: Manz.

1900–1. The Struggle for Rights (權利競爭論). Tokyo: n.p.

1913. Isaac Huski, trans. *Law as a Means to an End.* Boston: Boston Book Company.

1915. John J. Lalor, trans. *The Struggle for Law.* Chicago: Callaghan and Company.

Judge, Joan. 1997. Key Words in the Late Qing Reform Discourse: Classical and Contemporary Sources of Authority. *Indiana East Asian Working Paper Series.* Available at ⟨http://www.indiana.edu/~easc/pages/easc/working_papers/noframe_5_all.htm⟩, accessed 11/18/01.

Kamachi, Noriko. 1981. *Reform in China, Huang Tsun-hsien and the Japanese Model.* Cambridge: Council on East Asian Studies, Harvard University.

Kang Youwei. 1978. Li San-pao, trans. *Complete Book of Substantial Principles and General Laws. Zhongyan yanjiuyuan jindaishi yanjiusuo jikan* 7. 683–725.

Keenan, Barry. 1977. *The Dewey Experiment in China: Educational Reform and Political Power in the Early Republic.* Cambridge: Council on East Asian Studies, Harvard University.

Keith, Ronald C. 1995. The New Relevance of "Rights and Interests": China's Changing Human Rights Theories. *China Information* 10:2. 38–61.

Kent, Ann. 1993. *Between Freedom and Subsistence: China and Human Rights.* Hong Kong: Oxford University Press.

    1999. *China, the United Nations, and Human Rights: The Limits of Compliance.* Philadelphia: University of Pennsylvania Press.

Kitcher, Philip. 1985. *Vaulting Ambition.* Cambridge: M.I.T. Press.

Knoblock, John, trans. 1988, 1990, 1994. *Xunzi: A Translation and Study of the Complete Works*, 3 vols. Stanford: Stanford University Press.

Kuhn, Thomas S. 1970. *The Structure of Scientific Revolutions.* 2nd Edition. Chicago: University of Chicago Press.

    1983. Commensurability, Comparability, Communicability. *PSA 1982*, pp. 669–688.

Laski, Harold J. 1929. *A Grammar of Politics.* New Haven: Yale University Press.

Lau, D. C., trans. 1970. *Mencius.* London: Penguin.

    trans. 1979. *Analects.* London: Penguin.

    1991. On the Expression Zai You. In: Rosemont, Henry, ed. *Chinese Texts and Philosophical Contexts.* Chicago: Open Court. 5–20.

Lee, Theresa Man Ling. 1998. Local Self-Government in Late Qing Reform. *The Review of Politics* 60:1. 31–53.

Legge, James, trans. 1985 (1872). *The Ch'un Ts'ew with the Tso Chuen.* Taipei: Southern Materials Center.

Levenson, Joseph R. 1967. *Liang Ch'i-ch'ao and the Mind of Modern China.* Berkeley: University of California Press.

Lewis, Charlotte. 1976. *Prologue to the Chinese Revolution: The Transformation of Ideas and Institutions in Hunan Province, 1891–1907.* Cambridge: East Asian Research Center, Harvard University.

Lewis, David. 1975. Languages and Language. In: Gunderson, Keith, ed. *Minnesota Studies in the Philosophy of Science.* Minneapolis: University of Minnesota Press; vol. VII.

Li Buyun 李步云. 1992. On the Three Existential Types of Human Rights (論人權的三種存在形態). In: Legal Research Institute – Chinese Academy of Social Sciences, eds. *Contemporary Human Rights* (當代人權). Beijing: Chinese Academy of Social Sciences Press.

    1996. Individual Human Rights and Collective Human Rights (論個體人權與集體人權). In: Liu Nanlai et al., eds. *The Universality and Particularity of Human Rights* (人權的普遍性和特殊性). Beijing: Social Sciences Documents Press.

Li Disheng 李滌生. 1979. *Collected Interpretations of Xunzi* (荀子集釋). Taipei: Xuesheng shuju.

Li Hongzhang 李鴻章 et al. 1930. *The Complete Account of Our Management of Barbarian Affairs* (籌辦夷務始末). Beijing: n.p.

Liang Qichao 梁啟超. 1959 (1905). *Mirror of Ethical Education* (德育鑑). Taipei: Zhonghua shuju.

1989a (1896). China's Weakness Comes from Overcaution (論中國積弱由於防弊). In: Collected Works from an Ice-Drinker's Studio (飲冰室合集). Vol. 1:1. Beijing: Zhonghua shuju. 96–100.

1989b (1899). The Right of Strength (論強權). In: Collected Works from an Ice-Drinker's Studio (飲冰室合集). Vol. 6:2. Beijing: Zhonghua shuju.

1989c (1901). Intellectual Biography of Rousseau (盧梭學案). In: Collected Works from an Ice-Drinker's Studio (飲冰室合集). Vol. 1:6. Beijing: Zhonghua shuju.

1989d (1902–3). *On the New People* (新民說). In: Collected Works from an Ice-Drinker's Studio (飲冰室合集). Vol. 6:4. Beijing: Zhonghua shuju.

Liang Shuming 梁漱溟. 1921. *Eastern and Western Cultures and Their Philosophies* (東西文化及其哲學).

Lin Keyi 林可彝. 1922. How the Temple of Heaven Draft Constitution Ought to Be Amended (天壇憲法應該怎麼樣改正). *Dongfang Zazhi* (東方雜誌) 19:21.

Lin Yü-sheng. 1979. *The Crisis of Chinese Consciousness: Radical Antitraditionalism in the May Fourth Era.* Madison: University of Wisconsin Press.

Liu Huaqiu. 1995. Statement by Liu Huaqiu, Head of the Chinese Delegation. In: Tang, James T. H., ed. *Human Rights and International Relations in the Asia-Pacific Region.* London: Pinter. 213–7.

Liu, James T. C. 1967. *Ou-yang Hsiu: An Eleventh-Century Neo-Confucianist.* Stanford: Stanford University Press.

Liu Junning 劉軍寧. 1998. *The Beijing University Tradition and Modern China: Harbingers of Liberalism* (北大傳統與近代中國：自由主義的先聲). Beijing: Zhongguo renshi chubanshe.

Liu, Kwang-Ching 劉廣京. 1984. Written Opinions on "Gu Yanwu's View of Personal Benefit" (關於「顧炎武的私利觀」的書面意見). In: Institute of Modern History, Academia Sinica, eds. *Proceedings of the Conference on Modern Chinese Statecraft Thought* (近世中國經世思想研討會論文集). Taipei: Academia Sinica.

1990. Introduction: Orthodoxy in Chinese Society. In: Liu, Kwang-Ching, ed. *Orthodoxy in Late Imperial China.* Berkeley: University of California Press. 1–24.

1994a. The Beginnings of China's Modernization. In: Chu, Samuel C.; Liu, Kwang-Ching, eds. *Li Hung-chang and China'ss Early Modernization.* Armonk, NY: M. E. Sharpe.

1994b (1970). The Confucian as Patriot and Pragmatist: Li Hung-chang's Formative Years, 1823–1866. In: Chu, Samuel C.; Liu, Kwang-Ching, eds. *Li Hung-chang and China's Early Modernization.* Armonk, NY: M. E. Sharpe.

1994c (1967). Li Hung-chang in Chihli: The Emergence of a Policy, 1870–1875. In: Chu, Samuel C.; Liu, Kwang-Ching, eds. *Li Hung-chang and China's Early Modernization.* Armonk, NY: M. E. Sharpe.

1994d. A Preliminary Study of the Ideas on Human Rights in the Late Qing Period – With Comments on the Influence of Christian Thought (晚清人權論初探——兼論基督教思想之影響). *New Historiography* (新史學) 5:3.

Liu, Lydia H. 1995. *Translingual Practice: Literature, National Culture, and Translated Modernity in China, 1900–1937*. Stanford: Stanford University Press.

1999. Legislating the Universal: The Circulation of International Law in the Nineteenth Century. In: Lydia H. Liu, ed. *Tokens of Exchange: The Problem of Translation in Global Circulations*. Durham: Duke University Press. 127–164.

Liu Nanlai 劉楠來. 1996a. Developing Countries and Human Rights (論個體人權與集體人權). In: Liu Nanlai et al., eds. *The Universality and Particularity of Human Rights* (人權的普遍性和特殊性). Beijing: Social Sciences Documents Press.

1996b. Developing Countries and Human Rights. In: Baehr, Peter R.; van Hoof, Fried; Liu Nanlai; Tao Zhenghua, eds. *Human Rights: Chinese and Dutch Perspectives*. The Hague: Martinus Nijhoff.

Liu Shipei 劉師培. 1936a (1903). *The Essentials of the Chinese Social Contract* (中國民約精義). In: *The Collected Works of Liu Shipei* (劉申叔先生遺書). Shanghai: n.p.

1936b (1905). *Textbook on Ethics* (倫理教科書). In: *The Collected Works of Liu Shipei* (劉申叔先生遺書). Shanghai: n.p.

1936c (1905). *General Explanations of Neo-Confucian Terminology* (理學字義通釋). In: *The Collected Works of Liu Shipei* (劉申叔先生遺書). Shanghai: n.p.

Lovibond, Sabina. 1983. *Realism and Imagination in Ethics*. Minneapolis: University of Minnesota Press.

Lufrano, Richard John. 1997. *Honorable Merchants: Commerce and Self-Cultivation in Late Imperial China*. Honolulu: University of Hawaii Press.

Lukes, Steven. 1985. *Marxism and Morality*. Oxford: Oxford University Press.

Luo Mingda 羅明達; He Hangzhou 賀航洲. 1993. On the Individual-based Properties of Human Rights (論人權的個體屬性). *Zhengfa Luntan* 1. 56–61.

Luo Qinshun. 1987. Bloom, Irene, trans. *Knowledge Painfully Acquired*. New York: Columbia University Press.

Lyons, David. 1994. Utility and Rights. In: *Rights, Welfare, and Mill's Moral Theory*. Oxford: Oxford University Press.

MacIntyre, Alasdair. 1988. *Whose Justice? Which Rationality?* Notre Dame: University of Notre Dame Press.

1989. Relativism, Power, and Philosophy. In: Krausz, Michael, ed. *Relativism: Interpretation and Confrontation*. Notre Dame: University of Notre Dame Press. 182–204.

1991. Incommensurability, Truth, and the Conversation between Confucians and Aristotelians about the Virtues. In: Deutsch, Eliot, ed. *Culture and Modernity*. Honolulu: University of Hawaii Press.

Madsen, Richard. 1995. *China and the American Dream: A Moral Inquiry*. Berkeley: University of California Press.

Mao Zedong 毛澤東. 1991 (1940). On Policy. In: *Selected Works of Mao Zedong* (毛澤東選集). Shanghai: n.p.

    1976. Stuart R. Schram, ed. *Mao Tse-tung Unrehearsed, Talks and Letters: 1956–1971.* Harmondsworth: Penguin.

Martin, Michael. 1990. Review of *Thinking Through Confucius. Journal of Chinese Philosophy* 17:495–503.

Martin, W. A. P., trans. 1864. *General Laws of the Myriad Nations* (萬國公法). Beijing: n.p.

Martin, W. A. P., trans. 1878. *Introduction to International Law* (公法便覽). Beijing: n.p.

Marx, Karl. 1978a (1843). On the Jewish Question. In: Tucker, Robert C., ed. and trans. *The Marx-Engels Reader.* New York: W. W. Norton. 26–52.

    1978b (1859). Preface to *A Contribution to the Critique of Political Economy.* In: Tucker, Robert C., ed. and trans. *The Marx-Engels Reader.* New York: W. W. Norton. 3–6.

    1978c (1875). Critique of the Gotha Program. In: Tucker, Robert C., ed. and trans. *The Marx-Engels Reader.* New York: W. W. Norton. 525–41.

Masini, Federico. 1993. *The Formation of Modern Chinese Lexicon and Its Evolution Toward a National Language: The Period from 1840 to 1898. Journal of Chinese Linguistics.* Monograph Series Number 6.

Matsumoto Sannosuke. 1978. The Idea of Heaven: A Tokugawa Foundation for Natural Rights Theory. In: Tetsuo Najita; Scheiner, Irwin, eds. *Japanese Thought in the Tokugawa Period: Methods and Metaphors.* Chicago: University of Chicago Press. 181–199.

Metzger, Thomas A. 1977. *Escape from Predicament: Neo-Confucianism and China's Evolving Political Culture.* New York: Columbia University Press.

Midgely, Mary. 1999. Towards an Ethic of Global Responsibility. In: Dunne, Tim; Wheeler, Nicholas J., eds. *Human Rights in Global Politics.* Cambridge: Cambridge University Press. 160–174.

Min, Tu-ki. 1985. Late Ch'ing Reformists (1895–1898) and Rousseau: Min-Ch'uan versus Popular Sovereignty. *Tsing Hua Journal of Chinese Studies* 17:1–2. 199–209.

Mizoguchi Yuzo 溝口雄三. 1991. Special Characteristics of Chinese "People's Right" Thought (中國民權思想的特色). In: *Collection of Discussions of Chinese Modernization* (中國現代化討論會論文集). Taipei.

Morsink, Johannes. 1999. *The Universal Declaration of Human Rights. Origins, Drafting and Intent.* Philadelphia: University of Pennsylvania Press.

Motoyama Yukihiko. 1997. Meirokusha Thinkers and Early Meiji Enlightenment Thought. In: *Proliferating Talent.* Honolulu: University of Hawaii Press.

Munro, Donald J. 1988. *Images of Human Nature: A Sung Portrait.* Princeton: Princeton University Press.

    1996. *The Imperial Style of Inquiry in Twentieth-Century China: The Emergence of New Approaches.* Ann Arbor: Center for Chinese Studies, University of Michigan.

Najita, Tetsuo. 1987. *Visions of Virtue in Tokugawa Japan: The Kaitokudō Merchant Academy of Osaka.* Chicago: University of Chicago Press.

Narramore, Terry. 1983. Chinese Intellectuals and Politics: Luo Longji and Chinese Liberalism. M.A. thesis. University of Melbourne.

Nathan, Andrew J. 1985. *Chinese Democracy*. Berkeley: University of California Press.

    1986. Sources of Chinese Rights Thinking. In: Edwards, R. Randle; Henkin, Louis; Nathan, Andrew J., eds. *Human Rights in Contemporary China*. New York: Columbia University Press.

Ng, Wai-ming. 1995. The Formation of Huang Tsun-hsien's Political Thought in Japan (1877–1882). *Sino-Japanese Studies* 8:1. 4–21.

Ng, Wing F. 1998. To Rejuvenate an Old Civilization: Philosophical Aspects of Intellectual Change in China, 1895–1898. Wesleyan University Senior Thesis. Unpublished.

Nozick, Robert. 1974. *Anarchy, State, and Utopia*. New York: Basic Books.

Onogawa Hidemi. 1967. Liu Shih-p'ei and Anarchism. *Acta Asiatica* 12. 70–99.

Parekh, Bhikhu. 1999. Non-Ethnocentric Universalism. In: Dunne, Tim; Wheeler, Nicholas J., eds. *Human Rights in Global Politics*. Cambridge: Cambridge University Press. 128–159.

Peerenboom, Randall. 1993. What's Wrong with Chinese Rights? Toward a Theory of Rights with Chinese Characteristics. *Harvard Human Rights Journal* 6. 29–57.

    1995. Rights, Interests, and the Interest in Rights in China. *Stanford Journal of International Law* 31. 359–386.

    1998. Confucian Harmony and Freedom of Thought: The Right to Think Versus Right Thinking. In: de Bary, Wm. Theodore; Tu Wei-ming, eds. *Confucianism and Human Rights*. New York: Columbia University Press. 235–260.

Peng Kang 彭康. 1983 (1931). The Culture Movement and the Human Rights Movement (文化運動與人權運動). In: Cai Shangsi, ed. *Selected Materials on Contemporary Chinese Intellectual History* (中國現代思想史資料簡編), vol. 3. Hangzhou Zhejiang renmin chubanshe.

Pennock, J. Roland. 1981. Rights, Natural Rights, and Human Rights – A General View. In: Pennock, J. Roland; Chapman, John W., eds. *Human Rights: Nomos XXIII*. New York: New York University Press.

Pettit, Philip. 1987. Rights, Constraints, and Trumps. *Analysis* 47. 8–14.

    1988. The Consequentialist Can Recognize Rights. *Philosophical Quarterly* 38. 150.

Phillips, Anne. 1999. The Politicization of Difference: Does This Make for a More Intolerant Society? In: Horton, John; Mendus, Susan, eds. *Toleration, Identity, and Difference*. New York: St. Martin's. 126–145.

Pleister, Wolfgang. 1982. *Persönlichkeit, Wille und Freiheit im Werke Jherings*. Ebelsbach: Gremer.

Pong, David. 1985. The Vocabulary of Change: Reformist Ideas in the 1860s and 1870s. In: Pong, D.; Fung, E. S. K., eds. *Ideal and Reality: Social and Political Change in Modern China, 1860–1949*. Lanham, MD: University Press of America. 25–61.

Ramberg, Bjørn T. 1989. *Donald Davidson's Philosophy of Language*. Oxford: Basil Blackwell.

Rankin, Mary Backus. 1986. *Elite Activism and Political Transformation in China: Zhejiang Province, 1865–1911.* Stanford: Stanford University Press.

Rawls, John. 1993. The Law of Peoples. In: Shute, Stephen; Hurley, Susan, eds. *On Human Rights: The Oxford Amnesty Lectures, 1993.* New York: Basic Books. 41–82.

Raz, Joseph. 1984. On the Nature of Rights. *Mind* 93:215–229.

——— 1986. *The Morality of Freedom.* Oxford: Clarendon Press.

——— 1990. *Practical Reason and Norms.* Princeton: Princeton University Press.

——— 1992. Rights and Individual Well-Being. *Ratio Juris* 5:2. 127–142.

Ren Wanding. 1990. A Discussion of the Historical Tasks and Objectives of the April 1989 People's Democracy Movement. In: Han Minzhu, ed. *Cries for Democracy: Writings and Speeches from the 1989 Chinese Democracy Movement.* Princeton: Princeton University Press. 121–4.

Rorty, Richard. 1989. *Contingency, Irony, and Solidarity.* Cambridge: Cambridge University Press.

——— 1991. Cosmopolitanism without Emancipation: A Response to Jean-François Lyotard. In: *Objectivity, Relativism, and Truth.* Cambridge: Cambridge University Press. 211–222.

——— 1993. Human Rights, Rationality, and Sentimentality. In: Shute, Stephen; Hurley, Susan, eds. *On Human Rights: The Oxford Amnesty Lectures, 1993.* New York: Basic Books.

Rousseau, Jean-Jacques. 1987. On the Social Contract. In: Cress, Donald, trans. *The Basic Political Writings.* Indianapolis: Hackett.

Santoro, Michael A. 2000. *Profits and Principles: Global Capitalism and Human Rights in China.* Ithaca: Cornell University Press.

Schwartz, Benjamin. 1976. History and Culture in the Thought of Joseph Levenson. In: Meisner, Maurice; Murphey, Rhoads, eds. *The Mozartian Historian: Essays on the Works of Joseph R. Levenson.* Berkeley: University of California Press.

Sen, Amartya. 1999. *Development as Freedom.* New York: Anchor Books.

Seymour, James D., ed. 1980. *The Fifth Modernization: China's Human Rights Movement, 1978–1979.* Stanfordville, NY: Human Rights Publishing Group.

Shek, Richard H. 1976. Some Western Influences on T'an Ssu-t'ung's Thought. In: Cohen, Paul A.; Schrecker, John E., eds. *Reform in Nineteenth-Century China.* Cambridge: East Asian Research Center, Harvard University.

Shue, Henry. 1996 (1980). *Basic Rights.* Princeton: Princeton University Press.

Spar, Frederic J. 1992. Human Rights and Political Engagement: Luo Longji in the 1930s. In: Jeans, Roger B., ed. *Roads Not Taken: The Struggle of Opposition Parties in Twentieth-Century China.* Boulder: Westview Press.

Spence, Jonathan D. 1990. *The Search for Modern China.* New York: W. W. Norton.

Stout, Jeffrey. 1988. *Ethics After Babel.* Boston: Beacon Press.

Suzuki Shuji 鈴木修次. 1981. Terminology Surrounding the "Tripartite Separation of Powers" (「三権分立」にまつわる用語). In: *Japanese Terms in Chinese and China* (日本漢語と中國). Tokyo: Chūkō shinsho.

——— 1997. Fogel, Joshua A., trans. Terminology Surrounding the "Tripartite Separation of Powers." Unpublished.

Svarverud, Rune. 2000. Jus Gentium Sinese: The Earliest Translation of International Law with Some Considerations Regarding the Compilation of *Haiguo Tuzhi. Acta Orientalia* 61: n.p.

Svensson, Marina. 1996. The Chinese Conception of Human Rights: The Debate on Human Rights in China, 1898–1949. Ph.D. diss. Lund University.

1998. An Ambiguous Legacy: Contemporary Lessons from the Chinese Communists' Debate on Human Rights in the Pre-1949 Period. Unpublished.

In press. Debating Human Rights in China, 1899–1999: A Conceptual and Political History. Lanham, MD: Rowman and Littlefield.

Tam, Yue-him. 1991. The Intellectual Impact on Late Ch'ing China from Meiji Japan: The Case of Liang Ch'i-ch'ao Reconsidered. Unpublished.

Tan Mingqian 譚鳴謙. 1920. The Spirit of Contemporary Democracy (現代民治主義的精神). *New Tide* (新朝) 2:3.

Tang, James T. H., ed. 1995. *Human Rights and International Relations in the Asia-Pacific Region.* London: Pinter.

Tao Qing 陶清. 1997. *The Philosophy of Nine Great Ming Loyalists* (明遺民九大家哲學). Taipei.

Teng, Ssu-yu; Fairbank, John K. 1954. *China's Response to the West: A Documentary Survey 1839–1923.* New York: Atheneum.

Tillman, Hoyt Cleveland. 1982. *Utilitarian Confucianism.* Cambridge: Council on East Asian Studies, Harvard University.

1992. *Confucian Discourse and Chu Hsi's Ascendency.* Honolulu: University of Hawaii Press.

1994. *Ch'en Liang on Public Interest and the Law.* Honolulu: University of Hawaii Press.

Tuck, Richard. 1979. *Natural Rights Theories.* Cambridge: Cambridge University Press.

Tucker, John. 1996. People's Rights in Early Meiji Japan. Unpublished.

Twiss, Sumner B. 1999. Confucian Contributions to the Universal Declaration of Human Rights: A Historical and Philosophical Perspective (如學對世界人權宣言的貢獻：一種歷史與哲學的觀點). *International Confucian Research* (國際儒學研究). vol. 6.

Vattel, Emmerich de. 1820. *The Law of Nations.* Northampton, MA: S. Butler.

Wakabayashi, Bob Tadashi. 1984. Katō Hiroyuki and Confucian Natural Rights, 1861–1870. *Harvard Journal of Asiatic Studies* 44. 469–492.

Wakeman, Frederic, Jr. 1972. The Price of Autonomy: Intellectuals in Ming and Ch'ing Politics. *Daedalus*, pp. 35–70.

Waldron, Jeremy, ed. 1987. *Nonsense Upon Stilts: Bentham, Burke, and Marx on the Rights of Man.* London: Methuen.

Walzer, Michael. 1994. *Thick and Thin.* Notre Dame: University of Notre Dame Press.

1997. *On Toleration.* New Haven: Yale University Press.

Wang Kangnian. 1953 (1896). On the Benefits of Using People's Authority for China (論中國參用民權之利益). *Shiwu bao.* In: Jian Bozan 翦伯贊, ed. *Reform in 1898* (戊戌變法). Shanghai: Shenzhou guoguang she. Vol. 3, 147–148.

Wang Yangming. 1963. Chan, Wing-tsit, trans. *Instructions for Practical Living.* New York: Columbia University Press.

Watson, Burton, trans. 1968. *The Complete Works of Chuang-tzu.* New York: Columbia University Press.

Weatherley, Robert. 1999. *The Discourse of Human Rights in China: Historical and Ideological Perpsectives.* New York: St. Martin's.

Wei Jingsheng. 1980a. The Fifth Modernization. In: Seymour, James D., ed. *The Fifth Modernization: China's Human Rights Movement, 1978–1979.* Stanfordville, NY: Human Rights Publishing Group.

    1980b. Human Rights, Equality, and Democracy. In: Seymour, James D., ed. *The Fifth Modernization: China's Human Rights Movement, 1978–1979.* Stanfordville, NY: Human Rights Publishing Group.

    1997. Torgeson, Kristina M., ed. and trans. *The Courage to Stand Alone: Letters from Prison and Other Writings.* New York: Viking.

Wei Yuan 魏源. 1840. *Illustrated Compendium on Coastal Nations* (海國圖志).

Welchman, Jennifer. 1995. *Dewey's Ethical Thought.* Ithaca: Cornell University Press.

Wheaton, Henry. 1878 (1836). Boyd, A. C., ed. *Elements of International Law.* London: Stevens & Sons.

Wieacker, Franz. 1995. *A History of Private Law in Europe with Particular Reference to Germany.* Oxford: Oxford University Press.

Williams, Bernard. 1972. *Morality: An Introduction to Ethics.* New York: Harper & Row.

    1985. *Ethics and the Limits of Philosophy.* Cambridge: Harvard University Press.

    1996. Toleration: An Impossible Virtue? In: Heyd, David, ed. *Toleration.* Princeton: Princeton University Press. 18–27.

Wong, David B. 1984. *Moral Relativity.* Berkeley: University of California Press.

    In press. Rights and Community in Confucianism. In: Shun, Kwong-loi; Wong, David B., eds., *Confucian Ethics: A Comparative Study of Self, Autonomy, and Community.* Cambridge: Cambridge University Press.

Wood, Alan T. 1995. *Limits to Autocracy: From Sung Neo-Confucianism to a Doctrine of Political Rights.* Honolulu: University of Hawaii Press.

Wright, Crispin. 1992. *Truth and Objectivity.* Cambridge: Harvard University Press.

Wright, Stanley F. 1950. *Hart and the Chinese Customs.* Belfast: W. Mullan.

Xia Yong 夏勇. 1992. *The Origins and Foundations of Human Rights: A Chinese Interpretation* (人權概念起源). Beijing: Zhengfa University Press.

    1996. Human Rights and the Chinese Tradition (人權與中國傳統). In: Liu Nanlai et al., eds. *The Universality and Particularity of Human Rights* (人權的普遍性和特殊性). Beijing: Social Sciences Documents Press.

Xu Shen 許慎. 1981. *Annotated Explanations of Words and Phrases* (説文解字注). Shanghai: Shanghai guji chubanshe.

Xu Zhengxiong 許政雄. 1992. *The Development and Divergence of Late Qing People's Power Thought* (清末民權思想的發展與歧異). Taipei: Wenshizhe chubanshe.

Xue Fucheng 薛福成. n.d. Financial Control (利權). In: Chen Zhongyi, ed. *Statecraft Writings of the Imperial Dynasty, Third Series* (皇朝經世文三編). Taipei: Wenhai chubanshe. 1:5.

Xunzi Index (荀子引得). 1986. Shanghai: Shanghai Ancient Books Press.

Yan Fu 嚴復. 1986. *Collected Works of Yan Fu* (嚴復集). Beijing.

Yanabu Akira 柳父章. 1994. The Concept of "Right" (権利：権利の「権」, 権力の「権」). In: *Conditions Surrounding the Formation of Translated Terms* (翻訳語成立事情). Tokyo: Iwanami shinsho.

——. 1997. Fogel, Joshua A., trans. The Concept of "Right." Unpublished.

Yoon, Seungjoo. 2000. Limits of Interstitial Bureaucracy: Intern-Commissioners of the *Chinese Progress* (*Shiwu bao*) in Discord, 1896–1898. Unpublished.

Yu Yingshi 余英時. 1987. China's Modern Religious Ethics and the Merchant Spirit (中國近代宗教倫理與商人精神). In: *The Contemporary Interpretation of the Tradition of Chinese Thought* (中國思想傳統的現代詮釋). Taipei: Lianjing Press.

——. 1994. Roundtable Discussion of *The Trouble with Confucianism*. *China Review International* 1:1. 9–47.

Zarrow, Peter. 1990. *Anarchism and Chinese Political Culture.* New York: Columbia University Press.

——. 1996. Chen Duxiu: Human Rights and Politics in the New Culture Movement. Unpublished.

Zhang Qiyun 張其昀 et al. 1973. *Encyclopedic Dictionary of the Chinese Language* (中文大辭典). Taipei: Chinese Cultural University.

Zhang Wenxian 張文顯. 1992. On the Subjects of Human Rights and the Human Rights of Subjects (論人權的主體與主體的人權). In: Legal Research Institute – Chinese Academy of Social Sciences, eds. *Contemporary Human Rights* (當代人權). Beijing: Chinese Academy of Social Sciences Press.

Zhang Zhidong 張之洞. 1970 (1898). An Encouragement to Learning (勸學篇). In: Wang Shunian, ed. *Zhang Wenxiang Gong Chuanji*; vol. 1. Taipei: Wenhai chubanshe.

Zhou Dunyi 周敦頤. 1990. *Collected Works of Zhou Dunyi* (周敦頤集). Beijing: Zhonghua shuju.

Zhou Fohai 周佛海. 1928. The Basis and Particulars of the Principle of Democracy (民權主義的根具和特質). *New Life* (新生命) 1:2.

Zhu Xi 朱熹. 1974 (1710). Zhang Boxing 張伯行, ed. *Extended Reflection on Things at Hand* (續近思錄). Beijing: Shijie shuju.

——. 1983. *Classified Conversations of Master Zhu* (朱子語類). In: *Wenyuange Siku Quanshu* (文淵閣四庫全書). Taipei: Commercial Press. vols. 700–702.

——. 1991. Wittenborn, Allan, trans. *Further Reflections on Things at Hand.* Lanham, MD: University Press of America.

Zhu Xi; Lu Zuqian. 1967. Chan, Wing-tsit, trans. *Reflections on Things at Hand.* New York: Columbia University Press.

Glossary and Index

LaVergne, TN USA
15 July 2010
189562LV00004B/13/P